3

AVENUES
English Skills

Lynne Gaetz

TEACHER'S ANNOTATED EDITION

PEARSON
Montréal

Managing Editor
Sharnee Chait

Editor
Lucie Turcotte

Copy Editor
Esmé A. Vlahos

Proofreader
Mairi MacKinnon

Coordinator, Rights and Permissions
Pierre Richard Bernier

Art Director
Hélène Cousineau

Graphic Design Coordinator
Lyse LeBlanc

Book and Cover Design
Frédérique Bouvier

Book Layout
Interscript

Illustration
p. 38, Benoit Pitre

Cover Artwork
Pietro Adamo, *Citta Series*, 2009. Mixed media on paper, 36 x 24 inches. Courtesy of Progressive Fine Art and Galerie Beauchamp. © 2011 Artist Pietro Adamo.

ERPI publishes and distributes PEARSON ELT products in Canada.

5757 Cypihot Street
Saint-Laurent, Québec H4S 1R3
CANADA
Telephone: 1 800 263-3678
Fax: 1 866 334-0448
infoesl@pearsonerpi.com
http://pearsonelt.ca

Registration of copyright – Bibliothèque et Archives nationales du Québec, 2013
Registration of copyright – Library and Archives Canada, 2013

Printed in Canada 123456789 IO 17 16 15 14 13
ISBN 978-2-7613-5124-9 135124 ABCD ENV94

Acknowledgements

- Lucie Turcotte for her dedicated editing and her magnificent job of polishing this book;
- Sharnee Chait for her valuable expertise;
- Julie Hough for her enthusiastic words, which helped ignite this project;
- Frédérique Bouvier and Interscript for the creative layout;
- Esmé Vlahos and Mairi MacKinnon for their careful work on the manuscript and proofs;
- My students at Collège Lionel-Groulx for their insightful feedback;
- Diego Pelaez for his valuable contributions to the manuscript and the Companion Website;
- Rebeka Pelaez for her optimistic attitude as she worked on the transcripts and tests.

100 %
BIOGAS ENERGY

This book is printed on paper made in Québec from 100% post-consumer recycled materials, processed chlorine-free, certified Eco-Logo, and manufactured using biogas energy.

Preface

Avenues 3: English Skills is the third of a three-level series. Designed for high-intermediate and advanced students of English as a second language, *Avenues 3* is a comprehensive integrated skills text.

Avenues 3: English Skills is composed of eight chapters focusing on contemporary themes that will engage and challenge students. The Start-Up activity in each chapter introduces students to the chapter's theme. Vocabulary Boosts and online exercises help students develop a more varied vocabulary. Readings, which expose students to a variety of ideas and writing styles, include a blog post, an academic paper excerpt, novel and textbook excerpts, magazine and newspaper articles, and short stories. Students are expected to make inferences, to recognize tone and cultural context, and to think critically. In the Take Action! section near the end of each chapter, there are additional writing and speaking prompts. Scattered throughout the chapters, grammar tips remind students about key concepts. Chapters end with revising and editing practices that can help students improve their writing skills. At the end of the book, writing workshops contain detailed information about the academic essay. The final workshop guides students through the core elements of narratives and stories.

Avenues 3: English Skills is accompanied by a learning-centred website, the *Avenues 3: English Skills Companion Website Plus*. To provide maximum flexibility for teachers, every reading, watching, and listening activity in the skills book has two sets of different questions: 1) Textbook questions can be taken up in class; 2) Online questions can be assigned as homework or done in a classroom lab. The automated grading function allows students to check their results. Using the grade tracker, you can conveniently monitor their progress and verify that homework was done. Also, to help students do better in their reading tests, including Benchmark and TESOL tests, the website contains additional readings.

In the Teacher Section of the Companion Website, you will find a variety of class-tested reading and listening tests. If you want to modify a particular test, simply download the Word document and make adjustments. The Teacher Section also contains evaluation grids as well as transcripts for the audio and visual material.

Avenues 3: English Skills contains more material than you may need, thus allowing you to use different chapters when you've exhausted certain topics. Additionally, you can present chapters in whatever sequence you prefer.

Complementing the themes in this book is *Avenues 3: English Grammar*. If students have particular difficulties with a grammatical concept, they can try additional online exercises created for the *Avenues 3: English Grammar Companion Website Plus.*

Finally, I'm delighted with the decision to print my books on recycled paper.

Lynne Gaetz

Highlights

Warm-up activities provide a relevant introduction to each chapter's theme.

Speaking activities help students communicate confidently.

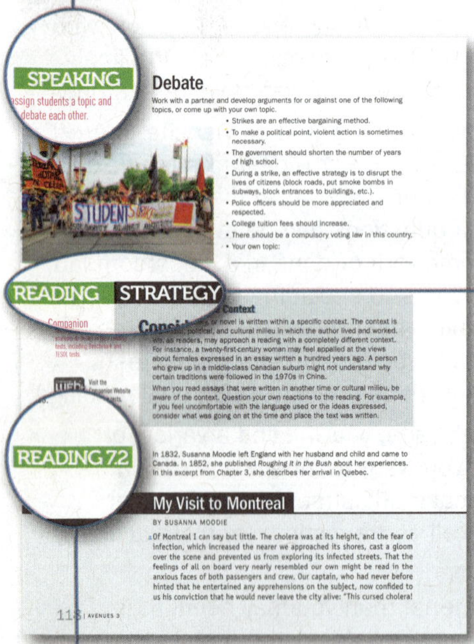

Effective strategies help students improve their reading skills.

Texts taken from a variety of sources expose students to different writing styles and ideas.

Online questions for all readings allow students to prepare for reading tests, including Benchmark and TESOL tests.

Throughout the book, Grammar Tips cover key concepts, which are further explored in *Avenues 3: English Grammar*.

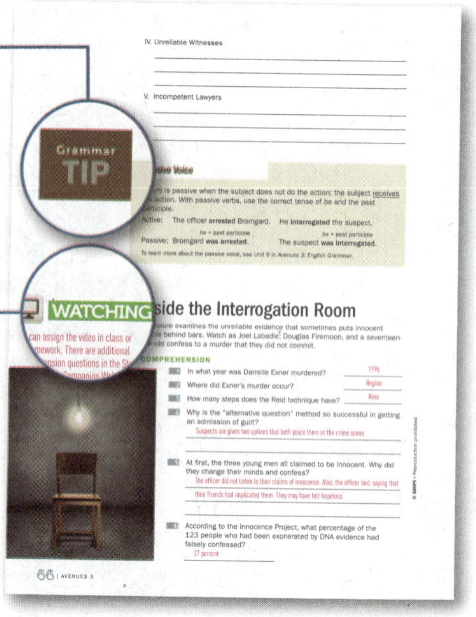

A variety of audio and video segments provide rich listening practice material.

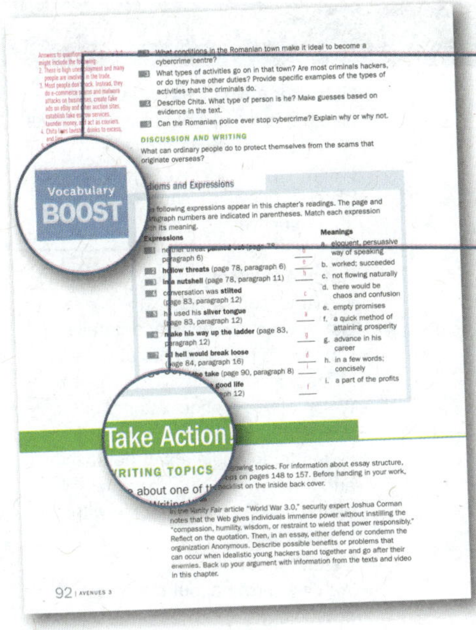

Vocabulary Boosts help students build their vocabulary.

In each chapter, the Take Action! section includes additional writing and speaking topics. Students are invited to research movies and television shows that relate to the chapter themes and to discuss them in essays and oral presentations.

The Revising and Editing section helps students to develop their writing skills and to prepare for writing tests, including the Benchmark and TESOL tests.

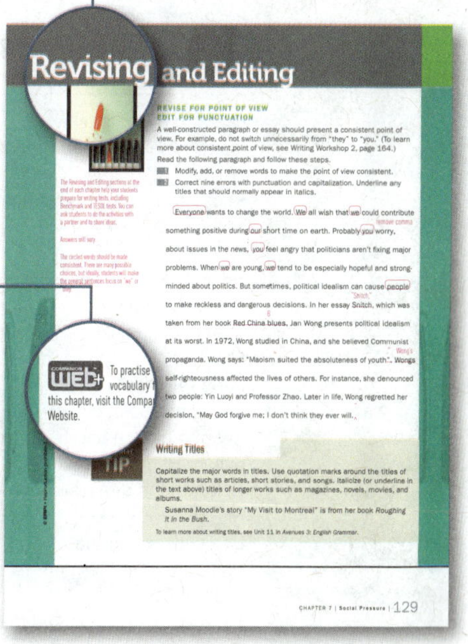

The *Avenues 3: English Skills Companion Website Plus* contains additional reading material for further practice. It also includes vocabulary exercises and extra comprehension questions for all the reading and listening activities in the book.

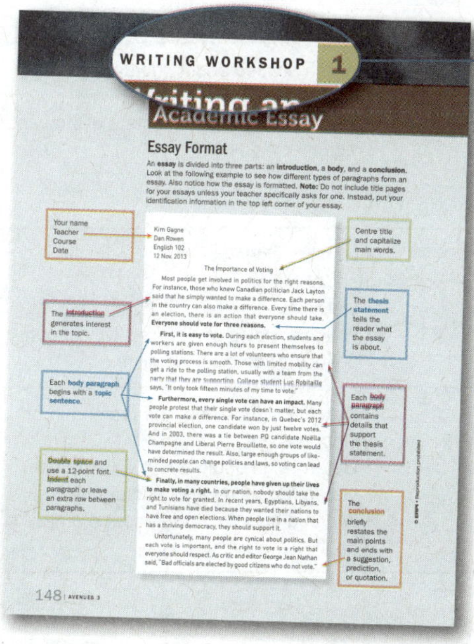

Four Writing Workshops provide detailed explanations about essay writing.

Scope and Sequence

	READING	WRITING	LISTENING/WATCHING
CHAPTER 1: Survivors	• Use context clues • Recognize cognates • Identify imagery • Read for main ideas and details • Read: an essay, two articles, and a book excerpt	• Write paragraphs • Use imagery • Take notes • Write questions • Write an essay • Write topic sentences	• Listen for main ideas and details • Listen to an audio about bear attacks • Watch a video about surviving a plane crash • Watch a television show or movie about survival
CHAPTER 2: Tolerance	• Learn how to summarize • Identify main ideas: recognize thesis statements and topic sentences • Read for details • Read three essays	• Write about stereotypes • Write summaries • Write an essay • Write to compare	• Watch a video about how Canadians see Americans • Listen for main ideas and details • Listen to a panel debate about gay heroes • Watch a movie about intolerance
CHAPTER 3: Mysterious Minds	• Learn to think critically: determine the purpose of a text and recognize bias • Identify main ideas and recognize details • Recognize tone • Read: an essay and two book excerpts	• Write paragraphs • Write an essay • Write a summary • Write an introduction	• Listen to an audio about neuroscience and the law • Watch a video about people with superior memories • Listen for details • Watch a movie about memory and psychology
CHAPTER 4: Crime and Punishment	• Learn to make inferences • Identify main ideas and understand details • Read: an article, a selection from a website, and an essay	• Prepare an outline • Write a summary • Write a short story • Write as a team • Write an essay	• Watch a video about false confessions • Listen to a clip about civilian crime fighters • Listen for details • Watch a television show or movie about crime and/or punishment
CHAPTER 5: Cybercrime	• Recognize irony • Use critical thinking • Learn to skim and scan • Read for details • Recognize point of view • Read: a blog, a book excerpt, two online articles and a research paper excerpt, and a research paper excerpt	• Write a paragraph • Write an essay • Compare and contrast in an essay • Write a conclusion	• Watch a video about hackers • Listen to a discussion about online crime • Listen for details • Watch a film about technology or cybercrime
CHAPTER 6: Viral Culture	• Use critical thinking • Understand literary genres and analyze fiction • Read for main ideas and details • Read: two online articles, a book excerpt, and a research paper excerpt	• Write arguments • Compare and contrast • Write questions • Write essays	• Watch a video about geotagging • Listen for details • Watch a film that presents a dystopian vision of the world
CHAPTER 7: Social Pressure	• Consider the context • Use critical thinking • Read for main ideas and details • Read: an online article and two excerpts from novels	• Write paragraphs • Use quotations • Write an essay	• Watch a video about the power of social roles • Listen for details • Watch a movie or documentary about politics or political idealism
CHAPTER 8: The Good Life	• Identify figurative devices • Analyze lyrics • Read: song lyrics, an essay, and an excerpt from a book • Read for main ideas and details	• Use similes, metaphors, and personification • Do freewriting and write lyrics • Practise academic writing • Summarize • Write essays	• Watch a video about the promotion of kindness • Listen to an audio about voluntourism • Listen for main ideas and details • Watch a classic movie about moral righteousness

SPEAKING/ PRONUNCIATION	VOCABULARY	GRAMMAR	REVISING AND EDITING
• Talk about risky situations • Discuss ways to survive a plane crash • Make an oral presentation	• Learn about vivid vocabulary that appeals to the senses • Identify cognates and false cognates • Define words from context	• Form questions using the present, past, and future tenses • Identity subject-verb agreement errors	• Revise for a main idea • Edit for subject-verb agreement and word choice
• Talk about: stereotypes; regional and national conflicts • Discuss ways to solve problems • Brainstorm • Make an oral presentation	• Define words from context • Correct slang terms • Use *say* and *tell* • Learn to use a variety of verbs	• Use the present perfect • Use the simple and progressive forms of present and past verbs • Ask and answer questions	• Revise for adequate support • Edit for verb tense
• Talk about life lessons • Make an oral presentation • Discuss brain games	• Define words • Distinguish between *memory*, *remind*, and *souvenir*	• Use subject and object pronouns • Ask and answer questions	• Revise for an introduction • Edit for spelling, pronoun, and modal errors
• Discuss possible criminal sentences • Make an oral presentation • Create a rant	• Do a crossword puzzle • Define phrases from context • Define verbs and act them out	• Recognize the passive voice • Learn about using *one of the ...* • Ask and answer questions	• Revise for transitional words and phrases • Edit for mixed errors
• Discuss the ethics of hacking • Make an oral presentation • Prepare an argument	• Define words from context; recognize parts of speech • Define idioms and expressions	• Learn about the past form of modals • Ask and answer questions • Identify idioms and expressions	• Revise for a conclusion • Edit for mixed errors
• Brainstorm • Talk about: words that describe your generation; peep culture • Make an oral presentation	• Invent new words • Define verbs and act them out • Define verbs from context clues • Distinguish between Canadian, American, and British spelling and language	• Learn about the comparative and superlative forms • Use subordinators	• Revise for sentence variety • Edit for repetitive words
• Develop arguments and debate • Explain your opinions • Make an oral presentation	• Define expressions • Define vivid verbs	• Learn to quote from a source • Use past forms of *should*	• Revise for point of view • Edit for punctuation
• Give and explain your opinion • Brainstorm • Describe your experiences • Make an oral presentation • Create a video • Compare two readings	• Differentiate between literary and academic English • Define expressions	• Learn about forming embedded questions • Learn about literary versus academic English	• Revise for a thesis statement • Edit for mixed errors

Table of Contents

CHAPTER 1

Survivors

"It is not the strongest of the species that survives, nor the most intelligent, but the one most responsive to change."

– CHARLES DARWIN, BRITISH NATURALIST

Our lives are an adventure, much like a road to be travelled. We all have setbacks and challenges. In this chapter, you will read about thrill-seekers and survivors.

START UP

Answers to the Start Up appear in the Companion Website, in Chapter 1. See the file "Start Up: Survival Strategies." You can introduce students to the website by getting them to search for the responses to this Start Up. Note that many of the answers to these questions also appear in Unit 1 of *Avenues 3: English Grammar.*

Survival Strategies

With a partner or a small group of students, discuss what you should do in the following circumstances. When you finish, check your answers by visiting the Companion Website.

- You are locked in a car trunk and someone is driving the car.
- You are caught in a riptide. A strong wave is pulling you back out to sea.
- You are in the middle of a club and there is a fire. The club is packed with people.
- You are driving on a quiet road when the brakes on your car suddenly stop working.
- You are bitten by a rattlesnake.
- You are on the 80th floor of a building when a large fire starts two floors below you. The building has 92 floors.

Vocabulary BOOST

Description

Descriptive writing contains imagery that appeals to the five senses: sight, smell, hearing, taste, and touch. Look at the following examples of imagery.

Sight: "The second car—it was a Trans-Am—was still running, its high beams washing the scene in a lurid stagy light."
T. Coraghessan Boyle, "Greasy Lake"

Hearing: "As the glass tinkled onto the cellar floor, he heard a low growl."
Christopher Morley, *The Haunted Bookshop*

Touch: "I felt a drop or two of blood from my head trickle down my neck."
Charlotte Brontë, *Jane Eyre*

Smell: "The perfume from a great bowl of lavender seemed to mingle curiously yet pleasantly with the half-musty odour of the old leather-bound volumes."
E. Phillips Oppenheim, "The Vanished Messenger"

Taste: The lozenge, which melted on my tongue, had the sweet chill of peppermint.

Also, to make a story more vivid, you can use the following strategies:

- Use **adjectives and adverbs.** Adjectives give more information about nouns. Adverbs give information about verbs.

  Boring: He spoke to the child.
  Vivid: The **well-dressed young** man spoke to the **squalling** child.

- Use **specific verbs**. For example, *gazed* is more specific than *looked.*

  Boring: She looked out the open window and exhaled.
  Vivid: She **gazed** out the open window and **sighed**.

- Add **details** to make the sentence more complete.

  Boring: The teacher looked at the bad student.
  Vivid: **Mrs. Normandeau**, a **nasty** teacher**, snapped her ruler on the child's desk** and **glared** at the **young offender**.

Answers will vary.

PRACTICE

1 Work with a partner. Using a thesaurus or dictionary, come up with two or three more specific and vivid verbs.

EXAMPLE: run: dash; sprint; jog

a) laugh: chuckle; snicker; roar; giggle

b) cry: bawl; sob; whimper; wail; snivel

c) look at: stare; glare; gaze; ogle; glance at

d) walk: stroll; saunter; stomp; step; march

2 With your partner, brainstorm ways to make the following sentences more descriptive and interesting. Provide details for each noun—such as a name and a physical description. Also use more specific and vivid verbs.

EXAMPLE: The baby cried.

Markie, the three-week-old newborn, bawled until his face turned red.

a) The boy fell. ______________________________

____

b) The boss was angry with the employee. ______________________________

____

c) The officer arrested the adolescent. ______________________________

____

3 Write a paragraph of about 150 words about a risky, frightening, or thrilling moment. Include a clear topic sentence (a sentence that expresses the main idea) and descriptive details. Include details that appeal to at least two of the following senses: sight, hearing, smell, touch, and taste. (See Writing Workshop 1, page 153, for more information about topic sentences.)

READING STRATEGY

Students can visit the Companion Website to practise their reading comprehension. Questions for all readings are structured to help students do better in their reading tests, including Benchmark and TESOL tests.

COMPANION WEB+ Visit the Companion Website to prepare for your reading tests. Online questions for all readings are structured to help you practise reading strategies.

Identifying Context Clues

1• Look at the parts of the word. You might recognize a part of the word and then be able to guess its meaning (**sun**screen). A **prefix** or a **suffix** also helps you understand the meaning. For instance, the prefixes *un–*, *dis–*, and *il–* mean "not." The prefix *multi–* means "many" and *anti–* means "against." The suffix *–less* means "without."

2• Determine the part of speech. Sometimes it helps to know a word's function. Is it a noun, verb, adjective, etc.? For example, in the sentence "He didn't trip on the carpet," it helps to recognize that *trip* is a verb.

3• Look at surrounding words and sentences. Other words in the sentence can help you. Look for a **synonym** (a word that means the same thing) or **antonym** (a word that means the opposite). Also look at surrounding sentences. These may give you clues to the word's meaning.

→

Recognizing Cognates

Many different languages share words that have the same linguistic root. Cognates—or word twins—are words that have a similar appearance and meaning in different languages.

EXAMPLE: *English: responsible* *French and Spanish: responsable*

False Cognates

Sometimes words in two languages appear to be similar, but they have completely different meanings. For example, the French word *fabrique* (meaning "factory") is a false cognate because it does not mean the same thing as the English word *fabric* (meaning "cloth").

PRACTICE

1 Work with a partner. Read the paragraph and define the words in bold. Use context clues.

On his world-record-breaking adventure, traveller Graham Hughes faced **formidable** logistical problems. One of the most frustrating was acquiring visas. "Working through all the **red tape** needed to get from one country to another is an absolute nightmare," he says. For instance, while waiting for his Papua New Guinea visa, he filled out numerous forms and met with a series of passive officials. After ten days of hearing empty promises, he was **seething**, but he made the **sensible** decision to be polite and to acquiesce to the bureaucrats' demands rather than to get **irate**.

Answers will vary.

a) formidable: significant

b) red tape: paperwork; bureaucracy

c) seething: furious

d) sensible: smart; reasonable

e) irate: angry

2 Which words in the paragraph are cognates? Circle three true cognates and at least one false cognate.

If you have a language lab, ask students to do Reading 1.1 in pairs. They can take turns reading paragraphs, and they can discuss the vocabulary together.

READING 1.1

What motivates some travellers to risk their lives in dangerous adventures? Read about international thrill-seekers.

On the line next to each word in bold, write a short definition, synonym, or translation. Use context clues to guess the meaning of each word.

International Thrill-Seekers

BY A. WINLAND

Answers will vary.

EXAMPLE: individuals

arrived

jumping with a parachute

1 There have always been those who are prepared to risk life and limb in an epic adventure. In the past, fearless **souls** set out to find the edge of the world and **landed** in America. More adventurers died in their search for the North Pole. Today, with no new unknown lands to conquer, adventure travellers find other ways to take risks and get an adrenaline high. They do off-track skiing in the Rockies, **skydiving** in Mexico, and mountain climbing in Nepal. There are some

distinct types of travellers who attempt death-defying endeavours: the adventurer, the revolution chaser, and the record breaker.

2 Adventurers want a fun and audacious personal challenge. Drew Hayden Taylor, a native of Curve Lake First Nations in Ontario, points out that aboriginal activities such as canoeing and skiing are "corrupted and marketed as something fun to do." What were once transportation and hunting methods have become amusing—but dangerous—adventures. Hayden Taylor wryly observes that Caucasians who throw themselves down "long stretches of roaring rapids, with large pointy rocks and lots of turbulent white water" are—well—**nuts**.

crazy

origins

jump

carry

descended quickly

3 Some of the most extreme travel activities have **roots** in New Zealand. The nation started bungee jumping, cave rafting, and zorbing, which is rolling down a hill in a giant inflatable ball. In an article in *The New York Times*, Ethan Todras-Whitehill describes how aboriginal bungee jumpers used vines to **leap** from high branches of trees. In 1988, a couple of entrepreneurs replaced the vine with a rubber cord, and installed a pulley system to **haul** the jumper back up to the top of the bridge. On the first day of their bungee jumping activity, about thirty people gave it a try. Now, every year, almost 100,000 tourists travel to Queensland, Australia, to leap off a bridge for fun. Avon Wade, a tourist from Halifax, describes his 2012 bungee jump: "Attached at the ankles, I **plummeted** down and the ground got close really fast. Then the harness pulled the skin on my ankles, and suddenly the earth retreated as I bounced back up." His shrieks echoed across the canyon.

endeavour

equipment

dead bodies

4 Some thrill-seekers just want to climb the highest mountain, but it is not a simple **feat**. Using a system of ropes, pulleys, hammers, and other specialized **gear**, they cling to rock faces at dizzying heights. In fact, those who climb Mount Everest must pass through a 26,000-foot-high "death zone." It is literally a field of **corpses** of those who did not survive their adventure. The bodies, dressed in snowsuits and frozen solid, are too heavy to remove from their perches on rocks or from their eternal beds in caves. Daniel Mazur, in an interview with *The Seattle Times*, says, "It's one of the most horrible, humbling experiences I've ever had, walking over those dead bodies."

look for

truly

knocked hard

violent protest

5 Some unusual and interesting thrill-seekers—known as "revolution chasers"—are adventure tourists who **seek out** places of war, revolution, and chaos. *ABC News* recently profiled a member of this group. British citizen Alistair Caldicott, thirty-three, says that he loves the moment when he is "**genuinely** uncertain" about whether or not he will survive. A few years earlier, he feared for his life when Afghan Taliban insurgents **pounded** on his hotel room door, trying to break into his room. Later, he was imprisoned in Bolivia and almost shot in Rio de Janeiro. In Pakistan, he sipped milky sweet tea with drug lords and gun suppliers. And in Budapest, Hungary, he joined a group of protesters who marched to the parliament buildings. As the **riot** escalated, he got caught in a cul-de-sac. Tear gas burned his eyes and left a bitter, pungent flavour in his mouth.

dangerous action

dangerous and stupid

6 Finally, there are those record-breaker travellers who hope to find some fame and notoriety by doing a travel **stunt.** A sixteen-year-old American, Abby Sunderland, wanted to break a world record and become the youngest person to sail around the world alone. Her **reckless** adventure ended badly. She was rescued thousands of kilometres west of Australia after her boat's mast broke during a fierce storm.

destined

bad smell

7 Graham Hughes, from Liverpool, England, wants to be the first person to set foot in every country without using air transport. When someone travels alone hauling a video camera to some of the earth's most dangerous destinations, he or she is **bound** to encounter some problems. Hughes was arrested and thrown into prison in Cape Verde, Africa, and then again in Congo. On his blog, he describes the experience: "The police took my shirt, shoes, socks, and even my f***ing glasses." He spent six days in a cell that had the **stench** of a rotting corpse. Eventually, a gentleman who worked for the British Consul came to his rescue.

forget

calmly

backbone

8 What many record-breaking travellers **neglect** to consider are the possible costs, should they face any problems. First, there is the financial cost. For instance, the Australian government paid over $300,000 to send a Quantas airplane and a fishing vessel in search of teen sailor Abby Sunderland. (Her family **placidly** conceded that they can't afford to reimburse the nation.) But more importantly, there are the physical costs. Bungee jumpers and skydivers have had severe **spinal** cord injuries that resulted in paralysis. In 2011, four American sailors, on a trip around the world, were killed off the coast of Somalia by pirates. And there are all of those bodies on Mount Everest.

9 So ultimately, why do so many people risk their lives to have dangerous travel adventures? Perhaps Alistair Caldicott says it best: "If you have lived with fear and survived, you can do anything."

(930 words)

Sources: "Bodies of Those Left Behind Offer a Macabre Reminder." *Seattle Times*. McClatchy Newspapers, 22 May 2007. Web.

Caldicott, Alistair. "Rioting in Budapest." Alistair Caldicott, 2008. Web.

Hayden Taylor, Drew. "This Boat Is My Boat." *This Magazine*. Red Maple Foundation, 2008. Web.

Hughes, Graham. "The Odyssey Expedition." Travel Blog, 2008. Web.

Todras-Whitehill, Ethan. "Extreme New Zealand, a Thrill-Seeker's Playground." *New York Times*. New York Times Company, 28 Jan. 2011. Web.

Students can read the essay in class or for homework. There are additional questions in the Student Section of the Companion Website. You can verify if students have read the essay by checking their scores with the grade tracker.

COMPREHENSION: IDENTIFY IMAGERY AND MAIN IDEAS

1 The writer uses words and phrases that appeal to the five senses: sight, hearing, smell, taste, and touch. Find some words or phrases that appeal to each sense. The paragraph numbers are in parentheses.

a) Sight (2 or 4): Caucasians throw themselves down long stretches of roaring rapids, with large pointy rocks and lots of turbulent water. (2) The bodies, dressed in snowsuits and frozen solid, are too heavy to move from their perches on rocks or from their eternal beds in caves. (4)

b) Touch (3): the harness pulled the skin on my ankles

c) Hearing (2, 3, or 5): roaring rapids (2); His shrieks echoed across the canyon (3); insurgents pounded on his hotel room door (5)

d) Taste (5): he sipped milky sweet tea; tear gas ... left a bitter, pungent flavour in his mouth

e) Smell (7): a cell that had the stench of a rotting corpse

2 Describe the three main types of thrill-seeking travellers identified in the reading. Give examples of people who belong to each type.

a) Adventurer: someone who tries off-track skiing, skydiving, mountain climbing, canoeing in rapids, bungee jumping, cave rafting, zorbing, etc. Examples: Daniel Mazur climbed Mount Everest, and Avon Wade tried bungee jumping.

b) Revolution chaser: someone who goes to places of war, revolution, and chaos. Example: Alistair Caldicott goes to areas of extreme conflict and enjoys the thrill of not knowing whether he will survive.

c) Record breaker: someone who wants to break a world record. Examples: Abby Sunderland tried to sail around the world, and Graham Hughes wants to visit every country without flying.

3 What are some of the dangers thrill-seekers face? List at least five risks.

freezing on a mountain; drowning; falling; getting shot; imprisonment; spinal cord injuries resulting in paralysis; getting killed; etc.

DISCUSSION AND WRITING

When people go into war zones or sail around the world or do off-track skiing, they may get into trouble. The costs for rescuing them can be very high. For example, the province of British Columbia spent $200,000 searching for just one off-track skier. (Costs include the dozens of police personnel, helicopter rental, etc.) Should thrill-seekers be forced to pay for their own rescue? Why or why not?

COMPANION WEB+ Answer additional questions for all the reading and listening activities. You can also access audio and video clips online.

SPEAKING

My Risky Adventures

You may refer students to the Companion Website to practise pronouncing past tense verbs. Appendix 2 on page 175 also summarizes the pronunciation rules for past tense verbs, third-person singular present tense verbs, words with silent letters, words containing *h* and *th*, and words with multiple syllables.

Work with a team of three or four students. Choose one student to begin. She or he will speak non-stop about one or more of the following topics. When the teacher flicks the lights, change speakers. You can speak about any of the topics when it is your turn.

- The time I got hurt
- A bad decision that I made
- A wild travel experience that I had
- A car, motorcycle, scooter, skateboarding, or bike accident that I had
- My dangerous hobby that I love (skiing, snowboarding, BMX biking, etc.)
- Reasons I don't risk my life

COMPANION WEB+ Visit the Companion Website to practise pronouncing past tense verbs. You can also practise pronouncing words with silent letters, words containing *h* and *th*, and words with multiple syllables.

LISTENING

Bear Attacks

In this segment, you'll hear from people who have had close encounters with bears.

You can assign this listening activity in class or for homework. There are additional comprehension questions in the Student Section of the Companion Website.

COMPREHENSION

1 Which is more dangerous: a male bear or a female bear? Explain your answer.

Although mother bears can be dangerous, the vast majority of attacks are by males. "It's a macho thing," says the expert.

2 Each year, how many people are killed by bears in North America? Two

3 What type of camper was Marci Bridges driving when she saw a bear?

a. Ford b. Chrysler (c.) Volkswagen

4 Describe what the bear was doing when Marci Bridges saw it.

The bear ran across the highway and then along the centre line beside her vehicle.

5 What was Dave Mitt doing when he first saw the bear?

(a.) urinating b. driving c. jogging

6 How did Dave Mitt get away from the bear?

He climbed on top of a train car.

7 Where does Jason Turnbull live? Sudbury, Ontario

8 What happened when Turnbull saw a bear?

He climbed a six-foot-high fence, then scaled the gutter of a neighbour's house.

DISCUSSION AND WRITING

Have you ever had an encounter with a wild animal? Describe what happened.

READING 1.2

In the next essay, read about boundary-pushing survivors. As you read, guess the meaning of the words in bold.

Redefining Who Lives

BY KATHRYN BLAZE CARLSON

1 Haiti's government declared the search-and-rescue operation over on January 23, 2009, but Evans Monsigrace was not done surviving. **Buried** alive in the earthquake that hit his country, he had already carried on for nine days under the wrecked market where he once sold rice. Mr. Monsigrace would stubbornly go on surviving another eighteen days. When his emaciated but living body was at last rescued on February 9, he emerged to a world that had mostly lost hope and had given up on the possibility that hearts still pounded under all that grey, amid all that death.

2 Six months later, pessimists would again be proven wrong: after seventeen days spent deep beneath the Earth's surface, a group of thirty-three Chilean miners

would offer their first **sign** of life—a note, passed upward to civilization through a 688-metre probe, that read, "All thirty-three of us are fine in the shelter." The men would all go on to survive another fifty-two days underground.

Earthquake in Haiti

3 And between and after those spectacular stories of survival, there are countless more. There were the three teenagers who drank rainwater and ate raw seagull flesh while surviving fifty days lost at sea in the South Pacific, and there was the Dutch boy who was pronounced the **sole** survivor of a plane crash that killed 103 passengers in Libya. A ninety-six-year-old mushroom-picker survived two nights in sub-zero temperatures on Oregon's Mount Hood. A ten-year-old Australian girl survived severe jellyfish stings not seen except on bodies in morgues.

4 Those **tales** have challenged our ideas about what can be survived. Could it be that our bodies and brains are capable of far more than we once thought? Could it be that simply hearing these stories will increase our individual chances of surviving a life-or-death situation? Can we now dismiss the so-called Rule of Three—the survival principle that says a person can survive roughly three minutes without air, three hours without **shelter** in extreme weather, three days without water, and three weeks without food?

5 "'Never give up'—and these stories are precisely why I say that," said Laurence Gonzales, author of *Deep Survival: Who Lives, Who Dies, and Why*. "You just don't know what's possible until you've seen it happen. Every time someone says, 'They'll never find anyone else,' they find someone else." Gonzales believes the boundary-pushing survival stories may actually have an effect on future casualty rates. "The next time somebody gets trapped in some situation where they would think they ought to expire, maybe they'll be sitting there thinking, 'Well, if the Chilean miners can do it, I can do it.' It has a **ripple effect**," he said.

6 Mr. Gonzales, whose father survived falling 27,000 feet in a spinning plane that crashed in Germany during the Second World War, pointed to history for evidence. On May 6, 1954, Sir Roger Bannister did the unthinkable: he ran a mile in less than four minutes—a feat doctors had said was impossible, maybe fatal. Two weeks later, an Australian shaved two seconds off Mr. Bannister's time, and then a month after that, the record was bettered once more. In the years since, the record has been beaten, only to be beaten again. "Surely, people haven't evolved that quickly," Mr. Gonzales said, citing the Mount Everest climb as another example of a once-impossible feat that inspired **copycats**. "What happened was that people figured out it was possible, and so they did it. ... The trick is to believe that you can survive."

7 Mr. Gonzales has deemed the Rule of Three a "statistical artifact" because the principle has been defied any number of times in recent decades: in 2010, there was the Los Angeles man who survived six days without water in the California

desert, and a skier lasted seventeen hours exposed to the extremes of an avalanche burial. According to Mr. Gonzales, the so-called rule is just an average that "might have nothing to do with you."

8 Dr. Christopher Van Tilburg, an emergency physician and the editor of *Wilderness Medicine* magazine, says it may be necessary to **tweak** rescue operations, which typically see the first three days as the most critical. "When we're searching for lost climbers, do we stop looking at day four? Day five? Day six?" he said, noting that this very topic is today being discussed in professional search-and-rescue circles. "These stories reinforce the idea that as long as we have the ability or resources, we should be looking long after five or six days."

9 For Dr. John Leach, head of survival research for the Norwegian military and author of *Survivor Psychology*, the Haitian man who held on for twenty-seven days is not the interesting case study. For him, it is the other unknown number of people who survived the physical trauma of the quake, but who ultimately succumbed to the psychological trauma sometime after. "Why did they die?" said Dr. Leach. "What about all those people who died within three days, but who could have survived twenty-seven days [physically speaking]?" He explained that of those who are going to die from physical trauma, 95 percent will die within the first three hours of sustaining physical harm that could kill them. If a person lives **beyond** those three hours, he or she has a good chance of surviving the physical trauma. Dr. Leach continued, "I have found that the people who will die by psychological trauma will die within three days because they cannot adapt to the new environment."

10 Death by psychological trauma? Researchers have learned that the brain is **impaired** in a disaster situation for about three days before it returns to proper function. During that time it may, in fact, start shutting the body down. Indeed, when it comes to survival, Dr. Leach said, "It's the brain that keeps you alive in your environment, much more than your body."

11 What is it about the brains of survivors that allows them to survive? For Aron Ralston—the backcountry climber whose excruciating survival story is the subject of the film *127 Hours*—the goal was two-fold: first, **saw** through his own right hand to free himself from an 800-pound boulder that was crushing his wrist; second, to return to his loved ones and someday find new love. Dr. Van Tilburg described that driving force as the "will to live."

12 And so, in hearing about survival stories, will people believe themselves more resilient than they had in years past? "I think we ought to," Mr. Gonzales said. "We should believe that we can get through it when we're facing adversity."

(1121 words)

Source: Blaze Carlson, Kathryn. "Redefining Survival 2010." *National Post*. Postmedia Network, 24 Dec. 2010. Web.

Students can read the essay in class or for homework. There are additional questions in the Student Section of the Companion Website. You can verify if students have read the essay by checking their scores with the grade tracker.

Answers will vary.

VOCABULARY AND COMPREHENSION

1 Use context clues to define each word. The words appear in bold in the text. The paragraph numbers are in parentheses.

EXAMPLE: buried (1): completely covered with broken parts of the building

a) sign (2): indication

b) sole (3): only

c) tales (4): anecdotes; stories

d) shelter (4): home or place to live

e) ripple effect (5): something that spreads more and more

f) copycats (6): people who do the same thing

g) tweak (8): modify

h) beyond (9): more than

i) impaired (10): not working properly

j) saw (11): cut through

2 What is the main idea of paragraphs 1 to 3?

a. There are many bad accidents in the world, and people suffer terribly.

b. The Chilean miners had an amazing experience when they survived for fifty-two days underground.

c. Survival is difficult.

(d.) Many people have surpassed expectations when they survived terrible ordeals.

3 Is the Rule of Three still relevant today? Explain your answer.

It is a statistical artifact. Many people have survived longer than the Rule of Three dictates.

For example, a man survived six days without water in the California desert.

4 Dr. Christopher Van Tilburg believes that rescue operations need to be changed. Why does he believe that?

People are surviving much longer than rescuers expect, so they should search for longer than a set period of days.

5 In paragraph 10, according to Dr. Leach, your ___ is your most important asset when trying to survive a disaster.

(a.) brain or mind b. family c. physical fitness

6 What is the principal or main idea of the essay?

Many past ideas about survival are no longer true or relevant because people can survive much longer than experts believed.

WATCHING

Surviving a Plane Crash

What are your odds of surviving a plane crash? Watch and find out.

You can assign the video in class or for homework. There are additional comprehension questions in the Student Section of the Companion Website.

COMPREHENSION

1 Why did the United Airlines plane start to drop?

There was an explosion in an engine.

2 Where was part-time pilot Upton Rehnberg seated? Row nine

3 How many pieces did the plane break into? Six

4 When the plane stopped, what position was Jerry Schemmel in?

a. flat on the floor

(b.) upside down in his seat

c. on the ceiling of the plane

5 When a plane is on fire, about how many seconds do people have to escape?

Ninety seconds

6 The plane contained 296 people. How many people survived the crash?

a. 85 (b.) 185 c. 250

7 What percentage of passengers have survived plane crashes in the last twenty years?

75 percent

8 What are some tips that can help you survive a plane crash? List at least three ideas. Answers will vary.

Have a plan and act on it. Wear natural fibres in case there is a fire. Read the safety card. Be alert during takeoffs and landings. Count the number of rows in front of and behind you to the nearest exits.

9 When do most survivable plane crashes happen?

During the first three minutes after takeoff and the last eight minutes before landing

READING 1.3

At the beginning of the twenty-first century, two commercial airliners flew into the World Trade Center in New York City. Read about one Canadian man's memories of that event. As you read, highlight examples of descriptive imagery.

Memories of 9/11

BY DOUGLAS QUAN

Some examples of descriptive imagery are underlined in red.

1 The way Brian Clark remembers it, the moment of impact from the second plane was like a double explosion—"a loud boom, boom." In an instant, the building torqued, the floor buckled, and the walls ripped at jagged angles. Lights, speakers and air-conditioning ducts dropped from the ceiling. Chalky, throat-burning dust filled the air. Then, for about five seconds, the building seemed to sway toward the Hudson River. Clark, a Toronto native and then executive vice-president of Euro Brokers on the 84th floor of the South Tower of the World Trade Center, braced himself. "The thought went through my mind: we're going to fall over."

2 For many who experienced first-hand the terror of two hijacked planes slamming into both towers of the World Trade Center on September 11, 2001, toppling both and killing nearly 3,000 people, the memories and emotions of that day have not faded.

3 They all remember the weather: blue-skied and sunny. Brian Clark was sitting at his desk in the South Tower when his peripheral vision glimpsed a swirl of flames just outside his window. Then he saw singed papers fluttering through the air. In those initial moments, his reaction wasn't panic but more a sense of wonderment. Did a welder just hit a gas line up above? Within minutes, television news reports suggested a small plane, possibly a Cessna, had crashed into the

North Tower. But Clark and his colleagues looked out their windows and saw the "ring of fire" around the upper—roughly 93rd to 99th—floors of the other tower and knew something bigger than a Cessna had just sliced into that building. His colleagues reported some people were jumping out of windows. Clark couldn't bear to look.

4 An announcement on the public address system said people in the South Tower were not in danger and could return to their desks. But most of the 250 people in Euro Brokers' offices that morning fled anyway. Clark was among the fifty or so who stayed behind. After the 1993 bombing at the World Trade Center, he had volunteered to be part of his office's fire-safety team. He called his wife to tell her that he was okay.

5 Minutes later, at 9:03 a.m., United Airlines Flight 175 crashed into the South Tower around the 78th floor, unleashing a fireball. Inside the Euro Brokers' office on the 84th floor, Clark, who had been talking to a colleague on the trading floor, braced himself in a football player's stance as he felt the building tilt to one side and then return to vertical. "Whether it really happened or not, I don't know, but it felt like a six to eight-foot swing. And for those ten seconds, I was terrified." He quickly whipped out the flashlight he'd put in his pocket earlier, and led a small group of co-workers through the gag-inducing dust and debris for one of the stairwells.

6 When Clark and his small group of co-workers from Euro Brokers reached the 81st floor, they encountered a heavy-set woman and man struggling to go up the stairwell. "No way you'll make it by going down," she told them. "Too much fire and smoke. The only way to go is up." While they debated what to do, Clark was distracted by a faint scream.

7 "Help, is anyone there?" the voice said. "I'm buried." The voice belonged to Stanley Praimnath, an executive of Fuji Bank, who worked on the 81st floor. Moments earlier, Praimnath had seen United 175 heading straight for the building and dove under his desk for cover just as the plane slammed into the building a few floors below him. Praimnath, temporarily deafened from the explosive impact, crawled across four office departments looking for a way out. He saw the flicker from Clark's flashlight.

8 Clark grabbed co-worker Ron DiFrancesco, a Hamilton, Ontario, native, and they headed toward the voice, pushing sideways through cracked drywall and debris. As they did, the other members of their group decided to follow the heavy-set woman's advice and go up instead of down. Clark would never see them again. The smoke was so thick, DiFrancesco stopped to catch his breath. He tried using the gym bag he was carrying to filter the air, but it didn't help. He retreated back to the stairwell and escaped on his own.

9 Somehow, Clark found himself in a bubble of fresh air and pushed forward. "Can you see my hand?"

10 Praimnath yelled out. Clark shone his flashlight down and onto his face. "Hallelujah, I've been saved!" Praimnath screamed.

11 Back on the 81st floor landing, Clark shone his flashlight down the staircase to see if it was safe to descend. There was smoke and lots of debris, but no flames. The pair decided to keep going down. When the pair reached ground level, a foreman told them if they went out the doors, they'd have to "go for it" because debris was falling from above. They made a run for it. One-and-a-half blocks later, they stopped at a deli where they were given food and water.

12 As they headed to nearby Trinity Church for shelter, Praimnath turned around and looked up at the burning tower from which they had just escaped. "That tower could come down," he said. Clark dismissed the suggestion. "It's a steel structure. It won't." Just at that moment—9:59 a.m.—the South Tower began its thunderous collapse. They ran into the lobby of a nearby building as a giant cloud of dust reached them. At 10:28 a.m., the second tower collapsed. Everything went dark again.

13 Clark, one of only four people working above the South Tower's 80th floor to survive, learned sixty-one Euro Brokers employees had died. Now retired, Clark says 9/11 taught him to live for today. "I've been blessed that the gift I've been given is that I don't dwell on the past, I don't worry about the future. It leaves me with the present. I live every day in the present. I appreciate every moment."

(994 words)

Source: Quan, Douglas. "Marked Forever by Memories of 9/11." *The Gazette* [Montreal]. Postmedia Network, 3 Sept. 2011. Web.

Students can read the essay in class or for homework. There are additional questions in the Student Section of the Companion Website. You can verify if students have read the essay by checking their scores with the grade tracker.

You might ask students to do this activity in pairs. With the class, identify imagery in the text.

Ask students to check a partner's questions for proper question form.

WRITTEN COMPREHENSION

Do the following activity on a separate sheet of paper.

1 Define ten words from the text. Write your definitions in English.

2 Identify and write examples of three different types of vivid imagery. To review the types of imagery, see the Vocabulary Boost on page 2.

3 Write fifteen questions about this text. Use the present, past, and future tenses in your questions.

DISCUSSION AND WRITING

On September 11, 2001, what factors helped Brian Clark to survive?

Grammar TIP

Question Forms

In questions, the auxiliary usually comes before the subject.

Why **does** he want to travel around the world?

In "subject" questions, the answer is the subject, and no auxiliary is needed.

Who went to Africa? Graham went to Africa.

To learn more about question forms, see Unit 2 in *Avenues 3: English Grammar*.

SPEAKING

Survival Challenge

Join a group of about five students and discuss the following situation.

You and your companions have just survived the crash of a small plane. Both the pilot and co-pilot were killed in the crash. It is mid-January, and you are in northern Canada. The daily temperature is -25°C, and the nighttime temperature is -40°C. There is snow on the ground, and the countryside is wooded with several creeks criss-crossing the area. The nearest town is 35 kilometres away, but you have no map and are unsure of how to get there. You are all dressed in city clothes appropriate for a business meeting. Your group of survivors has the opportunity to salvage **five** of the following items:

- A ball of steel wool
- A small axe
- A loaded .45-caliber pistol with three bullets
- A metal can of Crisco shortening
- Newspapers (one per person)
- Cigarette lighter (without fluid)
- Extra shirt and pants for each survivor
- A 20 x 20 foot piece of heavy-duty canvas
- A sectional air map made of plastic
- One quart of 100-proof whiskey
- A compass
- Family-size chocolate bars (one per person)

Your challenge: Determine which five items are the most valuable to help you survive. Later, your teacher will award points for each item. The winning team is the one that chooses the most useful objects.

The answers to this Survival Challenge appear in the Student Section of the Companion Website.

Source: Mark Wanvig, a former instructor in survival training for the Reconnaissance School of the 101st Division of the U.S. Army. This game is used in military training classrooms.

READING 1.4

Laurence Gonzales is an award-winning writer. The next excerpt is from his book, *Deep Survival*.

The Rules of Survival

BY LAURENCE GONZALES

1 As a journalist, I've been writing about accidents for more than thirty years. In the last fifteen or so years, I've concentrated on accidents in outdoor recreation, in an effort to understand who lives, who dies, and why. To my surprise, I found an eerie uniformity in the way people survive seemingly impossible circumstances. Decades and sometimes centuries apart, separated by culture, geography, race, language, and tradition, the most successful survivors—those who practise what I call "deep survival"—go through the same patterns of thought and behaviour, the same transformation and spiritual discovery, in the course of keeping themselves alive. It doesn't seem to matter whether they are surviving being lost in the wilderness or battling cancer; the strategies remain the same.

2 Survival should be thought of as a journey, a vision quest of the sort that Native Americans have had as a rite of passage for thousands of years. Once people pass the precipitating event—for instance, they are cast away at sea or told they have cancer—they are enrolled in one of the oldest schools in history. Here are a few things I've learned about survival.

Aron Ralston

Stay Calm

3 In the initial crisis, survivors are not ruled by fear; instead, they make use of it. Their fear often feels like (and turns into) anger, which motivates them and makes them feel sharper. Aron Ralston, the hiker who had to cut off his hand to free himself from a stone that had trapped him in a slot canyon in Utah, initially panicked and began slamming himself over and over against the boulder that had caught his hand. But very quickly he stopped himself, did some deep breathing, and began thinking about his options. He eventually spent five days progressing through the stages necessary to convince him of what decisive action he had to take to save his own life.

Think, Analyze, and Plan

4 Survivors quickly organize, set up routines, and institute discipline. When Lance Armstrong was diagnosed with cancer, he organized his fight against it the way he would organize his training for a race. He read everything he could about it, put himself on a training schedule, and put together a team from among friends, family, and doctors to support his efforts. Such conscious, organized effort in the face of grave danger requires a split between reason and emotion in which reason gives direction and emotion provides the power source. Survivors often report experiencing reason as an audible "voice."

5 Steve Callahan, a sailor and boat designer, was rammed by a whale, and his boat sank while he was on a solo voyage in 1982. Adrift in the Atlantic for seventy-six days on a five-and-a-half-foot raft, he experienced his survival voyage as taking place under the command of a "captain" who gave him his orders and kept him on his water ration, even as his own mutinous (emotional) spirit complained. His captain routinely lectured "the crew." Thus under strict control, he was able to push away thoughts that his situation was hopeless and take the necessary first steps of the survival journey: to think clearly, analyze his situation, and formulate a plan.

Celebrate Every Victory

6 Survivors take great joy from even their smallest successes. This attitude helps keep motivation high and prevents a lethal plunge into hopelessness. It also provides relief from the unspeakable strain of a life-threatening situation.

7 Lauren Elder was the only survivor of a light plane crash in the High Sierras. Stranded on a twelve-thousand-foot peak, one arm broken, she could see the San Joaquin Valley in California below, but a vast wilderness and sheer and icy cliffs separated her from safety. Wearing a wrap-around skirt and blouse but no underwear, with two-inch heeled boots, she crawled "on all fours, doing a kind of sideways spiderwalk," as she put it later, "balancing myself on the ice crust, punching through it with my hands and feet." She had thirty-six hours of climbing ahead of her—a seemingly impossible task. But Elder allowed herself to think only as far as the next big rock. Once she had completed her descent of the first pitch, Elder said that she looked up at the impossibly steep slope and thought, "Look what I've done! Exhilarated, I gave a whoop that echoed down the silent pass." Even with a broken arm, joy was Elder's constant companion. A good survivor always tells herself, "Count your blessings—you're alive."

Enjoy the Survival Journey

8 It may seem counter-intuitive, but even in the worst circumstances, survivors find something to enjoy, some way to play and laugh. Survival can be tedious,

and waiting itself is an art. Elder found herself laughing out loud when she started to worry that someone might see up her skirt as she climbed. Even as Callahan's boat was sinking, he stopped to laugh at himself as he clutched a knife in his teeth like a pirate while trying to get into his life raft. And Viktor Frankl ordered some of his companions in Auschwitz who were threatening to give up hope to force themselves to think of one funny thing each day. Singing, playing mind games, reciting poetry, and doing mathematical problems can make waiting tolerable, while heightening perception and quieting fear.

Never Give Up

9 Yes, you might die. In fact, you will die—we all do. But perhaps it doesn't have to be today. Don't let it worry you. Forget about rescue. Everything you need is inside you already. Dougal Robertson, a sailor who was cast away at sea for thirty-eight days after his boat sank, advised thinking of survival this way: "Rescue will come as a welcome interruption of ... the survival voyage." One survival psychologist calls that "resignation without giving up. It is survival by surrender."

10 Survivors are not easily discouraged by setbacks. They accept that the environment is constantly changing and know that they must adapt. When they fall, they pick themselves up and start the entire process over again, breaking it down into manageable bits. When Apollo 13's oxygen tank exploded, apparently dooming the crew, Commander Jim Lovell chose to keep on transmitting whatever data he could back to mission control, even as they burned up on re-entry. Elder and Callahan were equally determined and knew this final truth: if you're still alive, there is always one more thing that you can do.

(1066 words)

Source: Gonzales, Laurence. *Deep Survival: Who Lives, Who Dies, and Why*. NY: W. W. Norton, 2003. Print.

VOCABULARY AND COMPREHENSION

Students can read the essay in class or for homework. There are additional questions in the Student Section of the Companion Website. You can verify if students have read the essay by checking their scores with the grade tracker.

1 What is the meaning of *seemingly* in paragraph 1?

a. clearly (b.) apparently c. unlikely

2 Find a word in paragraph 5 that means "a floating platform (not a boat)."

raft

3 In paragraph 7, what is the meaning of *pitch*?

(a.) slope b. throw c. tone

4 In paragraph 9, what is the meaning of *sank*?

a. fell on its side b. ruptured (c.) submerged below the surface

5 Find a word in paragraph 10 that means "defeats or reverses."

setbacks

6 In this process essay, the author describes the experiences of several survivors. Briefly explain what challenge the following people faced.

a) Aron Ralston: His hand was trapped in a boulder and he had to decide how to free himself.

b) Lance Armstrong: He was diagnosed with cancer.

→

c) Lauren Elder: She survived a light plane crash and had to descend an icy peak.

d) Viktor Frankl: He survived being incarcerated in a concentration camp.

e) Dougal Robertson: He was cast away at sea for thirty-eight days.

7 a) What do most of the stories of survival have in common? What were these people surviving?

Most of the people were surviving a force of nature or a natural process (cancer). They were dealing with a great physical or psychological threat.

b) How is Viktor Frankl's situation different from those of the others mentioned in the essay?

Frankl had to survive a situation that was man-made, not created by the natural world.

COMPANION web+ Shaun Ellis decided to infiltrate a wolf pack and live among the wild animals. Read "My Life as a Wolf" and answer the comprehension questions.

8 What lessons does this essay have for the reader?

It shows how resilient the human spirit is. It reminds us that we can get through our ordeals if we follow the survival steps of staying calm, analyzing the situation, celebrating small successes, and so on.

Take Action!

WRITING TOPICS

Write about one of the following topics. For information about essay structure, see the Writing Workshops on pages 148 to 157. Before handing in your work, refer to the Writing Checklist on the inside back cover.

1 A Physical Ordeal

Describe a difficult physical or mental ordeal that you or someone you know went through. (Consider times in the past when you were challenged by an important or difficult event. It could be an activity—such as mountain biking, or an emotional trauma—such as a break-up.) What happened? What steps did you take to get through the ordeal? Include descriptive words and phrases.

2 The Reasons for Risk-Taking

Why do some people take dangerous risks? Think of two or three reasons for risk-taking behaviour. For your supporting ideas, you can refer to "International Thrill-Seekers." Also provide examples from the media, from your life, or from the lives of people you know.

3 Survival Lessons

Should schools provide compulsory courses on survival skills? Why or why not? Provide at least two reasons for your opinion. You can quote from this chapter's survival essays and discuss the information in the *Surviving a Plane Crash* video.

SPEAKING TOPICS

Prepare a presentation about one of the following topics. For details about preparing a speaking presentation, see Appendix 1 on page 174.

Need help with pronunciation? Visit the Companion Website and try the Pronunciation Workshops.

1 Emotional Survival Video

In a video or in a short performance, explain the steps people should take when they have an emotional crisis. Provide specific examples from your life or from the life of someone you know. For example, explain how someone can survive a break-up, a significant move to a new place, a failure in school, a public humiliation, being bullied, a heavy work and school schedule, a divorce, or the loss of a friend. Choose a topic that you know about. Provide at least three steps, and give examples to explain them.

Remind students to try the Pronunciation Workshops on the Companion Website.

2 Risk-Takers

Discuss risk-taking behaviour. Talk about one or more of the following.

- Present three possible reasons for risk-taking behaviour.
- Describe the different types of risks that people take, and provide examples for each category. (Use your own categories—do not copy the ideas from "International Thrill-Seekers.")
- Discuss the importance and value of taking risks.
- Describe someone you know who takes risks.

MEDIA LINK

Watch a television show or movie about survival. For example, you could watch a movie such as *Buried*, *127 Hours*, *Into the Wild*, or *The Panic Room*. You could also watch a movie about surviving a break-up or the death of a loved one. In an essay or in a speaking presentation, explain what the show or film demonstrates about survival. What steps did the main character go through? Make a connection between the message in the movie and at least one of the readings in this chapter.

Revising and Editing

REVISE FOR A MAIN IDEA
EDIT FOR SUBJECT-VERB AGREEMENT AND WORD CHOICE

The following short essay contains supporting details, but it has no main idea. The main idea is expressed in a topic sentence. Read the essay and follow these steps:

1. Underline the thesis statement. Then add a good topic sentence to the two body paragraphs. (For more information about topic sentences, see Writing Workshop 1, page 153.)
2. Underline and correct nine errors. There are eight errors with subject-verb agreement and one error with word choice.

Introduction

In high schools, students learn about science, mathematics, and literature. Students play team sports and exercise regularly in a gym. Some high schools have great art and music programs. High schools should also teach survival skills.

Topic sentence 1

First, students should know what to do when there is a fire in a crowded place.

The Revising and Editing sections help your students prepare for writing tests, including Benchmark and TESOL tests. You can ask students to do the activities with a partner and to share ideas.

Often, during such events, people smell the smoke and panic. Everyone ~~stare~~ stares and nobody ~~react~~ reacts. The majority of people ~~rushes~~ rush to the main exit. They don't look for emergency or back exits. Thus, during a fire in a crowded place, there ~~is~~ are often many deaths because people jam the main entrance in a panic to leave the premises. Also, smoke inhalation ~~contribute~~ contributes to many deaths.

Topic sentence 2

Additionally, students should learn about water safety.

You can ask students to remove this activity and hand it in. Note that in the student books, pages are perforated.

Rip currents are quite common and extremely dangerous, yet most beach goers don't know what to do when a strong current pulls them out to sea. Neither a lifeguard nor a strong swimmer necessarily ~~have~~ has the ability to save someone from a rip current. Teachers should ~~learn~~ teach students what to do: swim to the side until they are out of the current. Also, students should learn CPR so that they can save someone who is drowning.

Conclusion

An emergency situation makes people ~~panics~~ panic. Only a small percentage of the population ~~act~~ acts appropriately during a fire or in a strong ocean current. It is best if people have a plan of action in their heads before a dangerous situation occurs. Then they have a much better chance of surviving.

Grammar **TIP**

Subject-Verb Agreement

Ensure that your subjects and verbs agree. Be careful with expressions of quantity. For example, the verb agrees with the noun that follows the words *of the*.

The majority of the swimmers **panic**.
The majority of the crowd **panics**.

To learn more about subject-verb agreement, see Unit 1 in *Avenues 3: English Grammar*.

COMPANION WEB+ To practise vocabulary from this chapter, visit the Companion Website.

CHAPTER 2

"The test of courage comes when we are in the minority. The test of tolerance comes when we are in the majority."

– RALPH W. SOCKMAN, AUTHOR

Tolerance

What are some national stereotypes? What contributes to intolerance? This chapter looks at how people view each other.

START UP

National Identity

Discuss the UN joke with students. Are the stereotypes listed in the joke widely believed? Also ask students to debate if such jokes are offensive. They should explain why or why not.

Read the following joke, which was widely shared online.

> The United Nations attempted to conduct a worldwide telephone survey. The only question was: "Would you please give your honest opinion about solutions to the food shortage in the rest of the world?" The survey was a failure for the following reasons.
>
> In Eastern Europe, they didn't know what "honest" meant. In Western Europe, they didn't know what "shortage" meant. In Africa, they didn't know what "food" meant. In China, they didn't know what "opinion" meant. In the Middle East, they didn't know what "solution" meant. In South America, they didn't know what "please" meant. In the US, they didn't know what "the rest of the world" meant. And in Canada, they hung up because they couldn't understand the researcher's accent.

Stereotypes—quick and simplistic generalizations—become the easy way to sum up an entire culture. What are some stereotypes about people in North America? Create a list of stereotypes about Canadians, Americans, and Mexicans.

Canadians	Americans	Mexicans

DISCUSSION AND WRITING

- Why do people create stereotypes about other nationalities? What are the possible reasons for stereotyping others?
- What problems can stereotyping cause?

READING STRATEGY

Students can visit the Companion Website to practise their reading comprehension. Questions for all readings are structured to help students do better in their reading tests, including Benchmark and TESOL tests.

Summarizing

When you summarize, you condense a message into its basic elements. You restate what the author said using your own words.

How to Summarize

- Identify the author and the title of the source that you are summarizing. Later, you will include this information in the first sentence of your summary.
- Read the original text carefully. You will need a complete picture before you begin to write. Highlight the main and supporting ideas.
- Write your summary. You can keep common words and the names of people and places, but find synonyms for other words. Do not copy any phrases from the text.
- Verify that you used your own words and did not copy any sentences from the text. Also, do not include your opinion unless specifically asked to do so.

Important: Avoid Plagiarism

If you copy phrases and sentences from another work, it is considered plagiarism. When you use the exact words of an author, put them in quotation marks and mention the source.

COMPANION WEB+ Visit the Companion Website to prepare for your reading tests. Online questions for all readings are structured to help you practise reading strategies.

PRACTICE

Answers will vary.

Write a one- or two-sentence summary of the following paragraph.

> According to Statistics Canada, car crashes are the main cause of fatalities among youths aged sixteen to twenty-four. In 2012, their average annual motor vehicle accident rate was higher than the rate for all other age groups combined. Although younger drivers spend less time on the road than their elders, they are more likely to engage in reckless behaviour. Over 90 percent of young drivers report driving over the speed limit, and three-quarters of the youths admitted that they try to beat a yellow light.
>
> Michelle Roberge, "Youths and Driving"

Risk taking and lack of experience combine to make driving a deadly activity for many of the nation's youths. In fact, car accidents are the major killer of people in their late teens and early twenties.

READING 2.1

Heather O'Neill is a Montreal-based writer of the award-winning novel, *Lullabies for Little Criminals*. The next essay examines a cross-border adventure. As you read, notice the words in bold and guess their meanings.

Riff-Raff

BY HEATHER O'NEILL

1 I was nineteen and I lived in Montreal. I was in a horrible relationship with a boy named Leroy. He would cheat on me and be mean to me in every possible way. I prayed that I would have the strength to leave him, but I never did. I was almost at the end of my first year at McGill University when I met another boy on the school steps.

2 He was an American student. We hung around together for the last two weeks of school, and then he told me he was going back to New Mexico. He said that I should come and spend the summer with him. He gave me the address on a piece of paper. Then he kissed me, and the kiss was like spinach to Popeye. I was suddenly filled with the determination to change my life. The only way to get away from my mean Canadian boyfriend, I decided, was to **flee** to the American Southwest.

3 I told my dad about my great escape plan, and he bought me a Greyhound bus ticket to New Mexico. He'd been **begging** me to leave Leroy for years. I had saved up $100 from working at a restaurant. I went to the bank and exchanged it for $80 American currency. That would be enough to feed myself over the three-day bus ride and keep me going until I got work in New Mexico.

4 I packed up everything I owned, which was almost nothing, into a duffel bag. I kissed my roommates adieu and walked to the bus station. I was so excited. It was the first time I was going anyplace on my own. I was off to have the great American Experience. I felt like **Jack Kerouac**.

Jack Kerouac: the author of *On the Road*, a book about a trip across the US

5 When the bus reached St. Louis, I went to use the pay phone at the back of the station to call my dad. As I took out my wallet to find change, two men came up behind me and **shoved** me into the restroom. One of them banged my head against the wall and **yanked** my wallet from my hand. Then they ran out before I could figure out what had happened. I was so sad. It was all the money that I had in the world.

6 A few minutes later, I was sitting in a little office with the bus driver and a police officer. Some other people who worked at the bus station came into the office to take a look at me. "A Canadian," they kept saying.

7 A woman who worked at the canteen **squinted** at me and shook her head, as if I were a three-year-old that a drunken mother had let play outside unsupervised. "What is a wee Canadian doing here all by herself?" she asked. "That ain't right."

8 They treated me like I was innocent as freshly driven snow. Because I was from Canada, they seemed to think that I had never been exposed to riff-raff. I was like the dodo birds that lacked natural predators and so stood meekly as Europeans clubbed them to death. Listening to too much **Anne Murray** had made me soft.

Anne Murray: Canadian singer from Nova Scotia

9 "Don't you have a boyfriend to travel around wid you?" the bus driver asked. "If you was an American, you'd have a big-assed boyfriend. He'd carry around a baseball bat and, boom, he'd a popped off the heads of them thieves. An American man would've never let that happen to you."

10 "Yeah, what's your Canadian boyfriend doing up there?" the cop said, **grinning.** "Building himself an igloo. There's a time and place for building igloos, yes sir."

11 "There's a time and a place for peacekeeping," said a janitor, **leaning** on his mop.

12 A man with an iguana on his shoulder came into the office. He was holding my wallet. He had found it tossed on the floor by the entrance of the bus station. I opened it up. All that was left was a $5 Canadian bill that I hadn't changed into American money.

13 "What's that?" the janitor asked. "Monopoly money?" Everyone in the office **chuckled.**

14 "Well, at least you can buy yourself Park Place wid that," the bus driver said. "Come on, sweetie, let's get back on the bus."

15 All the other passengers were in their seats waiting for us. I walked back to my seat with tears in my eyes, having no idea how I was supposed to eat for the next two days. I **slouched** in my seat, dejected.

16 Then the bus driver picked up the loudspeaker. "Now listen here," the bus driver said. "This poor sweet little Canadian came down to this country to visit us, to come and see what America is all about. And we go and mug her in the bathroom. She's going to go back and tell every single Canadian that we are animals. Now I am passing around my hat. I am putting $5 in it. I suggest that all of you do the same. And then she will know that Americans can also be generous."

17 The bus driver passed his hat around the bus, and almost everyone put money in it. When it came back to me, I had $75. That turned out to be one of the best summers of my life. I have one photograph of me in New Mexico. In the picture, I'm grinning wildly and look only about sixteen years old. I look as innocent as freshly driven snow.

Students can read the essay in class or for homework. There are additional questions in the Student Section of the Companion Website. You can verify if students have read the essay by checking their scores with the grade tracker.

(927 words)

Source: O'Neill, Heather. "Riff-Raff," *Walrus*. The Walrus Foundation, July/Aug. 2010. Web.

COMPANION WEB+ Visit the Companion Website to practise using vivid verbs.

VOCABULARY AND COMPREHENSION

1 The following action verbs appear in bold in the essay. The paragraph numbers are in parentheses. Write the correct verb under each photo. Read the words in context before you make your guesses.

flee (2)	shove (5)	squint (7)	lean (11)	slouch (15)
beg (3)	yank (5)	~~grin (10)~~	chuckle (13)	

EXAMPLE: grin

a) slouch

b) shove

c) chuckle

d) yank

e) squint

f) beg

g) lean

h) flee

2 Often, writers use slang—or street language—to make dialogue sound authentic. Rewrite the underlined words in standard (conventional) English.

EXAMPLE: "What is a wee Canadian doing here all by herself?" she asked. — young; little

a) "That ain't right." — isn't

b) "Don't you have a boyfriend to travel around wid you?" — with

c) "If you was an American, you'd have a big-assed boyfriend." — were / large, strong

d) "He'd carry around a baseball bat and, boom, he'd a popped off the heads of them thieves." — would have hit the

3 At the bus station, what stereotypes do the Americans have about Canadians? List at least three stereotypes.

Canadians are innocent and naive (para. 8), not tough (para. 9), live in igloos (para. 10), are peaceful and not aggressive (para. 11).

COMPANION WEB+ Answer additional questions for all the reading and listening activities. You can also access audio and video clips online.

4 What is this narrative essay about? Write a two-sentence summary.

A Canadian girl was travelling on a bus to New Mexico, and on the way, she was robbed in a rest-stop bathroom. Showing that not all Americans are mean, the driver and passengers collected money and gave it to the girl.

WATCHING

You can assign the video in class or for homework. There are additional comprehension questions in the Student Section of the Companion Website.

How Canadians See Americans

How do Canadians really see Americans? Watch and find out.

VOCABULARY AND COMPREHENSION

1 When the host says Canadians feel "smug," she means they are ________.

(a.) confident of their superiority   b. afraid   c. amused

2 What course does Tracey Rainey teach? — Canadian studies

3 According to the video, how do Canadians view Americans? List at least five adjectives.

Answers will vary, but may include: pompous, ignorant, addicted to war, discriminatory, pushy, power hungry, arrogant, pathetic, backward, dumb.

4 Do recent immigrants to Canada also have negative feelings about Americans? ☑ Yes ☐ No

5 What is the program *Talking to Americans* about?

Rick Mercer makes fun of Americans by telling them ridiculous things and filming their responses.

6 Gordon Giffin, a former US ambassador, met frustrated Canadians who complained that Americans knew very little about their northern neighbour. What was his response?

He would ask Canadians what they knew about Kansas or other American states.

7 Which nationality gives more to charity? ☐ Canadians ☑ Americans

8 According to the video, who works harder? ☐ Canadians ☑ Americans

9 Generally, how do Americans see Canadians?

They make positive comments about Canadians; for example, that Canadians are generous, friendly, good neighbours, and quiet.

DISCUSSION

After assigning "Small Differences, Large Conflicts," ask students how the film relates to the reading.

Refer to your answers in the Start Up. Were any of your stereotypes about Americans mentioned in the film? If so, which ones?

READING STRATEGY

Students can visit the Companion Website to practise their reading comprehension. Questions for all readings are structured to help students do better in their reading tests, including Benchmark and TESOL tests.

Identifying Main Ideas

The main idea is the principal focus of a text. It may be expressed in the title, introduction, or conclusion. Look for a **thesis statement**, which is a sentence that expresses the main idea. The thesis is usually at the end of an introductory paragraph.

An essay is supported with facts and examples. Often, each body paragraph has a **topic sentence**. The topic sentence supports the thesis, and it expresses the main idea of the paragraph.

Sometimes writers do not write thesis statements or topic sentences. If you cannot find a statement with the main idea, then ask yourself *who*, *what*, *when*, *where*, *why*, and *how* questions. In a sentence or two, you can write your own statement of the main idea.

COMPANION WEB+ Visit the Companion Website to prepare for your reading tests. Online questions for all readings are structured to help you practise reading strategies.

READING 2.2

Paul K. Kim is a lawyer and an avid traveller. Read about how small differences contribute to significant conflicts.

Small Differences, Large Conflicts

BY PAUL K. KIM

1 In Greek mythology, Narcissus was a vain hero who fell in love with his own reflection. Sigmund Freud adopted the term "narcissism" to refer to intense self-love. Then, during the First World War, Sigmund Freud's idea, called "narcissism of the minor difference," encapsulated the concept that our most intense hatred is directed at people who most closely resemble us. Moreover, we feel inordinately proud about the small markers that distinguish us from the hated group. Travelling to infamously divided or occupied lands, it occurred to me how so many hostile pairs are, to outsiders, so similar.

2 In Israel, I travelled among Jewish Israelis and Muslim Arabs. Conservative factions of both groups—who often regard each other with unabashed hostility—have similar cultures and beliefs. For instance, both groups have relatively severe rules on gender, such as men and women worshipping apart. Neither group eats pork, both have dietary certification regimes (kosher and halal), and their languages are not horribly far apart. Indeed, many Jews and Arabs belong to the

Old Arab men playing backgammon in Jerusalem, Israel

same Semitic ethnic group. Is there any doubt that some Jews look like Arabs and some Arabs look like Jews, however offensive it may be to point this out to either such subgroup? Yes, they have different beliefs, yet even their religions have many shared points. They both have one god and believe that they come from the same family of Abraham.

3 Ever since 1947, when India was partitioned into two separate nations—India and Pakistan—the two nations have clashed. (Later, in 1971, Bangladesh split away from Pakistan.) Although Indians are primarily Hindus, and Pakistanis are primarily Muslims, the hostile neighbours share remarkably similar tastes. Pakistan's Punjab and Singh provinces have highly seasoned cuisine that is similar to that in Northern India. And according to the *Times of India*, Pakistan is one of Bollywood's top five markets. Also, the British game cricket is deeply loved in both nations. In March 2011, the presidents of the two countries sat together at a major cricket match as a rare show of solidarity. Nevertheless, these neighbours often eye each other with great suspicion.

4 Even when the religion is shared, minor differences in beliefs can exacerbate conflict. Some Iranians hate Israel and Zionists, but for whom do they reserve a perhaps deeper well of hate and mistrust? Sunni Saudis, who are fellow Muslims! Of course, most outsiders don't even know the distinction between Sunni and Shia Islam. And what minority in Iran suffers from the greatest discrimination? Probably the Afghanis face the greatest intolerance, yet they speak the same language and share much of the same culture as the Iranians.

5 In Cyprus, I viewed the Greeks and Turks. Despite all of the conflict between North and South Cyprus, a Greek Cypriot confirmed to us that the two communities are almost indistinguishable. For instance, he claims that it is almost impossible to physically identify a Cypriot as Greek or Turk. He explained that the two communities have intermarried for hundreds of years, often dividing up the children of a mixed marriage so that the boys became Christian and the girls Muslim, or vice versa. In fact, prior to the conflicts of the last forty years, Cypriots didn't even think of themselves as Greek or Turk, but only as Christian or Muslim—simply a difference of faith rather than ethnic identity. Both cultures dine on the small appetizers called meze, sip an anise liqueur called ouzo or raki, and drink a thick sludgy coffee called Turkish coffee or Greek coffee.

6 Sometimes, hostility between groups is so intense, it results in massacres. During Rwanda's 1992 genocide, many Tutsis murdered their Hutu neighbours. Tribal differences, so important to the people involved, seem incomprehensible to outsiders. In Sri Lanka, the Tamils share an island paradise with the Sinhalese. Yet intense jealousy and resentment have led to bloody conflicts. In Northern Ireland, the Catholics and Protestants bombed each other for decades, yet they have a shared history, appearance, and lifestyle.

7 In an essay for *Slate*, author Christopher Hitchens says, "One of the most unobtrusive differences in the world—the line that separates French from Flemish-speaking Belgians—is about to be forcefully reasserted in a bid to split

Belgium in two. If this secession occurs, then the headquarters country of NATO and the European Union will rather narcissistically cease to exist, undone by one of the smallest distinctions of all."

8 Perhaps, in the end, it could be all those years of living together, and all the similarities, that generate the antagonism. Cohabitation creates the opportunity for regretful incidents and periods of hostility for which grudges are held. Neighbours, with whom there were centuries of trade, cultural exchange, and even intermarriage, become mortal enemies. These opposing cultures are so similar, and to foster a sense of uniqueness in national identity, there is a constant need to emphasize differences **lest** identity become muddled.

lest: in case

Point out that *Homo sapiens* is the name of the species and as such, it is singular.

9 Christopher Hitchens points out that *Homo sapiens*, unlike other mammals, has "an amazing lack of variation between its different branches ... If we were dogs, we would be the same breed." Still, humans manage to find justifications for conflict and hate based on ridiculously minor differences in beliefs, lifestyle, language, or appearance. Perhaps we need to forget the past, focus on similarities with our neighbours, and spend more time thinking about how to work together to promote our mutual well-being.

(892 words)

Source: Adapted from Kim, Paul K. "Greeks and Turks." *Paul's Travel Blog*. 2008. Web.
Other sources: Goleman, Daniel. "Amid Ethnic Wars, Psychiatrists Seek Roots of Conflicts." *New York Times* 2 Aug. 1994. Web.
Hitchens, Christopher. "The Narcissism of the Small Difference." *Slate*. Slate Group, 28 June 2010. Web.

Students can read the essay in class or for homework. There are additional questions in the Student Section of the Companion Website. You can verify if students have read the essay by checking their scores with the grade tracker.

COMPREHENSION: IDENTIFYING MAIN IDEAS

1 Look at the introduction, and highlight the thesis statement. The thesis statement expresses the main or principal idea of the essay.

2 Underline the topic sentence in paragraphs 2 to 6 and 8. Be careful: the topic sentence may not be the first sentence in the paragraph.

3 In paragraph 7, what is Hitchens alluding to when he refers to "one of the most unobtrusive differences of all"?

Language

4 In paragraph 7, what is Hitchens' main point?

A difference in languages could cause the division of a nation, Belgium.

5 In paragraph 9, what point is Hitchens making about humans and dogs?

a. Humans are much more intelligent than dogs.
(b.) Dogs have much more variation between each other than humans do.
c. Humans, like dogs, need to learn to get along in harmony.

6 According to the author, why do small differences generate large conflicts?

People hurt each other and hold grudges. To create unique identities, groups may emphasize their differences from their neighbours.

7 How does the essay end?

(a.) with a suggestion   b. with a prediction   c. with a quotation

DISCUSSION

Does your region or country have conflicts with other regions or nations? If so, why?

SPEAKING

An International Hotel

Work with a team of about four students. Imagine that you have just been hired to manage an international hotel that is in your city or town. Discuss how to solve the following problems. Make a list of suggestions. You have about $5,000 to spend to solve the problems.

1 On *tripadvisor.com*, a review website, sixty people reviewed the hotel, and the average rating is 2 out of 5. Some guests made horrible comments.

2 Four of your most frequent business guests are very rude and racist. The men make loud comments, drink too much, and harass the female employees. The hotel's staff hates to serve them, and chambermaids are anxious about cleaning the rooms of the men. However, the guests travel together (they work in the same company), and they visit the hotel at least twice a month, often for three or four days. They rent four rooms and spend a lot of money at the hotel.

3 Many guests complain about the noise and disruption caused by the hotel bar in the lobby. Inebriated guests sing and shout in hallways. Some guests mention the loud music coming from the bar as their reason for never returning.

4 Guests are bored. Recently, some guests complained that there is nothing to do except watch TV or sit by the pool. You want to offer activities that will appeal to all your international clients.

LISTENING

You can assign the listening activity in class or for homework. There are additional comprehension questions in the Student Section of the Companion Website.

Gay Heroes

Do gay public figures have a moral obligation to come out? Listen as a panel from *Q* debates the issue.

COMPREHENSION

1 What prompted Rick Mercer's rant?

The suicide of a gay teenager

2 What is Mercer's point?

Gay public figures should come out.

3 What is the position of *The Globe and Mail* editorialist Karim Bardeesy?

Gay public figures should not be pressured or forced to come out. They might not be ready to come out. Everyone has multiple identities and should not have to prioritize one identity.

4 What is the position of Brenda Cossman?

Because of recent suicides of gay teens, she thinks that public figures should discuss their sexual orientation. It helps provide gay and lesbian teens with role models.

5 Does Cossman believe that public figures should be forced to come out? ☐ Yes ☑ No

6 What is New York mayor Ed Koch's position?

If politicians discuss their sexual orientation, it will become an issue and a constant discussion topic.

READING 2.3 In the following essay, Robert Fulford examines some profound changes in our nation and ourselves since 2001. As you read, identify main ideas.

How the World Has Changed

BY ROBERT FULFORD

Technically, *media* is the plural form of *medium*. However, many newspapers, magazines, and websites use *media* as a collective singular noun that encompasses both print and electronic media. In paragraph 1, *media* is used as a plural noun: "The mass media recovered their footing." Decide which usage you prefer and ask students to consistently consider *media* as singular or plural.

1 Nothing will ever be the same, some people said, but that turned out not to be quite true. A few months after 9/11, when even the most persistent of the fires at the Twin Towers were at last extinguished, the everyday flow of life picked up. The mass media recovered their footing. Soon politics in the US and Canada hardened into an intensified version of the familiar left-right struggles of the 1990s. While thousands of people bitterly mourned relatives and friends who were lost at Ground Zero, there were probably millions of others who turned away from their TV sets with a sharpened sense of life's cruel limits and a fresh awareness that even on the most beautiful day in early autumn, there is always the possibility that a catastrophe is waiting to happen.

2 Many tried to get over 9/11, to move on—and some believed they succeeded. Rich bankers discovered, to their delight, ways to get still richer. The sex lives of politicians recaptured the tabloid headlines. On college campuses, beer remained, just as before, a cherished focus of student life. People resumed their complaints over gas prices. The fall of the stock market in 2008 seized as much of our attention as the fall of the World Trade Center. Even so, a great deal has, in fact, changed. We have grown more cautious, more addicted to security, and more militant, and principles once considered firm have proven shaky. Our mindset, the standard equipment we bring to each new situation, has been fundamentally altered in different ways.

War and Peace

3 In the spring of 2011, we demonstrated how much we've changed in one crucial way. Canadians joined Americans and Europeans in a NATO mission to assist the Libyan rebels—and did it with hardly a moment's hesitation. In a stunningly brief period, talk about an innocent-sounding "no-fly zone" was followed by hundreds of bombing raids. Notably, no sizable group of Americans or Canadians objected. We were all appalled by the clowning Gaddafi; we were sure which side deserved our help, so we went briefly to war.

skirmish: conflict

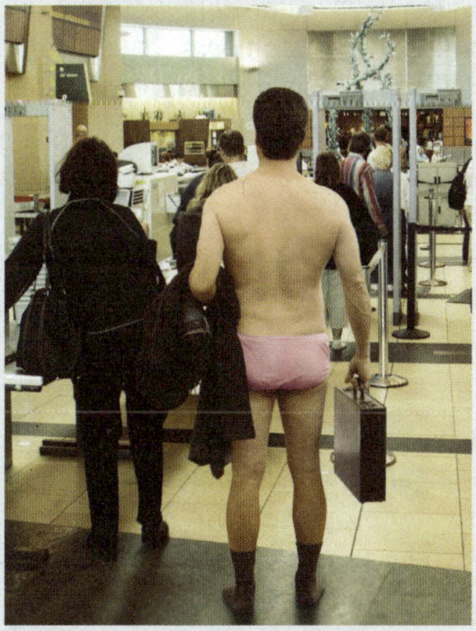

4 New and unexpected choices have been made. Our interest in maintaining our safety since 9/11 has weakened our interest in civil rights. When weighing the needs of security against traditional liberties, the public (perhaps after a brief moral **skirmish**) comes down firmly on the side of security. We are much more likely than before to acknowledge that, for everyone's sake, the government probably has to do what it does.

5 Every airport has become a theatre where we act out the details of our pathetic acquiescence. Herded by insolent guards, made to wait meekly for interminable periods, submitting to bizarre indignities, we tell ourselves that it doesn't matter all that much and perhaps it has to be this way, for security's sake, even as we watch a great-grandmother struggle out of her wheelchair to prove her underwear contains nothing combustible. Those of us who once looked forward to a plane trip don't bother to tell children how it used to be. They wouldn't believe us—and would find it hard to understand how much we have changed.

Multiculturalism in Question

6 At the end of the twentieth century, multiculturalism was an amiable, clearly hopeful idea. In the twenty-first century, multiculturalism has become shrouded in suspicion. We now speak of it warily as something that must be "handled" with care. Canadians, who once took it for granted that we know how to do this sort of thing, discovered that we don't. "Tolerance" is a much-loved word with a noble history, but it no longer does the job. For instance, these days Muslims sometimes claim they are the victims of Islamophobia. That word was seldom used before 9/11. Also, before 9/11, discussion of the **burka** was rare; many did not know what the word meant. Back in the 1990s, no one would have believed that Canadians would soon find themselves debating whether the nation should allow people to wear this or that garment on public streets. Most of us would have dismissed it as a personal matter, beyond the realm of public discussion.

burka: a loose garment, worn by Muslim women, that covers the body and face, with an opening for the eyes

Missiles, Human and Robotic

7 The nature of war has also changed radically. Suicide bombing, which was unknown in Islamic societies until the 1980s, was discouraged by most religious authorities. Today it's impossible to talk about the warriors of the Islamic jihad without mentioning those lonely young men (and a few women) who decide they can give meaning to their wretched lives by strapping on a suicide belt and going forth for one moment of glory. About three thousand terrorists, according to the best estimate, have died as suicide bombers in the past thirty years. With these human missiles, bin Laden turned American ingenuity and industry in on itself. In an unprecedented triumph of symbolism, he used one of the great American achievements, the commercial aircraft, to destroy an equally significant American success, the skyscraper.

8 The more we know of suicide bombers, the more trouble we have maintaining a good opinion of humanity. All of them are backed by elaborate and well-trained teams of instigators, financial backers, and coaches, several of whom have admitted with chilling frankness that they would never dream of killing themselves. The bombers are also backed, in many cases, by proud families, their mothers in the forefront, awaiting praise and financial compensation.

Predator drone

9 Partly in response to those human missiles, the US has developed a non-human missile of even greater force. Pilotless aircraft were barely in use in 2001. Now they routinely fly far out of sight, photograph on-the-ground details, send the pictures back to controllers in Nevada, then rain sudden death on selected targets. Drones and suicide bombers have major differences, but they are equally effective at sowing terror. The drones are expensive where the suicide bombers are cheap. They are usually precise in their effects where the suicide bombers kill at random. While the operators of the drones see only obscure figures on television monitors, the suicide bombers see many of their victims up close, for a moment. Each method seeks to deal sharp, swift blows.

The West's Future in Question

10 The West embodies, on its best days, the principles articulated in the eighteenth century by the Enlightenment, principles that are indispensable to our own lives—free speech, competitive politics, private property, and independent judges. Today, the West finds itself in an uncommonly weak position. It took success for granted too long and borrowed too much against it. Most of the democracies now suffer from disastrously wrong-headed national budgeting,

a persistent economic slump, and politicians driven to distraction by partisanship. With the help of the external threat from radicals, we may have reached one of those places where a civilization has to find a way to revive itself, or quietly accept that it has permanently lost its way.

(1139 words)

Source: Fulford, Robert. "How Can We Expect to Go On After This?" *National Post*. Postmedia Network, 10 Sept. 2011. Web.

Students can read the essay in class or for homework. There are additional questions in the Student Section of the Companion Website. You can verify if students have read the essay by checking their scores with the grade tracker.

Ask students to read the thesis and topic sentences out loud. Point out that such sentences of main idea sum up what the text is about.

COMPANION WEB+ Get more reading comprehension practice. Read "The Egalitarian Brain" and answer the comprehension questions.

For the discussion and writing question, possible answers are: there are better cellphones, e-readers, and technology that helps with revolutions (as in the Arab Spring); milder winters in the north (even if the flipside is global warming); more tolerance of homosexuality, etc.

COMPREHENSION: IDENTIFYING MAIN IDEAS

1. Look in the introductory section and highlight the thesis statement, which sums up the main idea of the essay. It may be in paragraph 1 or 2.
2. Underline the topic sentence in paragraphs 3 to 10.
3. How has the world changed since 2011, according to the author? Using your own words, summarize the author's main arguments. Follow the summary guidelines on page 23, and use the present perfect tense at least three times in your summary.

Answers will vary. Possible answer: North Americans have become less peaceful and have accepted, without very much questioning, the use of force in other nations. Citizens accept a lack of privacy and have shown less interest in civil rights. People have learned to tolerate silly rules in airports. They have also become less tolerant. The nature of war has changed with suicide bombing and drones.

DISCUSSION AND WRITING

How has the world improved during your lifetime? Brainstorm and list at least five ways in which the world has become a better place.

Grammar TIP

Present Perfect

The present perfect tense is used to

1) describe an action that began in the past and continues to the present time;

Since 2001, intolerance **has become** more common.

2) describe actions that occurred at unspecified past times.

I **have seen** the latest iPad, but I do not own one.

To learn more about the present perfect tense, see Unit 3 in *Avenues 3: English Grammar*.

Vocabulary BOOST

Verb Variety

Use the verb ***say*** in direct and indirect quotations. In direct quotations, follow ***say*** with a comma and the actual words that were said, and place those words inside quotation marks.

Fulford **says**, "The nature of war has also changed radically."

He **said** that people have become less tolerant.

You ***tell*** somebody something. The verb *tell* is followed by a noun or pronoun.

Aboud **told** the journalist about her experiment.

Also use ***tell*** in such expressions as *tell a lie*, *tell the truth*, and *tell a secret*.

PRACTICE

1 Fill in the blanks with the appropriate form of either *say* or *tell*.

Often, politicians ___tell___ a lie when they ___say___ that they will solve the nation's problems. They don't ___tell___ us about their inability to act because of financial restrictions. They rarely ___say___, "We must raise taxes to pay for our promises."

Answers will vary.

2 Write at least three synonyms for the following terms.

a) said: mentioned; stated; commented; observed

b) asked: questioned; queried; interrogated; inquired

3 Fill in the blanks with appropriate verbs. Do not use *say* or *tell*, and do not use the same verb twice.

Answers will vary.

Our leaders always ___promise___ to make positive changes. They ___warn___ us about the consequences of voting for the other parties. They rarely ___mention___ that all political parties have similar problems. They don't ___explain___ how to end corruption. They rarely ___admit___ that there is corruption in their own parties. Citizens should ___question___ their local political candidates and they should ___expect___ clear answers.

To learn more about word choice, see Unit 12 in *Avenues 3: English Grammar*.

Take Action!

WRITING TOPICS

Write about one of the following topics. For information about paragraph and essay structure, see the Writing Workshops on pages 148 to 157. Before handing in your work, refer to the Writing Checklist on the inside back cover.

1 Compare Places

Compare your country with another nation or compare two provinces or states. How are they similar or different? Do they have conflicts based on small differences? You can include anecdotes about your personal experiences. Also refer to readings or the video in this chapter.

2 Nationalism

Define nationalism. Then explain how nationalism can be harmful or helpful. Provide two or three supporting ideas, and give specific examples to back up your main points. Include information from the readings in this chapter.

3 The World

In an essay, explain how life has become better or worse during your lifetime. Give specific supporting examples from your experiences, from the news, and from readings in this chapter. If you quote from a specific reading, remember to cite the source and to punctuate your quotation correctly.

SPEAKING TOPICS

Prepare a presentation about one of the following topics. For details about preparing a speaking presentation, see Appendix 1 on page 174.

1 Stereotypes

Discuss stereotypes about people from your nation, gender, or religion. You can also discuss stereotypes that are associated with certain professions. Contrast the stereotypes with the reality.

COMPANION WEB+ Need help with pronunciation? Visit the Companion Website and try the Pronunciation Workshops.

2 My Home

Critically evaluate your city, province, state, or country. What are some of the worst problems? What are some of the best features? Provide specific examples and relevant statistics to support your points. If you use outside sources, acknowledge them during your presentation.

Remind students to try the Pronunciation Workshops on the Companion Website.

3 Tolerance

In your life, you have probably heard people make intolerant comments about someone of another religion, nationality, language, sexual orientation, or social class. Consider a specific type of intolerance. Prove that stereotypes about that group are not valid. Then explain how the government, schools, or the media can contribute to creating a more tolerant society. Present specific recommendations.

MEDIA LINK

Watch a movie that deals with the theme of intolerance. For example, you could watch *Brokeback Mountain, Gran Torino, Milk, Fire,* or a classic film such as *To Kill a Mocking Bird*. In an essay or in a speaking presentation, explain what the movie demonstrates about tolerance. Begin with a very brief summary. Then explain the message of the film. Make a connection between the message in the movie and at least one of the readings in this chapter.

Revising and Editing

The Revising and Editing sections at the end of each chapter help your students prepare for writing tests, including Benchmark and TESOL tests. You can ask students to do the activities with a partner and to share ideas.

REVISE FOR ADEQUATE SUPPORT
EDIT FOR VERB TENSE

In an essay, the body paragraphs should have adequate support. Always include specific examples from your life, this book's readings, or events in the media. (For more information about essay structure and adequate support, see Writing Workshops 1 and 2 at the back of this book.)

Practise your revising and editing skills. Read the body paragraphs and follow these steps:

1. Add supporting ideas to the two body paragraphs. You can insert specific examples and anecdotes.
2. Edit for verb tense errors. Underline and correct four errors, not including the example.

Last summer, I <u>was driving</u> (drove) across Canada. I expected the trip to be long and boring, but instead, I had a great time. I met people from Newfoundland

Ask a student to read the paragraphs aloud. Then, after students complete the exercise, ask another student to read them again with the supporting ideas. Students should recognize that specific details make the paragraphs stronger.

You can ask students to remove this activity and hand it in. Note that in the student books, pages are perforated.

to British Columbia, and everywhere they were surprising (surprised) me with their warmth and hospitality. But I also noticed some problems in this country. There are advantages and disadvantages to living in Canada.

Living in Canada has many clear advantages. First, the country boasts some of the most beautiful scenery in the world. There is (are) amazing waterfalls, forests, and mountains. ______________________________

____

____

People from around the world visited (visit) Canada. Tourists enjoy the festivals in the cities and the relatively low crime rates. ______________________________

____

____

On the other hand, like all nations, Canada has problems. People do not really trust the government. There are many allegations of corruption. Also, both federal and provincial governments made (make / have made) some bad decisions.

____

____

Furthermore, the health care system is in crisis. ______________________________

____

____

Unlike many nations, Canada has beautiful seasons, a lot of natural resources, and great landscapes. The country also faces political problems that it must address. Nevertheless, it is a great place to live. An American actress, J. Fonda, once said, "When I'm in Canada, I feel this is what the world should be like."

Grammar TIP

Simple or Progressive Forms

Use the simple tense to discuss current or past facts, habits, or customs. Use the progressive form only when an action is (or was) in progress at a particular moment.

Tourist are liking (like) to see glaciers. These days, ice melts (is melting) in the Arctic.

To learn more about verb tenses, see Unit 2 in *Avenues 3: English Grammar*.

COMPANION web+ To practise vocabulary from this chapter, visit the Companion Website.

CHAPTER 3

"Biology gives you a brain. Life turns it into a mind."

– JEFFREY EUGENIDES, WRITER

Mysterious Minds

How does the mind process what the eye sees? How does memory work? This chapter examines facets of our mysterious minds. It also looks at the importance of our memories to provide us with life lessons.

START UP

Brain Games

Try the following puzzles. Then share answers with a partner.

Students can measure both tables, or they can outline the top of one of the tables on a thin piece of paper, and move it over the other table to see for themselves.

1 Which table would fit through a door more easily?

A. **B.**

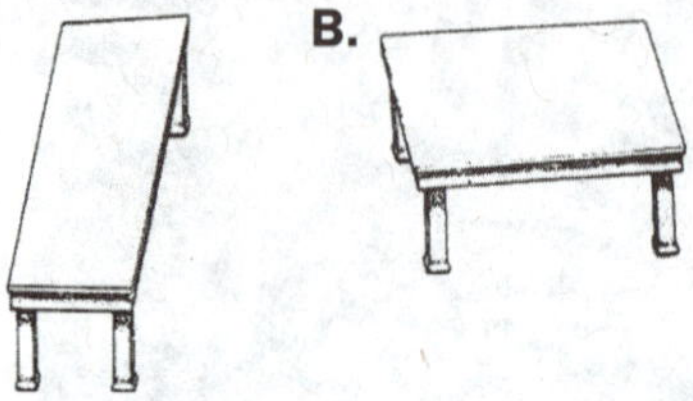

Source: Shepard, R. N. "Turning the Tables." *Mind Sights: Original Visual Illusions, Ambiguities, and other Anomalies.* NY: WH Freeman and Company, 1990. Print.

Answer: Both tables are the same size.

2 What word do you see?

Answer: LIFT (The letters are in the white space.)

3 Which image is the real "loonie"? Do not cheat and look at a coin! Make a guess based on your memory of handling coins every day. E

A **B** **C** **D** **E**

People tend to forget the 9 in 91, 92, etc.

People tend to see "of" as one symbol.

For question 6, give students the clue: My Very Educated Mother Just Served Us Nachos.

4 How many 9s appear between 1 and 100? 19

5 How many *f*'s do you see in this sentence? 10

After I finished reading the last pages of the terrific novel of my friend, I felt like drinking two cups of coffee.

6 What are the names of the eight planets in the solar system? List them quickly in order of the nearest to the farthest from the sun.

Mercury, Venus, Earth, Mars, Jupiter, Saturn, Uranus, and Neptune

For question 7, none of the words appears in the passage. Interpreting the story as one about medicine makes it more understandable, but it also contributes to inaccurate recall.

7 Read the following passage carefully.

Dr. Rashid Kumar, an experienced surgeon, carefully scrubbed her hands. Then she snapped on her rubber gloves. An elderly man lay sleeping on the table, under anaesthesia. Dr. Kumar carefully made an incision on the lower left side of the man's abdomen. An eager assistant gently pulled back the skin to expose the bowels. The medical team gasped. Attached to the man's intestine was a large growth of about 10 cm in circumference. It appeared to be malignant. An entire section of the bowels would have to be removed.

Now cover the text with one hand. With the other hand, underline the words below that appear in the passage. (Do not look back at the text!)

clean scalpel patient tumour cancer nurse

READING 3.1

Joseph T. Hallinan was a journalist for *The Wall Street Journal*, and he has won the Pulitzer Prize for Investigative Reporting. Read this excerpt from his book, *Why We Make Mistakes*.

Why We Make Mistakes

Images from the door-change blindness experiment. Source: Adapted, with permission, from Simons, D. J., and D. T. Levin. "Failure to Detect Changes to People during a Real-World Interaction." *Psychonomic Bulletin and Review* 5 (1998): 644-649. Print.

BY JOSEPH T. HALLINAN

1 We all know the cliché "To err is human," and it is true enough. When something goes wrong, the cause is overwhelmingly attributed to human error: airplane crashes (70 percent), car wrecks (90 percent), workplace accidents (also 90 percent). You name it, and humans are usually to blame. Many of our most common errors can be attributed to three things: not really seeing, not really paying attention, and trying to do too many things at once.

2 Every day, we look, but we do not always see. In fact, we often have startling kinds of blindness. One type is called "change blindness." About ten years ago, Daniel Simons and Daniel Levin, of Cornell University, designed an experiment. They had "strangers" on campus ask pedestrians for directions. The experiment involved a twist. As the stranger and the pedestrian talk, they are rudely interrupted by two men who pass between them while carrying a door. The interruption is brief—lasting just one second. But during that second, something important happens. One of the men carrying the door trades places with the "stranger." When the door is gone, the pedestrian is confronted with a different person who continues the conversation as if nothing had happened. Would the pedestrians notice that they were talking to someone new? Only seven of the fifteen pedestrians noticed the change. When the actor dressed as a construction worker, and he was changed for another person dressed in the same clothing, even fewer people noticed the change. Seeing, it turns out, is very hard work.

3 Seeing is especially difficult when people are asked to look for things that usually aren't there. Dr. Jeremy Wolfe, a professor of ophthalmology at Harvard Medical School, has done experiments showing that observers have "quitting thresholds." He asked volunteers to look at busy, filled images and to find a tool, such as a wrench or hammer. If the tool was in the image 50 percent of the time, the volunteers were correct 93 percent of the time. When the tool was rarely present—in one out of a hundred images, their error rate soared. They sped up and quit earlier, spending less time on each image. According to Wolfe, humans are hard-wired to quit early when the target is unlikely to be there. And most of the time, that works well enough.

4 So, what happens if someone's job is to find a gun or a tumour? Both baggage screeners at airports and radiologists at hospitals spend the bulk of their time looking for things they rarely see. In the case of radiologists, routine mammograms reveal tumours just 0.3 percent of the time. In other words, 99.7 percent of the time, radiologists won't find what they are looking for. Not surprisingly, radiologists have considerable error rates. Several studies suggest the "miss" rate hovers in the 30 percent range. In one study, doctors at the Mayo Clinic went back and checked the previous "normal" chest X-rays of patients who subsequently developed lung cancer. What they found was horrifying: up to 90 percent of the tumours were visible in the previous X-rays.

Not only that, the researchers noted, the cancers had been visible "for months or even years." The radiologists had simply missed them.

5 Keep in mind that these are trained professionals dealing with life or death issues. What about you or me? How good are we at seeing the important things around us? Did you try the loonie test [see page 38]? Likely, you don't recognize the correct image even though you handle coins daily. And do you have trouble remembering names? Names are a bit like the features of a loonie. They don't mean much, and as a consequence, we tend to forget or confuse them. When we create passwords, many of us soon can't recall them. For instance, *The New York Times*, whose customers include some of the most well-educated readers in the world, reported that one thousand online readers each week forget their password. By one estimate, up to 80 percent of all calls to corporate computer help desks are for forgotten passwords.

6 There are some tricks that can help us see—and remember—a little more easily. One way to overcome forgetting is to reframe otherwise meaningless information in a way that imbues it with meaning. For instance, try to memorize the following string of meaningless numbers: 218671945. Now break it up into three meaningful segments. There are "two" dates: 1867 and 1945. That makes it much easier to remember, right? If you have to remember words, try using mnemonics. For instance, to memorize the names of the five Great Lakes, use the acronym HOMES, which consists of the first letter of each word: Huron, Ontario, Michigan, Erie, Superior.

7 Finally, it helps to slow down. Multi-tasking is, for most of us, a mirage. Although we think we are focusing on several activities at once, our attention is actually jumping back and forth between the tasks. There are strict limits to the number of things we can do at one time. Consider the case of Captain Robert Loft, the pilot of Eastern Airlines Flight 401. While making his final approach to Miami International Airport, he noticed that the landing gear was down, but the indicator light didn't come on. He circled around, levelled off at one thousand feet, and decided to have a look. He couldn't figure it out, so he called in the first officer, and then the flight engineer. Even a flight mechanic from Boeing was flying that day and he, too, came to take a look. Soon, nobody was flying the plane. It went lower and lower. Suddenly, the captain shouted, "What's happening here?"

8 Those were his last words. Five seconds later, the plane plowed into the Everglades and burst into flames, killing everyone on board. A study later determined that the crew had become so engrossed in the task that they had lost awareness of their situation, all because of a $12 light bulb.

9 The crash wasn't a fluke. The experience of flying a perfectly good airplane into the ground is so common that an engineer from Honeywell coined a term for it: "Controlled Flight into Terrain" (CFIT). It is one of the most lethal hazards in aviation, and accounts for 40 percent of all aircraft accidents. Why? Pilots had "task saturation"—trying to do too many things at one time.

10 Divided attention can produce a dangerous condition known as inattention blindness. In this condition, it is possible for a person to look directly at something and still not see it. For instance, a bus driver near Washington, DC, was talking on a cellphone to his sister when he drove into a bridge and sheared the top of the bus off. Glass

and metal rained down on the passengers. The driver later told investigators that *he had failed to see the bridge*.

11 There are small things we can do to become less error prone. First, we should get enough sleep. Sleepy people make mistakes. It also helps to change our habits and try to look at things afresh. Habit saves us time and mental effort, but it can kill our ability to perceive novel situations. After a while, we see only what we expect to see. Finally, we need to slow down. Multi-tasking is one of the great myths of the modern age.

(1196 words)

Source: Hallinan, Joseph T. *Why We Make Mistakes*. NY: Broadway Books, 2009. Print.

Students can read the essay in class or for homework. There are additional questions in the Student Section of the Companion Website. You can verify if students have read the essay by checking their scores with the grade tracker.

COMPREHENSION

1 Underline the thesis statement. The thesis sums up the main idea of the essay.

2 In paragraph 2, in the "door" experiment, who is not an actor?

a. The man carrying a door

(b.) The person answering the questions

c. The person asking for directions

3 Paragraph 2 describes "change blindness." Why didn't people notice when the stranger changed into another person? Make a guess.

They were probably thinking about other things and not concentrating. People are preoccupied, and they don't really look at the person they are talking to.

4 Why do radiologists often fail to see tumours? Explain the problem.

Radiologists must constantly look for something that is not often there. Most people have quitting thresholds and stop looking for a target that rarely shows up.

5 In paragraph 4, why is the word *normal* in quotation marks?

The X-rays really weren't normal; tumours were visible in most of them.

6 According to the text, what are two strategies that can help people remember? See paragraph 6.

Give meaning to a series of numbers by breaking it into segments. Use acronyms to remember lists of words.

7 Find a word in paragraph 10 that means "sliced; cut off." sheared

8 What point is the writer making about multi-tasking?

It isn't really possible to do several things well at the same time.

Companion Web+ Answer additional questions for all the reading and listening activities. You can also access audio and video clips online.

DISCUSSION AND WRITING

1 Under what circumstances are you most likely to make inattention mistakes? What are some inattention mistakes that you commonly make?

2 Our lives are filled with PIN numbers and passwords. What are some good strategies to remember them?

LISTENING

You can assign the listening activity in class or for homework. There are additional comprehension questions in the Student Section of the Companion Website.

Neuroscience and the Law

What happens to justice when the courts can read your mind? On CBC's *Quirks and Quarks*, Bob McDonald discusses the brain.

COMPREHENSION

1 Fill in the missing words. Be careful of your spelling.

Ladies and Gentlemen of the jury, you are assembled here in the *Quirks and Quarks* courtroom to deliberate over the following legal dilemma. Our judicial system is increasingly faced with a new type of evidence: evidence coming from laboratories and research institutes, evidence that may challenge our concepts of guilt and responsibility. That evidence is emerging from the field of neurobiology, which allows us to look at the brain in much more detail than we ever could before. We're even developing techniques for figuring out what people are thinking, or whether they're telling the truth.

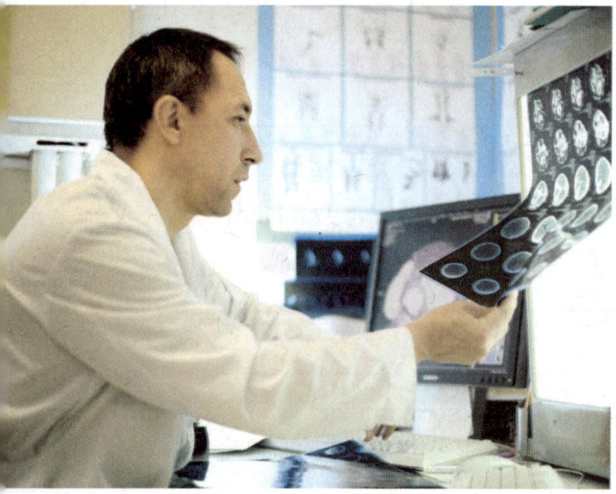

2 What may have caused the man's sudden interest in pedophilia?

He had a large tumour in a part of the brain that is associated with inhibition.

3 What happened after the man had surgery?

He went back to normal.

4 Why is evidence from lie detectors usually not accepted in courtrooms?

It relies on indirect methods such as the sweat on a person's palms or the heart rate. It might be misinterpreted.

5 What is a "guilty knowledge test"? Provide an example.

It shows a person's reaction to objects from the crime scene, such as the murder weapon. A guilty person would react differently to a picture of the murder weapon than an innocent person would.

6 Why is Functional Magnetic Resonance Imaging (FMRI) more reliable in a courtroom than traditional lie detectors?

FMRIs are not subjective since they look directly at brain activity. The suspect cannot control his brain's reaction when he sees a crime-scene object, for example.

DISCUSSION AND WRITING

The audio text describes a man who suddenly acted as a pedophile because of a brain tumour. Based on the information in the audio segment, should the man be convicted for his crime? Why or why not?

READING STRATEGY

Students can visit the Companion Website to practise their reading comprehension. Questions for all readings are structured to help students do better in their reading tests, including Benchmark and TESOL tests.

Thinking Critically

There are several things to consider when evaluating a text critically.

- **What is the author's purpose?**

  When you read, consider the author's purpose or intent. Most authors write for one of the following reasons:

  - **To inform:** Authors use facts to educate the reader.
  - **To persuade:** Authors use facts and opinions to argue a point. They hope to influence the reader.
  - **To entertain:** Authors narrate a story or describe something, hoping to get an emotional response from the reader. The text may evoke laughter, tears, anger, frustration, or shock.

- **Is it fact or opinion?**

  A **fact** is something that can be proven to be true or false. It is based on evidence and on personal observation. An **opinion** is a statement of personal feeling or judgment, and it cannot be proven right or wrong.

  Fact: Some women give birth to their babies at home.
  Opinion: A hospital is not the best place for a child to be born.

- **Is the writing clearly biased?**

  Everyone has biases or preconceived opinions. Our age, gender, and racial, financial, and cultural background influence our ideas about issues. Nonetheless, many newspaper, magazine, and textbook authors try to appear objective when they write informative articles. When you read, ask yourself if the writer is biased. To recognize a one-sided view, do the following.

  - **Ask yourself who might benefit from the article.** For example, if the story is about a political situation, determine if the article favours one side over the other. If it is about a survey, determine who paid for the survey.
  - **Consider the evidence.** Determine if there is clear, supporting evidence. Also, ask yourself if the evidence comes from a trustworthy source.
  - **Look for biased language.** Signs of the author's bias include the use of words that have strong emotional connections. For example, the following italicized words show bias: "The *white-trash* mother *abandoned* her son."

COMPANION WEB+ Visit the Companion Website to prepare for your reading tests. Online questions for all readings are structured to help you practise reading strategies.

PRACTICE

Read the following paragraphs and answer the questions.

1 The closest most people will come to having a "photographic memory" is a flashbulb memory, an exceptionally clear recollection of an important and emotion-packed event. Most of us harbour several such memories: a graduation, a tragic accident, a death, or a big victory. It feels as though we made a flash picture in our mind of the striking scene.

Source: Zimbardo, Philip G. *Psychology, Core Concepts*. Boston: Pearson, 2012. Print.

1. What is this an example of? ☑ fact ☐ opinion
2. What is the purpose? ☑ to inform ☐ to persuade ☐ to entertain
3. Does the text show evidence of bias? ☐ Yes ☑ No

   If you answered "yes," underline the words or phrases in the paragraph that show bias.

→

4. What is the paragraph about? Sum it up in one sentence.

Most people have "flashbulb memories," which are sharp recollections of highly intense moments.

2 It wasn't too long ago when there was much <u>hoopla</u> involving something called Recovered Memory Syndrome. Along with a few professionals, a whole slew of <u>marginally qualified</u> therapists and counsellors came forward to treat this <u>questionable</u> condition. The basic plot involved a repressed memory of some traumatic event (almost always of a sexual nature) that was now causing whatever it was the patient had ... or <u>could be convinced</u> she had. Many people were actually told that if they didn't remember being molested as a child, it was proof positive that they had been. Lawyers and law enforcement then <u>joined the bandwagon</u>, and a <u>full-fledged witch hunt</u> began.

Source: Mason, Stephen, Ph.D. "Recovered Memory Syndrome." *Psychology Today*. Sussex Publishers, 6 Jan. 2010. Web.

1. What is this an example of? ☐ fact ☑ opinion
2. What is the purpose? ☐ to inform ☑ to persuade ☐ to entertain
3. Does the text show evidence of bias? ☑ Yes ☐ No

   If you answered "yes," underline the words or phrases in the paragraph that show bias.
4. What is the paragraph about? Sum it up in one sentence.

   Recovered Memory Syndrome is not valid, and in the past, it led to unjust criminal investigations against innocent people.

READING 3.2

Chuck Klosterman is an author and essayist who has written best-selling works, including *Sex, Drugs, and Cocoa Puffs: A Low Culture Manifesto* and *The Visible Man*. The following essay first appeared in *Esquire* magazine.

Amnesia Is the New Bliss

BY CHUCK KLOSTERMAN

1 Last November, an episode of *60 Minutes* examined a prescription drug called propranolol. Lesley Stahl's report was the first time I'd ever heard of propranolol, and I haven't seen any major news source mention the drug since that evening. But propranolol might be the most philosophically vexing pharmaceutical since Prozac: it openly questions the significance of reality. This seems wonderful and terrifying at the same time. Propranolol is the closest society has come to making the 1996 film ***Brain Candy*** seem prophetic.

Brain Candy: a Canadian film about a pill that makes people remember their happiest memory

2 Understanding propranolol begins with understanding adrenaline, specifically how adrenaline impacts memory. Try to recall the most intense moments of your life (car accidents, fistfights, over-the-top sexual encounters, etc.). In most cases, you will remember the details from those events far more vividly than

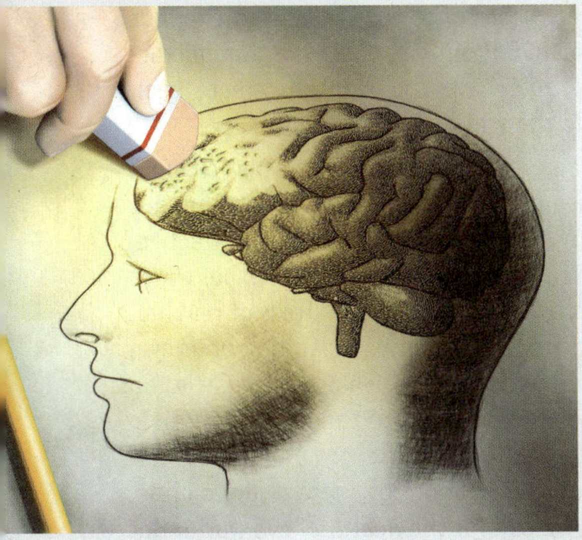

less meaningful, more conventional episodes from everyday existence. This is—at least partially—the product of adrenaline; the cerebral rush of adrenaline that accompanies intense circumstances burns those memories into your brain. Adrenaline makes us remember things.

3 When humankind was young, this process offered a sociobiological evolutionary advantage: if an early human got especially freaked out by a tiger attack, that hard-wiring taught him or her to stay out of tiger country. However, tigers are no longer a pressing issue in modern life. Today, adrenaline more often makes humans remember the events they'd most like to forget. This is why there are disorders like post-traumatic stress. Many people, such as war veterans, cannot psychologically overcome the worst moments from their life; the experiences never stop seeming vivid. Adrenaline has galvanized memories they don't want to recall.

4 This brings us to propranolol. If a surplus of adrenaline makes us remember, it stands to reason that a deficit of adrenaline would help us forget. And this is what propranolol does. It inhibits the chemical rush that makes memories hyperconcrete. It doesn't *erase* memories, but it makes them more abstract and less painful. In theory, giving accident victims immediate doses of propranolol could dramatically change how lucidly they remember the horror of a specific experience. What's even crazier is the possibility of propranolol working retroactively. It appears that patients might be able to erode traumas from the *distant* past by ingesting the drug and self-triggering memories on purpose (i.e., they repeatedly take propranolol and fixate on something that happened twenty years ago—over time, that specific memory grows hazy and normative).

5 It is hard to imagine how propranolol, used judiciously, wouldn't be good for society. It's impossible to justify why a nine-year-old who watched his parents get murdered needs to remember precisely what that looked and felt like. I'd feed that theoretical kid a cereal bowl of propranolol. But the problem, of course, is that our society is traditionally terrible at judicious drug use. And while the application of propranolol almost always seems reasonable on a case-by-case basis, the *idea* of propranolol is significantly more complicated.

rhetorical: expressed with no expected answer

6 How big are our lives? That is neither a **rhetorical** nor impossible question. The answer is easy: our lives are as big as our memories. Forgotten actions still have an impact on other people, but they don't have an impact on us. Reality is defined by what we know, and we obviously can't know what we don't remember. What this means is that propranolol provides an opportunity to shrink reality. It doesn't make past events wholly disappear from the mind, but it warps their meaning and context. So if people's personalities are simply the aggregation of their realities (and if reality is just an aggregation of memories), it can be argued that propranolol is a drug that artificially makes people's lives smaller.

7 As is so often the case with scientific innovations that feel like hypothetical problems, it's easy to imagine dystopian worst-case scenarios involving propranolol. What if the government used this drug to intensify the brutality of warfare, knowing the long-term cost on soldiers could be chemically mitigated? What if people used it simply because they didn't want to fixate over ex-girlfriends? It would seem that propranolol—like virtually everything else invented by man—has a short-term upside and a long-term consequence. The small picture provides benefits for victims of genuine pain; the big picture

suggests a confused society that consciously elects to expunge the pain that makes us human. But perhaps there is a third picture that's even bigger: do people have the right to create their reality? Who gets to decide the size of someone's life?

8 For a variety of reasons, the premise of taking a pill that changes our relationship with a memory seems scary. But we are already doing this all the time; our current means are just less effective. People get drunk in order not to care about things. People watch escapist movies to distract themselves from the stress of real life. Most significantly, we all distort the emotive meaning of our own past, usually without even trying; that's what nostalgia is. So let's assume that propranolol was abused to the highest possible degree; let's assume people started taking propranolol to edit every arbitrary memory that contained any fraction of mental discomfort. Ideologically, this would almost certainly be bad for the health of the world. But I still don't think it's something we could ethically *stop* people from doing.

9 The risk, I suppose, is that average people might behave differently if they had no fear of remorse or humiliation. Instead of thinking, "I will regret this in the morning," they might think, "I better remember to make myself forget this in the morning." Few things have been worse for society than the cultural evolution away from personal responsibility; I have no doubt that the world would be better off if more people felt guiltier about more things. But that sentiment is only *my* reality, and it's a specific reality I have created.

(986 words)

Source: Klosterman, Chuck. "Amnesia Is the New Bliss." *Esquire*. Hearst Communications, 10 Apr. 2007. Web.

Students can read the essay in class or for homework. There are additional questions in the Student Section of the Companion Website. You can verify if students have read the essay by checking their scores with the grade tracker.

VOCABULARY AND COMPREHENSION

1 Find a word in paragraph 6 that means "to make smaller."

shrink

2 In paragraph 7, what does *mitigated* mean?

a. removed (b.) made less severe c. accelerated d. qualified

3 What is the meaning of the word *means* as it is used in paragraph 8?

(a.) methods b. signifies c. angers

4 What is the main purpose of this essay: to inform, to persuade, or to entertain? Explain your answer.

To persuade: the author expresses the opinion that memory-erasing drugs can have negative consequences.

5 How did intense, adrenaline-fuelled memories help early humans?

The strong memories helped early humans protect themselves from dangers.

6 How does propranolol work?

It reduces the adrenaline "chemical rush" that makes memories very intense.

7 What effects of propranolol are most worrisome, according to the author? Think of at least two effects.

It makes people's lives smaller—they lose memories of intense moments.

People might feel less remorse after acting badly.

People will take less personal responsibility for their actions.

8 Klosterman suggests that people already have ways to forget bad memories, even without propranolol. How do people do this?

People abuse alcohol, watch escapist movies, and reframe past events with nostalgic memories.

9 In paragraph 9, Klosterman says "the world would be better off if more people felt guiltier about more things." Why is guilt important, in his opinion?

Guilt makes people less willing to repeat irresponsible behaviour. If they have no guilt, remorse, or humiliation, they may just repeat their actions.

DISCUSSION AND WRITING

1 What main point is Klosterman making about memory drugs? Explain why he is opposed to them.

2 Explain why you would or would not take a drug to erase a difficult memory.

3 Should memory-erasing drugs be readily available? Why or why not?

SPEAKING

What I've Learned

In an interview with *Esquire*, called "What I've Learned," Chuck Klosterman described some life lessons. Among his insights were the following:

- A friend is someone I would immediately contact if I got cancer.
- I can't play anything, and I can't sing.
- There are a lot of great Alice Cooper songs, but not "School's Out." That's an Alice Cooper song for people who don't like Alice Cooper.
- I don't have any big regrets, because I'm pretty happy with my life. But I have lots of minor regrets. I always order the wrong dish in restaurants. Always, no matter what I order, somebody else orders something that is better.[1]

Work with a team of three to five students. Scrunch up a piece of paper. When someone throws the paper at you, you must speak non-stop about something that you've learned. It can be a serious or a silly lesson. Just say the first ideas that come to your head. After you've spoken for at least ten seconds, you can throw the paper to someone else in the group.

To help get ideas flowing, you can consider categories such as love, family, arts and entertainment, school, food, and so on.

1. Source: Klosterman, Chuck. "What I've Learned." *Esquire*. Hearst Communications, 22 Dec. 2008. Web.

Vocabulary **BOOST**

Memory, Remind, and *Souvenir*

Memory is a noun meaning "the capacity to retain past impressions." It can also refer to the past impressions themselves.

I have great **memories** of my trip to Spain.

Remind is a verb meaning "to cause a person to remember something."

Remind me to bring my keys with me.

A ***souvenir*** is a memento that you buy to remind yourself of a special place.

We bought key chain **souvenirs** when we went to Banff.

You can practise using these terms in Unit 12 of *Avenues 3: English Grammar*.

PRACTICE

Fill in the blanks with *memory*, *remember*, *remind*, or *souvenir*. You can use the plural form of the nouns, and remember to conjugate verbs.

1 Because of a motorcycle accident, Kent Cochrane cannot create new ___memories___. When researchers visit Kent, they ___remind___ him of his contributions to science. Kent does not ___remember___ the visits.

2 When Kent went to London with his mother, he brought back a plastic ___souvenir___ of the London Bridge. His mother also bought two ___souvenirs___. Although his mother has great ___memories___ of the sites and sounds of London, Kent doesn't ___remember___ anything about England. He doesn't even know where his plastic ___souvenir___ came from.

Online, students can read more about Kent and about famous cases of people who have lost their memories. "Memory Makes Us Human" can serve as a practice reading test.

COMPANION WEB+ Read more about Kent Cochrane and others who have lost their memories. See "Memory Makes Us Human" on the Companion Website.

WATCHING

Endless Memory

There are some people who have what is known as "superior autobiographical memory." They are not geniuses; they are ordinary people with an extraordinary ability to remember almost every day of their lives in perfect detail. Watch and learn about people with extraordinary memories.

COMPREHENSION

1 Which person seems to be very uncomfortable with the steady stream of memories?

a. Brad Williams (b.) Jill Price c. Marilu Henner

2 What is physically different in the brains of people with superior memories?

Some parts of the brain are significantly larger.

3 How is Marilu Henner's closet unusual?

She is obsessive about the organization. Shoes are colour-coded, and she can see the toe and heel of every pair of shoes.

4 In Dr. McGaw's rat experiment, he injects adrenaline to help the rats remember. What role does adrenaline play in memory?

When we experience highly emotional events, adrenaline helps us remember them.

5 How do the people with endless memory appear to contradict the findings of the rat experiments?

They don't need adrenaline to help them remember. They remember "ordinary, non-emotional events."

6 Do these people with amazing memories have cluttered brains? ☐ Yes ☑ No

7 Of the five subjects with amazing memories who agreed to be interviewed, how many are married? One

8 According to Louise Owen, what is a positive benefit of having a superior memory?

It makes her live with more intention and joy, and she attempts to make every day significant.

You can assign the video in class or for homework. There are additional comprehension questions in the Student Section of the Companion Website.

DISCUSSION

With a partner, discuss whether you would like to be able to remember everything. Explain why or why not.

READING STRATEGY

Students can visit the Companion Website to practise their reading comprehension. Questions for all readings are structured to help students do better in their reading tests, including Benchmark and TESOL tests.

COMPANION WEB+ Visit the Companion Website to prepare for your reading tests. Online questions for all readings are structured to help you practise reading strategies.

Recognizing Tone

When people speak, their tone of voice betrays their mood. It is relatively easy to determine whether the person is feeling angry, joyful, sarcastic, or serious. While you read, you must look for written clues that help you determine the writer's overall mood, attitude, or feeling. Some clues about the author's tone can be found in the choice of language. For example, an author's tone could be one or more of the following:

angry	distant	lighthearted	sarcastic	silly
critical	frustrated	nostalgic	serious	sympathetic

READING 3.3

David Sedaris is an award-winning humour columnist. His acclaimed story collections include *Me Talk Pretty One Day* and *Barrel Fever*. In this story from *Naked*, he recalls episodes from his childhood.

Cyclops

BY DAVID SEDARIS

1 When he was young, my father shot out his best friend's eye with a BB gun. That is what he told us. "One foolish moment and, Jesus, if I could take it back, I would." He winced, shaking his fist as if it held a rattle. "It eats me alive," he said. "I mean to tell you that it absolutely tears me apart."

2 On one of our summer visits to his hometown, my father took us to meet this guy, a shoe salesman whose milky pupil hugged the corner of his mangled socket.

Capezios: a shoe brand (His father's friend is a shoe salesman.)

I watched the two men shake hands and turned away, sickened and ashamed by what my father had done.

3 Our next-door neighbour received a BB gun for his twelfth birthday and accepted it as a personal challenge to stalk and maim any living creature: sunbathing cats, sparrows, slugs, and squirrels—if it moved, he shot it. I thought this was an excellent idea, but every time I raised the gun to my shoulder, I saw my father's half-blind friend stumbling forth with an armload of **Capezios**. What would it be like to live with that sort of guilt? How could my father look himself in the mirror without throwing up?

4 While watching television one afternoon, my sister Tiffany stabbed me in the eye with a freshly sharpened pencil. The blood was copious, and I rode to the hospital knowing that if I was blinded, my sister would be my slave for the rest of her life. Never for one moment would I let her forget what she'd done to me. There would be no swinging cocktail parties in her future, no poolside barbecues or episodes of carefree laughter, not one moment of joy—I would make sure of that. I'd planned my vengeance so thoroughly that I was almost disappointed when the doctor announced that this was nothing but a minor puncture wound, located not on, but beneath the eye.

5 "Take a look at your brother's face," my father said, pointing to my Band-Aid. "You could have blinded him for life! Your own brother, a Cyclops; is that what you want?" Tiffany's suffering eased my pain for an hour or two, but then I began to feel sorry for her. "Every time you reach for a pencil, I want you to think about what you've done to your brother," my father said. "I want you to get on your knees and beg him to forgive you."

6 There are only so many times a person can apologize before it becomes annoying. I lost interest long before the bandage was removed, but not my father. By the time he was finished, Tiffany couldn't lift a dull crayon without breaking into tears. Her pretty, suntanned face assumed the characteristics of a wrinkled, grease-stained bag. Six years old and the girl was broken.

7 Danger was everywhere, and it was our father's lifelong duty to warn us. Attending the country club's Fourth of July celebration, we were told how one of his Navy buddies had been disfigured for life when a cherry bomb exploded in his lap. "Blew his balls right off the map," he said. "Take a second and imagine what that must have felt like!" Racing to the farthest edge of the golf course, I watched the remainder of the display with my hands between my legs.

8 Fireworks were hazardous, but thunderstorms were even worse. "I had a friend, used to be a very bright, good-looking guy. He was on top of the world until the day he got struck by lightning. It caught him right between the eyes while he was trout fishing, and cooked his brain just like you'd roast a chicken. Now he's got a metal plate in his forehead and can't even chew his own food; everything has to be put in a blender and taken through a straw."

9 If the lightning was going to get me, it would have to penetrate walls. At the first hint of a storm, I ran to the basement, crouching beneath a table and covering my head with a blanket. Those who watched from their front porches were fools. "The lightning can be attracted by a wedding ring or even the fillings in your teeth," my father said. "The moment you let down your guard is guaranteed to be the day it strikes."

10 In junior high, I signed up for shop class, and our first assignment was to build a napkin holder. "You're not going to be using a table saw, are you?" my father

asked. "I knew a guy, a kid about your size, who was using a table saw when the blade came loose, flew out of the machine, and sliced his face right in half." Using his index finger, my father drew an imaginary line from his forehead to his chin. "The guy survived, but nobody wanted anything to do with him. He turned into an alcoholic and wound up marrying a Chinese woman he'd ordered through a catalogue. Think about it." I did.

11 After a while, we began to wonder if my father had any friends who could still tie their own shoes or breathe without the aid of a respirator. With the exception of the shoe salesman, we'd never seen any of these people, only heard about them whenever one of us attempted to deep-fry chicken or operate the garbage disposal. "I've got a friend who buys a set of gloves and throws one of them away. He lost his right hand doing the exact same thing you're doing. He had his arm down the drain when the cat rubbed against the switch to the garbage disposal. Now he's wearing clip-on ties and having the restaurant waiters cut up his steak. Is that the kind of life you want for yourself?"

12 He allowed me to mow the lawn only because he was too cheap to pay a landscaper and didn't want to do it himself. "What happened," he said, "is that the guy slipped, probably on a pile of crap, and his leg got caught up in the blade. He found his foot, carried it to the hospital, but it was too late to sew it back on. Can you imagine that? The guy drove fifteen, twenty miles with his foot in his lap."

13 Regardless of the heat, I mowed the lawn wearing long pants, knee-high boots, a football helmet, and a pair of goggles. Before starting, I scouted the lawn for rocks and dog feces, slowly combing the area as if it were mined. Even then, I pushed the mower haltingly, always fearing that this next step might be my last.

14 Nothing bad ever happened, and within a few years I was mowing in shorts and sneakers, thinking of the supposed friend my father had used to illustrate his warning. I imagined this man jumping into his car and pressing on the accelerator with his bloody stump, a warm foot settled in his lap like a sleeping puppy. Why hadn't he just called an ambulance to come pick him up? How, in his shock, had he thought to search the weeds for his missing foot? It didn't add up.

15 I waited until my junior year of high school to sign up for driver's education. Before taking to the road, we sat in the darkened classroom, watching films that might have been written and directed by my father. *Don't do it*, I thought, watching the prom couple attempt to pass a lumbering dump truck. Every excursion ended with the young driver wrapped around a telephone pole or burned beyond recognition, the camera focusing in on a bloody corsage littering the side of the highway.

16 I drove a car no faster than I pushed the lawn mower, and the instructor soon lost patience. "That license is going to be your death warrant," my father said on the day I received my learner's permit. "You're going to get out there and kill someone, and the guilt is going to tear your heart out."

17 The thought of killing myself had slowed me down to five miles per hour. The thought of killing someone else stopped me completely.

18 My mother had picked me up from a play rehearsal one rainy night when, cresting a hill, the car ran over something it shouldn't have. This was not a brick or a misplaced boot, but some living creature that cried out when caught beneath the tire. "Shit," my mother whispered, tapping her forehead against the steering wheel. "Shit, shit, shit." We covered our heads against the rain and searched the darkened street until we found an orange cat coughing up blood into the gutter.

19 "You killed me," the cat said, pointing at my mother with its flattened paw. "Here I had so much to live for, but now it's over, my whole life wiped out just like that." The cat wheezed rhythmically before closing its eyes and dying.

20 "Shit," my mother repeated. We walked door to door until we found the cat's owner, a kind and understanding woman whose young daughter shared none of her qualities. "You killed my cat," she screamed, sobbing into her mother's skirt. "You're mean and you're ugly, and you killed my cat."

21 "She's at that age," the woman said, stroking the child's hair.

22 My mother felt bad enough without the lecture that awaited her at home. "That could have been a child!" my father shouted. "Think about that the next time you're tearing down the street searching for kicks." He made it sound as if my mother ran down cats for sport. "You think this is funny," he said, "but we'll see who's laughing when you're behind bars awaiting trial for manslaughter." I received a variation on the same speech after sideswiping a mailbox. Despite my mother's encouragement, I surrendered my permit and never drove again. My nerves just couldn't take it. It seemed much safer to hitchhike.

Central Park, New York

23 My father objected when I moved to Chicago and waged a full-fledged campaign of terror when I announced I would be moving to New York. "New York! Are you out of your mind? You might as well take a razor to your throat because, let me tell you something, those New Yorkers are going to eat you alive." He spoke of friends who had been robbed and bludgeoned by packs of roving gangs, and sent me newspaper clippings detailing the tragic slayings of joggers and vacationing tourists. "This could be you!" he wrote in the margins.

24 I'd lived in New York for several years when, travelling upstate to attend a wedding, I stopped in my father's hometown. We hadn't visited since our grandmother moved in with us, and I felt my way around with a creepy familiarity. I found my father's old apartment, but his friend's shoe store had been converted into a pool hall. When I called to tell him about it, my father said, "What shoe store? What are you talking about?"

25 "The place where your friend worked," I said. "You remember, the guy whose eye you shot out."

26 "Frank?" he said. "I didn't shoot his eye out; the guy was born that way."

27 My father visits me now in New York. We'll walk through Washington Square, where he'll yell, "Get a look at the ugly mug on that one!" referring to a three-hundred-pound biker with grinning skulls tattooed like a choker around his neck. A young man in Central Park is photographing his girlfriend, and my father races to throw himself into the picture. "All right, sweetheart," he says, placing his arm around the startled victim, "it's time to get comfortable." I cower as he marches into posh grocery stores, demanding to speak to the manager. "Back home, I can get this exact same cantaloupe for less than half this price," he says. The managers invariably suggest that he do just that. He screams at waiters and cuts in line at **tony** restaurants. "I have a friend," I tell him, "who lost his right arm snapping his fingers at a waiter."

28 "Oh, you kids," he says. "Not a one of you has got so much as a teaspoon of **gumption**. I don't know where you got it from, but in the end, it's going to kill you."

tony: classy and stylish

gumption: courage; guts

(2125 words)

Source: Sedaris, David. "Cyclops." *Naked*. NY: Little Brown and Co., 1997. Print.

Students can read the essay in class or for homework. There are additional questions in the Student Section of the Companion Website. You can verify if students have read the essay by checking their scores with the grade tracker.

The Companion Website includes a reading test for this chapter.

VOCABULARY

1 Match each vivid action verb with its meaning. Write the letter of the correct answer in the space. Before you make your guesses, read the words in context. The paragraph numbers are in parentheses.

Terms		Definitions
1. wince (1)	c	a) cut grass with a machine
2. stalk (3)	f	b) cut a piece of something
3. maim (3)	d	c) shrink back in pain or distress
4. stab (4)	g	d) wound or injure seriously
5. crouch (9)	h	e) breathe with difficulty, making a whistling sound
6. slice (10)	b	f) follow obsessively
7. mow (12)	a	g) pierce with a pointed weapon
8. wheeze (19)	e	h) squat or bend down close to the ground

WRITTEN COMPREHENSION

On a separate piece of paper, answer the following questions. For each answer, write a short paragraph (about 50–80 words).

1 What is the writer's mood or tone? Is he frustrated, serious, lighthearted, or critical? Defend your answer with evidence from the text.

2 What was the author afraid of during his childhood? List some things that scared him.

3 Describe the personality of the writer's father. Look in paragraph 27 for ideas.

4 What was wrong with the father's parenting strategy? How was it misguided? In your answer, discuss the ending of the story.

Take Action!

WRITING TOPICS

Write about one of the following topics. For information about essay structure, see the Writing Workshops on pages 148 to 157. Before handing in your work, refer to the Writing Checklist on the inside back cover.

1 **A Letter to the Past**

If you could go back in time, what would you tell your twelve-year-old self? Write a letter to your younger self with suggestions and advice.

2 **Mistakes**

How do our mistakes inform or educate us? Describe three lessons people learn when they make different types of mistakes. You can consider mistakes made in social relationships, in academic life, and in lifestyle. Develop your ideas by referring to the readings or the video from this chapter. Also refer to events in the media, in your life, or the lives of people you know.

SPEAKING TOPICS

Prepare a presentation about one of the following topics. For details about preparing a speaking presentation, see Appendix 1 on page 174.

Need help with pronunciation? Visit the Companion Website and try the Pronunciation Workshops.

Remind students to try the Pronunciation Workshops on the Companion Website.

1 Parenting Mistakes

In "Cyclops," David Sedaris describes his father's parenting ideas. Present some common parenting mistakes. Provide specific examples from your life, from the media, and from the essay "Cyclops."

2 A Life-Changing Lesson

> "Two roads diverged in a wood, and I—I took the one less travelled by, and that has made all the difference."
>
> – Robert Frost, poet, "The Road Not Taken"

Respond to the quotation. Describe how something—it could be a proud moment, a bad decision, or a shocking event—made a difference in your life.

MEDIA LINK

Watch a movie that discusses memory or psychology. For example, you could watch *Donnie Darko*, *Eternal Sunshine of the Spotless Mind*, *Fifty First Dates*, or *Memento*. You could also do an Internet search for movies about psychology, and then choose one. Prepare an essay or a speaking presentation about humans and memory. Begin with a very brief summary of the film (four to six sentences maximum). Then explain the message of the film. Make a connection between the message in the movie and at least one of the readings in this chapter.

Revising and Editing

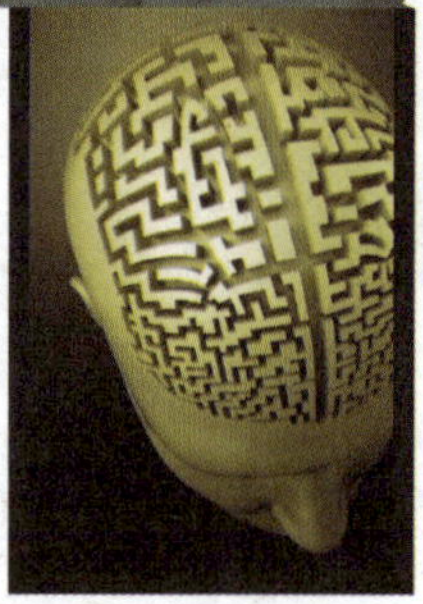

The Revising and Editing sections at the end of each chapter help your students prepare for writing tests, including Benchmark and TESOL tests. You can ask students to do the activities with a partner and to share ideas.

REVISE FOR AN INTRODUCTION
EDIT FOR SPELLING, PRONOUN, AND MODAL ERRORS

A piece of writing should begin with an introduction that captures the reader's attention. (To learn more about introductions, see page 150 in Writing Workshop 1.)

Read the short essay and follow these steps:

1. Underline and correct ten errors. Correct four spelling errors and four pronoun errors. Also correct two errors with modal forms.
2. Write a short introduction. Begin with general or historical information, an anecdote, a definition, or a contrasting position.

Introduction: ______________________________

First, a significant parenting mistake people make is trying to be friends rather then [than] authority figures. Many parents want their children to like them, so they refrain from setting boundaries. My aunt, for exemple [example], does not provide a regular bedtime for my ten-year-old cousin Julian. Him [He] and his little sister stay up as late as the adults. He is overtired, so he acts hyper and rude, but nobody disciplines him. My aunt should give him boundaries.

Another common mistake parents make is to lie to theirs [their] children. Parents often believe that they are protecting their children when they hide significant problems. If the issues are not identified and discussed, the child may be confused and anxious. My parents, for instance, divorced when I was thirteen. Before the divorce, they pretended that everything was fine, and they rarely fougth [fought] in front of my brother and I [me]. When they told us about their plans for the divorce at the last moment, we were devastated. They should of [have] been more open and honest. My brother and me [I] could have handle [handled] the truth.

Becoming a parent is a person's most significant life responsability [responsibility]. However, many people do not take the time to learn about good parenting. Too many children are raised without solid boundaries and in houses filled with lies. Perhaps colleges should provide students with compulsory parenting courses.

Grammar **TIP**

Subject or Object Pronoun

When a pronoun is paired with another noun, the correct pronoun isn't always obvious. A simple way to determine the correct pronoun is to repeat the sentence using just one pronoun.

Mr. Reed asked my friend and (**I** or **me**?) for some help.

Possible choices: Mr. Reed asked **I** ... / Mr. Reed asked **me** ...

Correct answer: Mr. Reed asked my friend and **me** for some help.

To learn more about pronouns, see Unit 8 in *Avenues 3: English Grammar*.

COMPANION WEB+ To practise vocabulary from this chapter, visit the Companion Website.

CHAPTER 4

Crime and Punishment

"The common argument that crime is caused by poverty is a kind of slander on the poor."

– H. L. MENCKEN, WRITER

What are some problems with the criminal justice system? Does our nation need to get tougher on crime? This chapter examines issues surrounding crime and punishment.

START UP

Crime Crossword

Make the Start Up a contest. Ask students to work with a partner or team, and the first team to complete the puzzle wins.

Work with a partner or team, and complete the crossword. Unravel the clues to guess the crime vocabulary. You can use a dictionary if necessary.

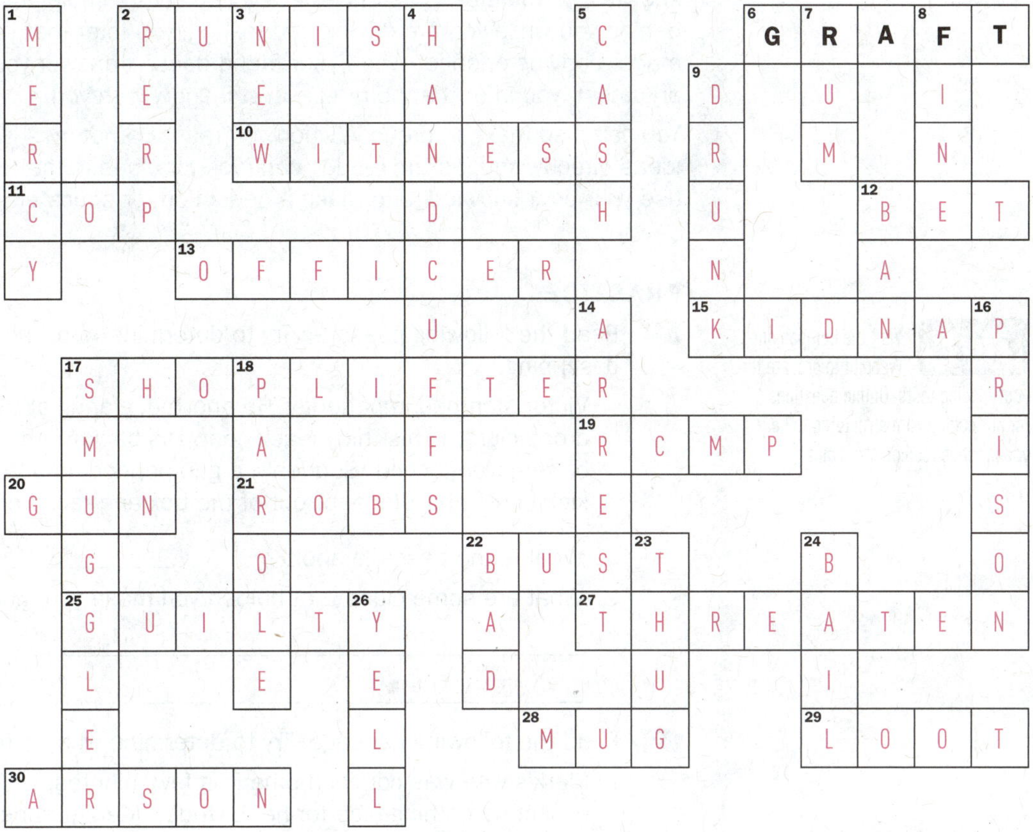

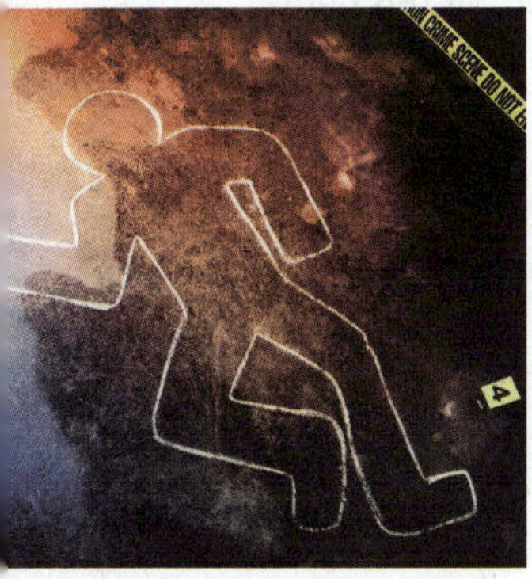

Across

2 ▶ To inflict a penalty
6 ▶ The practice of bribery and corruption
10 ▶ Someone who sees an illegal act
11 ▶ A slang term for "police officer"
12 ▶ To place a wager when gambling
13 ▶ A police ___ protects citizens
15 ▶ To abduct and confine another person
17 ▶ Someone who steals from a store
19 ▶ The abbreviation for Royal Canadian Mounted Police
20 ▶ A weapon that shoots
21 ▶ Another word for "steals"
22 ▶ A slang term meaning "to arrest"
25 ▶ Not innocent
27 ▶ To menace
28 ▶ To attack and rob someone in a street
29 ▶ To plunder or steal (e.g., during a riot)
30 ▶ An intentionally set fire

Down

1 ▶ Another term for "clemency"
2 ▶ The short form of "perpetrator"
3 ▶ The opposite of "old"
4 ▶ The police place these on a suspect's wrists.
5 ▶ A slang term for "money"
7 ▶ An alcoholic beverage that is often mixed with Coke
8 ▶ A sum of money paid as a penalty for breaking a law
9 ▶ Inebriated
12 ▶ To prohibit or interdict
14 ▶ To apprehend a suspect
16 ▶ Another word for "jail"
17 ▶ A person who brings contraband items over an international border
18 ▶ A conditional release from jail
22 ▶ The opposite of "good"
23 ▶ A tough, violent criminal
24 ▶ Money paid to a court to temporarily release a suspect
26 ▶ To shout or talk very loudly

READING STRATEGY

Students can visit the Companion Website to practise their reading comprehension. Questions for all readings are structured to help students do better in their reading tests, including Benchmark and TESOL tests.

Making Inferences

When you infer, you make an educated guess based on the evidence and prior knowledge. You make inferences every day. For example, if you hear a siren behind you while you are driving and texting, you infer that you might have made a driving offence. When your friend doesn't answer your calls after an argument, you infer that he or she is still angry with you.

You can also make inferences when you read. Sometimes, writers do not state ideas directly. You, as the reader, can look for clues in the text, and you can use your prior knowledge to make a deduction, or educated guess.

COMPANION web+ Visit the Companion Website to prepare for your reading tests. Online questions for all readings are structured to help you practise reading strategies.

PRACTICE

1 Read the following passage. Try to determine what the writer is describing.

Victor stomped impatiently. He snorted, glaring at the horizon. Rain drops clung to his thick black coat. His back tooth, which needed to be removed, ached. Suddenly, a gun popped, and Victor felt the hard kick in his ribs. He leapt out of the box and raced down the track.

1. What is the passage about? A horse at a race course
2. What are some clues that helped you make your guess?
   stomped; snorted; thick black coat; gun popped; hard kick in his ribs; leapt out of the box; raced down the track

2 Read the following passage. Try to determine what is really happening.

Mark's wife was coming home in a few minutes, and she would expect something nice for her birthday. Mark grabbed a piece of paper. Thinking quickly, he wrote a few lines. He would call it a love poem. As soon as she opened the door, Mark put down his pen and smiled. In his pocket, he fingered a box that enclosed a thin gold necklace, but it was not for the woman entering the room.

Reading between the lines, what inferences can you make about the man?
Mark is thoughtless, he forgot about his wife's birthday, and he is probably having an affair.

READING 4.1

Should Canada's government strengthen crime laws? In this article from *The Globe and Mail*, Ian Brown explains his views.

Why Are Canadians Afraid?

BY IAN BROWN

1 If you ever ask your fellow Canadians why they support getting tough on crime, you will have the following conversation over and over again.

2 **Host:** Why do you want the government to get tough on crime when the crime rate's already down?

3 **Citizen:** But the violent crimes are going up.

4 **Host:** Actually, they're not.

5 **Citizen:** But the really violent criminals get out after two or three years. The judges let them out because there isn't any room in the jails.

6 **Host:** Not the really violent guys.

7 *[Pause]* **Citizen:** Okay, maybe it's not so much in Canada. But people get beheaded with machetes in other countries.

8 We might want to ask ourselves why we seem to feel such a burning desire to be tougher on crime. The crime rate has been dropping for a decade. The crime-severity index is 22 percent lower than it was in 1999. Statistics Canada's 2009 criminal-victimization survey (of nearly two thousand Canadians aged fifteen and over) found that 93 percent of us feel "somewhat" or "very" safe from crime, a number that hasn't changed in five years. About 90 percent of us feel fine walking alone in the dark, and 83 percent aren't afraid to be at home alone at night.

9 But those are dreary surveys. To see what I mean, let me take you to booming Abbotsford, BC, an hour's drive west of Vancouver. For two years, in 2008 and 2009, Abbotsford had the highest murder rate of any community in Canada over 100,000 people—5.22 murders per 100,000 residents. A deeply religious town with more than eighty churches, the town straddles a long stretch of undefended border. It's a Tunnel of Love for drug smuggling and gang activity. Pot, meth, and E go south; coke, guns, and freshly laundered cash come back. Eight of the nine murders that occurred in 2009 were gang-related.

10 Yet if you imagine Abbotsford as a hideous bullet-pocked hole, you are very wrong: it's a pleasant, friendly, middle-class suburban city. The parking lots are stuffed with brand new trucks. Herds of good-looking families roam the sidewalks. The city library is luxurious and bustling. Only a brochure pinned to the message board advertising a "support group for people grieving the loss of those who died by homicide" hints at the city's shadow.

11 No one I meet professes to be alarmed by the city's criminals. In the food court of the local mall, an eighty-nine-year-old woman says she's never concerned for her own safety. "I just keep my head down and my nose clean."

12 "I don't think anyone worries about it," her companion, a man in his seventies, adds. "Nowadays, with cellphones, you can get a hold of the cops pretty quick."

13 Then I run into Bill and Pam, a couple who own and operate five long-haul semis. They earn upwards of half-a-million dollars a year. Bill is in his sixties and full of news: three of his pals have just been sentenced to sixty years in the US for smuggling cannabis. Bill has been tempted to smuggle, too, but he likes his freedom too much. "It's so easy to get away with. You can make $75,000 a trip. Seven hockey bags will bring you 50 **grand**." He guesses the cops catch 10 percent of what crosses the border.

grand: thousand dollars

14 Bill's buddy, Ted, was nabbed with 1300 kilos under the floor of a cattle truck, hidden under a messy spot the border guards normally don't search. Some smugglers stuff drugs in PVC pipe, cover it with wood chips, and haul it under the city garbage. But even though meth labs have blown up across the street from where he and Pam were standing, Bill has never "particularly worried"

he might be a crime victim. "Most of the murders are targeted," Pam explains. Her fingers are thick with nice gold rings.

15 It's becoming clear that what makes people susceptible to "tough-on-crime" talk is more complicated than fear. It's also more evasive than facts. As personally unthreatened by crime as they say they are, everyone I meet wants the government to be tough on crime. Darshan Singh Dheliwal and his pals think Canada "has to be more like America." And Bill says things like, "If you get fifteen years, you should serve fifteen years."

16 If you think this is just socially conservative Abbotsford speaking, go to Vancouver South. There's extraordinarily little crime to be found—mostly break-ins (down 7 percent last year) and stolen cars (down 20 percent). In a pharmacy down the street from the Chong Lee Market, Dan Huzyk, sixty-four, laughs and tells me he can remember only two crimes in the nearly forty years he has lived here.

17 Our government can throw as many people as it wants into jail, but it won't affect crime rates. Until recently, the rate at which Canada incarcerated prisoners was restrained. For more than a century, we incarcerated between 80 and 110 adults per 100,000 people. The United States started out where we did, but today it has 760 prisoners per 100,000 people, which is the highest rate in the world. Even China runs a distant second. If it were true that jailing more criminals made society safer from crime, the US should have seen greater rates of decline in its crime than we have. But the fluctuation in the US homicide rate mirrors ours. In both countries, homicide rates peaked in 1975 and have declined ever since.

18 Incarceration doesn't improve crime rates. Neither do the longer sentences or mandatory minimum sentences, which can interfere with rehabilitation. So why has crime dropped? Excellent question. Theories abound. Neil Boyd, a criminologist at Simon Fraser University, credits the aging baby boom. "There were twice as many young men in the population in the 1970s as there are now." Young men commit most crimes.

19 James Hackler of the University of Victoria thinks, "the strongest answer to crime rates is equality of income." Countries such as Scandinavia and Japan, where the ratio between CEO pay and worker pay is smaller than it is here, have lower crime rates.

20 Another theory points to the birth control pill and even legalized abortion. [In 1969, Canada's abortion law was thrown out, and in 1973, the US Supreme Court ruled that women have the right to an abortion. The argument put forth by John J. Donohue and Steven D. Levitt, a pair of American economists, is that fewer young single mothers means fewer unwanted children roaming the streets. The crime rates dropped in the 1980s, right about the time those unwanted children would have become teens.]

21 Just before the 2010 election, egged on by the victims of Montreal fraudster Earl Jones, Stephen Harper's government eliminated automatic parole review (APR). That will keep Mr. Jones in the slammer a little longer. But it will, much more seriously, affect many young, first-time, non-violent offenders (drug charges, break-ins) who will now serve longer sentences and run greater risks of reoffending when they get out, which APR was meant to prevent. "Being in prison doesn't make you a good citizen," Graham Stewart, the retired director of a prisoner-rights organization, explains. Furthermore, Ed McIsaac, the national

director at John Howard, estimates that housing those prisoners for the extended time could cost $47 million a year. That's about the same amount Mr. Jones stole from his victims over the course of twenty-five years.

22 Tough-on-crime sentiment may be difficult to justify logically, but it is easy to feel. One reason, of course, is that crime victimizes people, and happens uncontrollably, and so it scares us—if not personally, then existentially. Things that actually reduce crime—sophisticated parole programs, rehabilitation systems, anti-poverty initiatives, education, mental-health centres, retraining—cost money and time, but they are not political quick fixes. For many years, Canada relied less on prison and more on rehabilitation, on changing people. But now we seem to be headed the other way.

(1312 words)

Source: Brown, Ian. Abridged from "What Are Canadians Really Afraid of When It Comes to Crime?" *The Globe and Mail* [Toronto]. The Globe and Mail Inc., 9 Apr. 2011. Web.

Students can read the essay in class or for homework. There are additional questions in the Student Section of the Companion Website. You can verify if students have read the essay by checking their scores with the grade tracker.

COMPREHENSION: MAKING INFERENCES

1 What is the writer's tone?

(a.) frustration b. nostalgia c. sympathy d. sadness

2 Why does the writer begin with an imaginary conversation? Make an inference.

He wants to show that people are irrational when they support "tough-on-crime" policies.

3 What is the writer's purpose?

a. To explain why Canadians are afraid and show reasons for their fear

b. To provide solutions that will lower the crime rate and make people feel safer

(c.) To suggest that Canada is relatively safe and there is no reason to be tougher on crime

4 Describe the town of Abbotsford. What is unusual about the town?

Answers will vary. It is pleasant, friendly, and middle-class, yet there are many drug smugglers and gang-related murders in town.

5 In paragraph 14, explain why the place where Ted hid drugs is called a "spot the border guards normally don't search." Make an inference.

The sub-floor of a cattle truck is full of manure, so nobody would want to look there.

6 Which nation in the world has the highest incarceration rate per 100,000 people?

a. Canada (b.) the United States c. China

7 In paragraphs 18 to 20, the author provides possible explanations for the drop in the crime rate. What are the three theories?

There are fewer young men now than there were in the 1970s.

Equality of income results in lower crime rates.

With birth control pills and legalized abortion, fewer unwanted children means fewer criminals.

8 In 2010, the Canadian government eliminated automatic parole review (APR). What problems could that decision cause? See paragraph 21, and make some inferences.

Young offenders might spend more time in jail and become better criminals. Also, costs associated with housing more criminals can drive up Canada's debt.

DISCUSSION AND WRITING

Companion Web+ Answer additional questions for all the reading and listening activities. You can also access audio and video clips online.

1 Have you ever felt angry with the criminal justice system? Discuss a time when you thought that the courts were too lenient or too strict.

2 In paragraph 15, the writer says that our susceptibility for tough-on-crime talk "is more complicated than fear" and "more evasive than facts." So why do many people support tougher crime laws? Think of some possible reasons.

SPEAKING

Crime and Punishment

Work with a team of students and discuss the following scenarios. What should the sentence be?

Before doing this activity, you could give students the "Flogging" listening test. They could also discuss the validity of flogging as a punishment.

1 In Winnipeg, a fifteen-year-old boy and a fourteen-year-old girl went on a vandalism spree. They entered a local school and caused $82,000 in damage. They broke windows, smashed doors, and poured paint on computer equipment, office printers, and photocopiers. The school's insurance company is suing the children's families for $50,000 each.

What should the judge do? Discuss the following options and give reasons for your opinion.

- Force the parents to pay for the damage.
- Shame the teens. Force them to wear large signs saying, "I'm a vandal" and make them stand in a public place during daylight hours for two weeks. (Passers-by would probably make comments to the culprits.)
- Put the teens in prison for three months.
- In some countries, people are flogged (whipped) for minor crimes. Flog the teens with ten lashes.
- Let the teens off with a warning. Tell them to never do it again.
- Your solution.

2 Seventeen-year-old Miranda is a chronic shoplifter. She has robbed clothing from numerous clothing retailers in a local shopping mall. The stores compared surveillance camera videos and have evidence that she has robbed over $9,000 in merchandise.

Which punishment would be the most effective? Discuss the following options and give reasons for your opinion.

- Force Miranda to wash the floors in the mall and in the stores, for no pay, for three months.
- Force Miranda to appear in print and television ads admitting to her crime and publicly apologizing. The goal is to make her feel ashamed.
- Put Miranda in jail for six months.
- In some countries, people are flogged (whipped) for minor crimes. Flog Miranda with ten lashes.
- Let Miranda off with a warning. Force her to get some counselling.
- Your solution.

READING 4.2 Read about some of the reasons why innocent people are convicted in this selection from the *Innocence Project* website.

The Causes of Wrongful Conviction

ADAPTED FROM *THE INNOCENCE PROJECT*

1 In recent years, wrongful convictions have revealed some upsetting realities about our criminal justice system. In each case where DNA has proven the innocence of a convicted felon beyond a doubt, an overlapping array of causes for the conviction has emerged—from mistakes to misconduct, to factors of race and class.

Eyewitness Misidentification

2 Eyewitness misidentification is the single greatest cause of wrongful convictions, playing a role in approximately 75 percent of convictions overturned through DNA testing.[1] While eyewitness testimony can be persuasive evidence before a judge or jury, thirty years of strong social science research has proven that eyewitness identification is often unreliable. The human mind is not like a video camera. Instead, witness memory is like any other evidence at a crime scene; it must be preserved carefully and retrieved methodically, or it can be contaminated. Hundreds of scientific studies have affirmed that eyewitness identification is often inaccurate and that it can be made more accurate by implementing specific identification reforms.

3 Variables that can influence eyewitness misidentification include simple factors like the lighting when the crime took place, or the distance from which the witness saw the perpetrator. Identifications have proven to be less accurate when witnesses are identifying perpetrators of a different race. Rod Lindsay, a professor at Queen's University, notes that stress narrows our attention. Thus, witnesses often remember a gun, for instance, more clearly than they remember the suspect. Elizabeth Loftus, a memory expert, notes that misinformation after an event can become integrated into a witness's memory.

4 The ways that law enforcement agencies retrieve and record witness memory can also influence accuracy. Ideally, photos should be presented to witnesses sequentially, instead of a single array of six or twelve (which make witnesses feel compelled to choose one from the group). If the questioning officer has a suspect in mind, he or she can subtly and inadvertently influence the witness's choice. An officer who doesn't know the identity of the suspect should administer the lineup.

5 Police departments can take steps to minimize errors in eyewitness identification. For instance, after the wrongful conviction of Thomas Sophonow, Vancouver police implemented new procedures. Now they only use sequential lineups. The person doing the questioning of witnesses follows a script and does not know the identity of the suspect. And the police will not rely only on eyewitness testimony to charge a suspect.

Invalidated Forensic Science

6 In approximately 50 percent of DNA exonerations, improper forensic science contributed to the wrongful conviction.[2] Experts estimate that only 5 to 10 percent of all criminal cases involve biological evidence that can be subjected

1-2. Statistics apply to US cases.

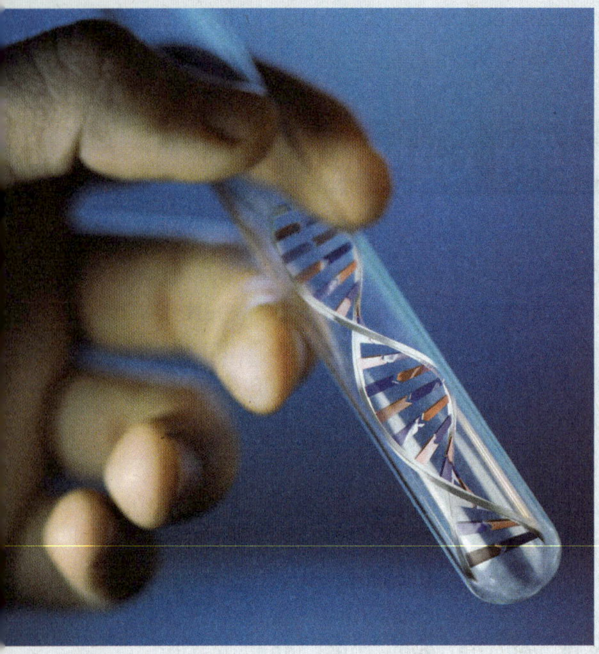

to DNA testing. Furthermore, forensic analysts sometimes testify in cases, without a proper scientific basis for their findings. For example, efforts to match a defendant's teeth to marks on a victim, or to compare a defendant's voice to a voicemail recording, may seem like science, but they lack even the most basic scientific standards.

7 Sometimes, forensic scientists are incompetent. In Ontario, Canada, Dr. Charles Smith worked as a pathologist with the Coroner's Office from the early 1980s to 2001. During that time, according to the *National Post's* Tom Blackwell, Smith "made errors and delivered inaccurate and inflammatory testimony in twenty death investigations." For instance, Sherry Sherrett-Robinson was convicted after her four-month-old son became tangled in bedclothes and died. She was jailed, and her other child was seized and put up for adoption. At an enquiry, a judge declared that Dr. Smith had misinterpreted the evidence. Dr. Smith had very little expertise, often neglected to visit crime scenes, and misinterpreted information.

Unreliable Witnesses

8 In some wrongful conviction cases, an informant or jailhouse snitch testified against the defendant. Snitches might be paid to testify, and they frequently receive a reduced sentence or an early release from prison for their testimony. Testifying falsely—in exchange for money or a sentence reduction—is often the last resort for a desperate inmate. Also, for someone who wants to avoid being charged with a crime, providing snitch testimony may be the only way to avoid a prison sentence. Sometimes law enforcement officials seek out snitches and give them extensive background on cases—essentially training them to give the false testimony the police need to charge a suspect when no other evidence is available.

9 In some cases, the snitch testimony is the only evidence of guilt. According to the Center on Wrongful Convictions at the Northwestern University School of Law, snitch testimony put thirty-eight innocent Americans on death row. In Canada, Guy Paul Morin was wrongfully convicted of the rape and murder of an eight-year-old girl in 1984. Much of the evidence against Morin was provided by two jailhouse snitches who falsely testified that Morin had confessed to committing the murder. (In 1995, DNA evidence exonerated Morin of the crime.)

Incompetent Lawyers

10 The justice system can be unfairly tilted against poor defendants. Because they cannot afford to hire decent legal council, they may be represented by an incompetent or overburdened defence lawyer. The failure of overworked lawyers to investigate, call witnesses, or prepare for trial has led to the conviction of innocent people.

11 In some of the worst cases, lawyers have slept in the courtroom during trial, failed to investigate alibis, failed to consult experts on forensic issues, and even failed to show up for hearings. The expression "you get what you pay for" seems to apply as much to our criminal justice system as anything else.

12 The exoneration and release of Jimmy Ray Bromgard from a Montana prison provides a sobering view of the effects of incompetent legal counsel. When Bromgard was eighteen, he was convicted for the brutal rape of an eight-year-old girl. He spent fifteen years in prison. A post-conviction DNA test proved he was innocent. Bromgard's trial attorney performed no investigation, filed no pre-trial

motions, gave no opening statement, did not prepare for closing arguments, and provided no expert to refute the fraudulent testimony of the state's hair microscopy expert. The forensic expert testified that there was less than a one in ten thousand (1/10,000) chance that the hairs did not belong to Bromgard. This sealed the deal for the prosecution, but the number was a fabrication, taken out of thin air.

13 Incompetent lawyers aren't only a danger south of the border. In Nova Scotia, Donald Marshall Jr. was wrongfully convicted of the murder of a seventeen-year-old acquaintance in 1971—largely because his lawyer declined to interview witnesses or demand disclosure of the Crown prosecutor's evidence. A later study of the case suggested his own lawyers seemed to believe that Marshall was guilty.

14 These factors are not the only causes of wrongful conviction. Each case is unique, and many include a combination of the above issues. We must strive toward a justice system that is more fair and transparent.

Contributing Causes of Wrongful Convictions (first 225 DNA exonerations)

Total is more than 100% because wrongful convictions can have more than one cause.

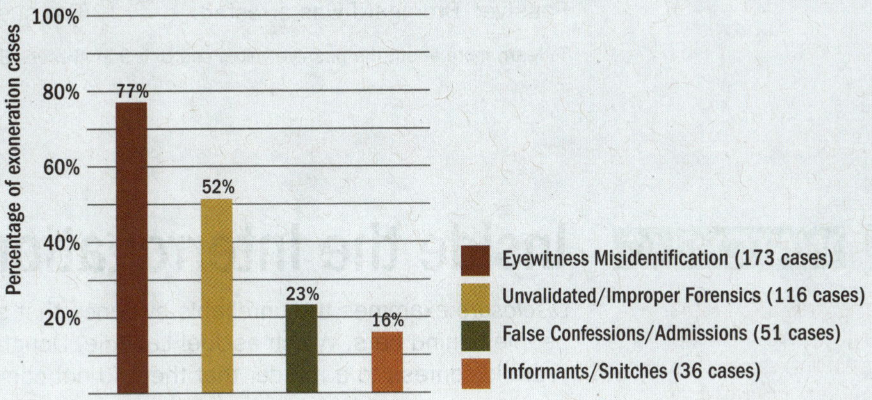

(1194 words)

Source: Abridged and adapted from "Understand the Causes." *The Innocence Project.* Innocence Project, n.d. Web.

Students can read the essay in class or for homework. There are additional questions in the Student Section of the Companion Website. You can verify if students have read the essay by checking their scores with the grade tracker.

Answers will vary.

COMPREHENSION: PREPARING AN OUTLINE

Prepare an outline for "The Causes of Wrongful Conviction." Under each heading, list three or four of the most important ideas in that section. For more information about preparing an outline (essay plan), see page 155 in Writing Workshop 1.

The Causes of Wrongful Conviction

I. Introduction

II. Eyewitness Misidentification

____

____

____

III. Invalidated Forensic Science

____

____

____

IV. Unreliable Witnesses

V. Incompetent Lawyers

Grammar TIP

Passive Voice

A verb is passive when the subject does not do the action; the subject receives the action. With passive verbs, use the correct tense of *be* and the past participle.

Active: The officer **arrested** Bromgard. He **interrogated** the suspect.

be + past participle

Passive: Bromgard **was arrested.** The suspect **was interrogated.**

To learn more about the passive voice, see Unit 9 in *Avenues 3: English Grammar*.

WATCHING

You can assign the video in class or for homework. There are additional comprehension questions in the Student Section of the Companion Website.

Inside the Interrogation Room

Disclosure examines the unreliable evidence that sometimes puts innocent people behind bars. Watch as Joel Labadie, Douglas Firemoon, and a seventeen-year-old confess to a murder that they did not commit.

COMPREHENSION

1 In what year was Darrelle Exner murdered? 1996

2 Where did Exner's murder occur? Regina

3 How many steps does the Reid technique have? Nine

4 Why is the "alternative question" method so successful in getting an admission of guilt?

Suspects are given two options that both place them at the crime scene.

5 At first, the three young men all claimed to be innocent. Why did they change their minds and confess?

The officer did not listen to their claims of innocence. Also, the officer lied, saying that their friends had implicated them. They may have felt hopeless.

6 According to the Innocence Project, what percentage of the 123 people who had been exonerated by DNA evidence had falsely confessed?

27 percent

7 British authorities determined that one in ... people are vulnerable to making wrong confessions.

(a.) five b. ten c. one hundred

8 Three young men confessed to Exner's murder. What detail about the murder did they not know?

They didn't know how she was murdered.

9 How long did the three young suspects spend in jail? Four and a half months

10 Why were the three young suspects eventually released from prison?

The DNA of Kenneth Patton, the man who found the girl's body, matched that of her rapist. Also, he pled guilty to the crime.

DISCUSSION AND WRITING

1 Why did the three young men confess to the murder? Explain what happened to them during the interrogation.

2 During the questioning of the young men, what should have alerted police to the fact that the confessions were false? What should the police have done?

3 In your opinion, should police departments continue to use the Reid interrogation method? Why or why not? What could they do to help ensure that there are fewer false confessions?

READING 4.3 Yirga Gebremeskel wrote the following essay while studying at college. Read about his experience in prison. Later, you will act out the words in green.

My Prison Story

BY YIRGA GEBREMESKEL

1 On November 8, 2005, my life completely changed. I was seventeen years old, and I was heading for disaster before I was wrongfully convicted of assault and battery. The terrible experience I went through made me a better person and helped me realize that life is too short and beautiful to be wasted.

2 Growing up, I found myself constantly getting in trouble. Trouble was like the sun. I started off by stealing candy and getting into fights in school. As I got older, my troubles progressed. I hung around with the wrong group of people and experimented with marijuana. My academic work declined because school was the last thing on my mind. All I wanted to do was hang out with the crew. I started to get in trouble with the law, but I never went to prison. My mother constantly lectured me, but her words went in one ear and out the other. No matter what she said, I always did what I wanted to do.

3 On November 8, my friend Malcolm invited me to hang out downtown. We planned to meet up in Downtown Crossing in Boston. I went, and I brought my little brother, Samson, with me. Malcolm's friend, Roger, was also there. We joked around and went window shopping before heading to a friend's house on Tremont Street. On the way, we felt thirsty, so we stopped into a 7-Eleven to get drinks.

4 I **strolled** to the back to get a beverage. When I got to the counter to pay, I looked through the glass doors and saw a cop cruiser pull up. I continued to pay for my item, but I felt like someone was watching me. When I **glanced** outside again, I found myself eye to eye with the officer occupying the cruiser. He pointed toward me, and my heart started to pound. I heard my brother asking, "Does he want you?" I looked the officer in the eye, and pointed toward myself to make sure he was talking to me. The officer **nodded** and signalled me to come outside.

5 When we got outside, the officer stepped out of the cruiser and **strutted** up to us. His first question was, "Where are you guys coming from?" We told him from downtown. He asked if we had any weapons, and we told him that we didn't. I thought nothing of it, at first, because getting harassed by the police was not a big deal. The cop said that someone had just been assaulted, and I fit the description. I protested that there had to be a mistake, but he put me against the wall and **patted** me **down**. Malcolm and my brother asked why, but the officer ignored them. The officer read me my rights and reached for his handcuffs, and he **shoved** me into the cruiser.

6 At the station, I was placed in a freezing little cubicle. It had a toilet and a sink, and it smelled like piss. I tried hard not to lean on anything. A while later, a different officer came over and took me to get my fingerprints taken. I explained that there was a mistake, and I didn't belong there. He **mumbled** that I would have to talk to my attorney. Then it was back to the dungeon. I lay down on the cement bed and kept promising myself that everything would be okay. My eyes were closed when I heard the officer's harsh voice: "Get up. You made bail." Those words were music to my ears.

7 My brother Samson had gone home and told my mother everything that had happened. She came to bail me out, like always. The bail was $2,500. My mother works hard for her money, so seeing her put up that much money really saddened me. She wasn't mad at me this time because she knew I was innocent.

8 The next morning, I had to be at court. I couldn't afford a lawyer, so the court gave me a court-appointed attorney. After he heard my story, the attorney explained that the man who had been assaulted was going to testify against me. How was that possible? I asked if I could speak to my accuser, but the attorney told me there was no way this could happen.

district attorney: In the United States, the district attorney is the state's prosecutor.

9 Four months later, my lawyer arrived one morning and said, "The **district attorney** is ready to go to trial today." I told him we couldn't because my brother, who was my most important witness, was at school. But my lawyer insisted that there could be no delays. He wouldn't give my mother enough time to find Samson. Very quickly, he prepared my friend Malcolm and me to answer questions. That was the first time that we had done any pre-trial preparation. Roger, Malcolm's friend, also knew the truth, but he was incarcerated. According to my attorney, there was no point in bringing Roger to testify because he wouldn't be credible.

10 The actual trial was very brief. It was hard for me to take it seriously; I felt like any moment the victim would realize his mistake. My attorney went first and argued my case. I took the stand, and so did my friend Malcolm. But Malcolm **trembled** and was really nervous on the stand, so maybe that looked bad to the jury.

11 After my attorney finished, the prosecution presented its case. The victim took the stand, and I saw my accuser for the first time. While the victim was describing what had happened, he seemed earnest. It was clear that he was not lying. He really believed that I was his attacker.

12 There was no other evidence. After what felt like forever, the jury came back with the verdict: "Guilty."

13 I couldn't believe my ears. I was going to jail! How could this be happening? I turned around to look at my mother's face, and there were tears coming down her cheeks. She knew that I was innocent.

14 The judge gave me my sentence. I would serve six months in prison with an additional two years on probation. My eyes got watery. The court officer **clutched** my arm. I asked him if I could hug my mother, and he allowed me to. She held me like she was trying to hold on. Then the officer escorted me through a side exit.

15 The first couple of days in the correctional facility were tough. I couldn't sleep; I **tossed** and turned all night. Soon, I fell into the boring routine of daily prison life. From 6:30 to bedtime, there was a schedule of breakfast, lock-in in the cell, some recreation time, back to the cell, and so on. Small things were the most difficult. The food was horrible. I missed being able to open a fridge. Sometimes I got cellmates who wouldn't shower, so the cell smelled bad. And it was loud; voices echoed as people talked and argued constantly. Even at night, people would **holler** through the doors, or my cellmates would **bicker**.

16 At times, it was hard talking to my family or friends on the phone because they were getting ready to go to a party or just a simple walk to the park, but I was going back to my cell. I started to read books to escape the environment I was in. At least when I read, it felt like I was somewhere else.

17 The most frustrating part of being in jail was wasting time that I could never get back. My mother had to take care of four kids on her own. Since I couldn't help her, she had to work two jobs. The stress was eating me up inside. Most people gain weight in prison, but I lost twenty pounds.

18 One great piece of advice I got was to do the time and not let the time do me. I started to make better use of my days. I read business books, a subject I had a lot of interest in. I spent nights thinking about my life and where I was heading, and how I could never come back to this place.

19 When my time was up, and I could head home, I was the happiest man in the world. I vowed to become a better person and to live my life to the fullest. Now I'm going to school, and I have given up drugs. To this day, I can't explain why the victim identified me. Probably I look like the person who assaulted him. I wonder how accurate visual memory is? Still, my incarceration changed my life in a positive way. I believe everything happens for a reason. If I met the eyewitness who completely changed my life, I would even say, "Thank you."

(1440 words)

Students can read the essay in class or for homework. There are additional questions in the Student Section of the Companion Website. You can verify if students have read the essay by checking their scores with the grade tracker.

VOCABULARY AND COMPREHENSION

1 What do the following phrases mean? Look at the context before you make your guess. (The paragraph numbers are in parentheses.)

a) hang out with the crew (2)

Spend time with my friends or gang

b) her words went in one ear and out the other (2)

I didn't pay attention or act on her words.

c) we went window shopping (3)

We looked at a store window display without buying anything.

d) Those words were music to my ears. (6)

The words made me feel happy.

e) I took the stand (10)

I went in front of the courtroom to testify.

f) I couldn't believe my ears. (13)

I couldn't believe what I was hearing.

2 In paragraph 5, the writer says that "getting harassed by the police was not a big deal" for him and his friends. What does that suggest about the writer's life?

He was often in trouble with the law.

3 Before the court case mentioned in the text, did the writer's mother previously pay bail for him? Explain your answer.

Yes. In paragraph 7, he writes, "She came to bail me out, like always," and "She wasn't mad at me this time because she knew I was innocent."

4 The writer didn't do the crime, and he had an alibi. Why was he sent to prison anyway? List at least three possible reasons.

He had had previous problems with the law. He couldn't afford a good lawyer. His defence attorney did not seem very competent. His most credible witness, his brother, wasn't there. The eyewitness was mistaken.

Answers will vary.

5 Yirga describes prison. What images stand out and make an impression? List some ideas.

The routine was boring. The food was horrible. The cellmates smelled because they didn't bathe. It was loud (voices echoed). It was hard to hear about the plans of family and friends.

6 Yirga spent six months in jail, but he was innocent. Today, why isn't he angrier? Why isn't he fighting to clear his name? Make some inferences (guesses) based on the text.

The prison term had a positive effect on his life and helped him change. Maybe he feels that he has no chance to clear his name.

DISCUSSION

COMPANION WEB+ For more reading practice, read "Types of Correctional Officers" on the Companion Website.

1 Yirga's story happened in Boston. If he had lived in Canada, what would his punishment have been? Make a guess based on your knowledge of the Canadian justice system.

2 Yirga was punished for something he didn't do, but it made him a better person. Is it a good idea to send youths to prison? Why or why not?

Vocabulary **BOOST**

Visit the Companion Website to practise using vivid verbs.

Vocabulary Boosts expand students' vocabulary. You might ask students to write a paragraph that includes some of the verbs in these lists.

Act It Out

The verbs listed below appear in the essay, "My Prison Story." Half of the class will define the words in column A, and the other half will define the words in column B.

- Working with a partner, define the words in your column using context clues and a dictionary. (The paragraph numbers are indicated in parentheses.)
- Then, act out your verbs for a pair of students who worked on the other column. Do not use any words. Instead, show the action.

A		B	
stroll (4):	____________	mumble (6):	____________
glance (4):	____________	tremble (10):	____________
nod (4):	____________	clutch (14):	____________
strut (5):	____________	toss (15):	____________
pat down (5):	____________	holler (15):	____________
shove (5):	____________	bicker (15):	____________

LISTENING

You can assign the listening activity in class or for homework. There are additional comprehension questions in the Student Section of the Companion Website.

Superhero Justice

Do we need civilian crime fighters—dressed as costumed superheroes—patrolling our city streets? Listen and find out.

COMPREHENSION: WRITING A SUMMARY

Summarize the information in the audio segment. In your summary, include the following information:

- Describe the superhero movement.
- Discuss Phoenix Jones. Who is he and why is he in trouble?
- Describe Mr. Extreme. Where is he located and how do the police view him?
- Why do ordinary people decide to become superheroes?

DISCUSSION

Go to YouTube and watch a short video about a real-life superhero. Then report back to your group and describe what happened. What are some problems with superhero justice?

WRITING

Superhero Story

PART A

In this activity, you are going to write a short story about an imaginary superhero.

First, choose the name, costume, and secret power of your superhero. Also consider where he or she is located. Brainstorm some ideas.

On a separate sheet of paper, write your name. Then write the following information:

superhero name | costume | secret power | specific location

Under that information, write the first sentence of your short story. Write the first thing that comes to your mind. Then join a team of students and sit in a circle. Your team is going to help you develop your story. Pass your sheet of paper to the student on your right. You will have someone else's sheet of paper in front of you. Add another sentence to that student's story. Keep writing sentences and passing your sheets of paper. Each person in your team will end up with his or her own unique story.

Don't spend too much time thinking. Just write the first idea that comes to your mind.

PART B

For homework, flesh out your short story to make it more complete. You can add or remove details. Include at least six lines of dialogue.

Take Action!

WRITING TOPICS

Write about one of the following topics. For information about essay structure, see the Writing Workshops on pages 148 to 157. Before handing in your work, refer to the Writing Checklist on the inside back cover.

1 My Prison Story

In "My Prison Story," Yirga Gebremeskel explains how he was arrested and convicted of a crime that he did not commit. Using information from "The Causes of Wrongful Conviction," give two or three possible reasons for Gebremeskel's conviction. If you quote from any articles, ensure that you use quotation marks properly and cite your source.

2 False Confessions

Why do people give false confessions? Give two or three reasons. You can consider ideas from the video *Inside the Interrogation Room*, and you can discuss the cases of Joel Labadie and Douglas Firemoon.

3 Superheroes

Write about the real-life superhero phenomenon and express your views about it. Begin by explaining why some ordinary people decide to become real-life superheroes. Does our society need such vigilante justice? Explain why or why not. Refer to the audio segment "Superhero Justice."

SPEAKING TOPICS

Companion Web+ Need help with pronunciation? Visit the Companion Website and try the Pronunciation Workshops.

Prepare a presentation about one of the following topics. For details about preparing a speaking presentation, see Appendix 1 on page 174.

1 My Rant

Brainstorm about things you find annoying. Then create a rant about something that bothers you. (A rant is a short but passionate speech.) Provide clear examples to explain why it bothers you.

Remind students to try the Pronunciation Workshops on the Companion Website.

2 A Problem and a Solution

Speak about an issue or problem that interests you. The problem could be personal, in your college, or in your town, city, province, or country. You are only speaking for five or six minutes, so try to narrow your topic. For example, you should not discuss organized crime in general, but you could present information about corruption that occurred during a particular government project. The problem can be serious (drug use, drinking and driving), or silly (a complaint about parking rules at the college). If you do research, mention your sources during your presentation.

- **Introduce your topic** with an anecdote, or general or historical background information. Include your thesis statement. In other words, state your point of view about the problem.
- **Prove that there is a problem:** Explain why it is a problem.
- **Explain how to solve the problem:** Suggest at least two actions that individuals, schools, governments, or others can do to solve this problem or to improve the situation.
- **Conclude** your presentation. End with a prediction, suggestion, or quotation.

MEDIA LINK

Watch a television show or a movie about crime and/or punishment. For example, you could watch *The Avengers* or a classic such as *The Shawshank Redemption*, *The Godfather*, or *The Hurricane*. (You could also do an Internet search for shows or movies about crime.) Prepare an essay or a speaking presentation about the show or movie and its relationship to crime and punishment. Begin with a very brief summary. Then explain the message of the movie or show. Make a connection between its message and at least one of the readings in this chapter.

Revising and Editing

The Revising and Editing sections at the end of each chapter help your students prepare for writing tests, including Benchmark and TESOL tests. You can ask students to do the activities with a partner and to share ideas.

REVISE FOR TRANSITIONAL WORDS AND EXPRESSIONS
EDIT FOR MIXED ERRORS

Your writing should be coherent, and connections between ideas should be logical. Transitional words and expressions help the reader follow the ideas. (To learn more about coherence, see page 161 in Writing Workshop 2.)

Read the short essay and follow these steps:

1 Underline and correct eight errors. Look for mistakes with plurals, adjectives, and adverbs.

2 Add logical transitional words and expressions. Choose from the words provided below. Use each word once.

additionally	for example	however	naturally
first	furthermore	meanwhile	therefore

Introduction

Answers will vary.

Since the early 1930s, people have been fascinated with superheroes. In 1936, one of the most popular radio show (shows) was *The Green Hornet*. The first Superman comic came out in 1938. ____Naturally____, such heroes are fictional, with their costumes and specials (special) powers. ____However____, they have a real (really) important role to play in the collective subconscious.

Body paragraph 1

First, superheroes, unlike the celebrities and politicians that fill the news, have a strong moral code and do not expect a reward for their service. People crave such goodness. Additionally, such characters have a human side that individuals can identify with. For example, Peter Parker is a seventeen-~~years~~ year-old high school student who feels lonely and inadequate until he puts on his costume. As Spider-Man, he doesn't expect money or popularity. His only desire is to help others: "With great power there must also come great responsibility!"

Body paragraph 2

Furthermore, superheroes play the roles of gods, and the villains are contemporary devils. Throughout history, people have created mythical half-humans who combat evil. The ancient Greeks had gods such as Apollo and Zeus. In India, Hindus celebrate deities such as the multi-armed Kali. In contemporary storys (stories), the Avengers battle the evil warmonger Loki, and Batman fights deranged criminals such as the Joker. The worse (worst) villains represent dark human impulse (impulses) of hate and greed. Katherine Monk, in an article for *Canada.com*, says, "Forever trapped in the timeless battle between good and evil, superheroes allow mere movie-going mortals a chance to dissect the human condition on an extra-large scale." Therefore, each superhero and villains (villain) has an important symbolic role.

Conclusion

You can ask students to remove this activity and hand it in. Note that in the student books, pages are perforated.

In their daily lives, people read about corrupt politicians, murder, and war. Meanwhile, film and comic superheroes provide an alternative, showing a model of selflessness. According to Monk, "It's not superpowers that make the superhero. In fact, it's quite the opposite." She argues that human love and compassion "are what truly make a hero."

Grammar TIP

One of the ...

Always use a plural noun after "one of the ..."

One of the best ~~superhero~~ superheroes is Wonder Woman.

To learn more about plural nouns, see Unit 8 in *Avenues 3: English Grammar*.

COMPANION WEB+ To practise vocabulary from this chapter, visit the Companion Website.

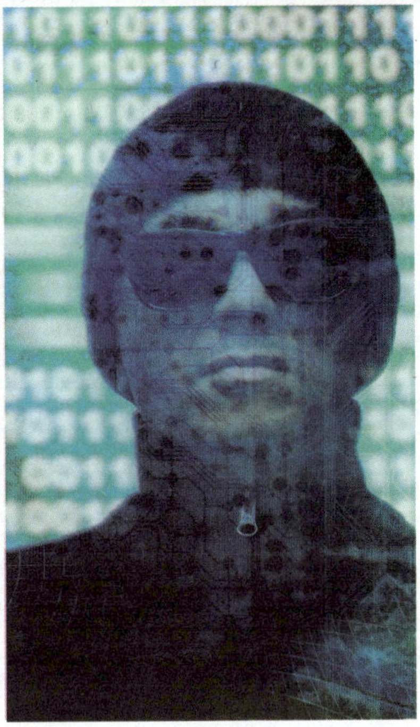

CHAPTER 5

"The War for the Internet was inevitable—a time bomb built into its creation."

- MICHAEL JOSEPH GROSS, WRITER OF "WORLD WAR 3.0"

Cybercrime

What types of cybercriminals stalk the Internet? In this chapter, you will learn about the world of cybercrime.

START UP

Black Hat Hacking

Kevin Poulsen is a reformed "black hat" hacker. He is now an editor for *Wired.com*'s "Threat Level" blog. In an interview with *Vanity Fair* magazine, Poulsen describes the level of difficulty of the following actions. Guess what his answers are.

	Relatively easy	Very difficult
1. Gain complete access to someone's computer	☑	☐
2. Siphon a few million dollars out of companies and transfer the money to a Swiss bank account	☑	☐
3. Shut down the power grid in the country	☐	☑
4. Take over someone's computer and use it to launch cyberattacks	☑	☐
5. Fix the Academy Awards so your choice of movie will be the winner	☐	☑
6. Put your image onto a giant screen at a sports stadium	☑	☐
7. Launch a nation's nuclear weapon	☐	☑
8. Publish your message on the front page of the *New York Times*' website	☑	☐
9. Install software to take over someone's online banking and mask the theft (the user will log on and not notice that money is missing)	☑	☐
10. Find your home address by looking at your online photos	☑	☐

DISCUSSION AND WRITING

Do you do online banking? Why or why not? What precautions do you take?

READING STRATEGY

Students can visit the Companion Website to practise their reading comprehension. Questions for all readings are structured to help students do better in their reading tests, including Benchmark and TESOL tests.

Recognizing Irony

Irony is a technique that some writers use to make a point. When an author is being ironic, he or she says one thing but really means the opposite. There are many types of irony.

Situational irony: There is a difference between how an event looks on the surface and what is going on underneath. Expectations and reality differ because there is a contrary—and often appropriate—turn of events.

EXAMPLES:
- Nathan is robbing a house. At that same moment, someone is robbing Nathan's apartment.
- Town residents, fed up with the constant "caw-caw" of crows, hire someone to solve the problem. Every morning, the crow controller fires cannons and sets off firecrackers to scare away the crows.

Dramatic irony: This type of irony is used in plays, stories, and novels. The audience knows something that the characters don't, which makes the characters' actions more tragic, humorous, or poignant.

EXAMPLE: In Shakespeare's *Romeo and Juliet*, Romeo kills himself because he believes that Juliet swallowed poison and died. The audience knows something that Romeo does not: Juliet is still alive because she really took a sleeping drug, not poison.

COMPANION WEB+ Visit the Companion Website to prepare for your reading tests. Online questions for all readings are structured to help you practise reading strategies.

Verbal irony: There is a contrast between what the writer or character says and what the writer or character means. The author uses an ironic tone and does not intend the reader to interpret the words literally. Sarcasm is a type of verbal irony.

EXAMPLE: An overworked employee says, "I can't wait to start working on those twenty reports that are due next week."

READING 5.1 Anonymous, the loose hacking collective, carried out its first coordinated cyberattack in 2006. Read about some of the problems with the group.

The Problem with Anonymous

BY ANDRES GUADAMUZ

1 Remember, remember, the fifth of November
Gunpowder, treason, and plot.
We see no reason
Why gunpowder treason
Should ever be forgot!

2 It is a heartening example of this age (or a sad indictment, depending on one's world view) that one of the most famous hacktivist collectives in the world—Anonymous—takes its imagery from the graphic novel and eponymous film *V for Vendetta*. This should come as no surprise, however. To the Internet activist masses, the novel's hero V has become a powerful symbol of collective action against the establishment. V, who wears the **Guy Fawkes** mask made famous by the film, has become the face of Anonymous. In the novel, Evey, the protagonist, finds the hero V lying on the floor dying. She realizes that V is not simply the masked person lying on the floor; V is everyone who believes the ideas he espouses. This is treated in the film in a more cinematic—and dare I say, ham-fisted manner—when large parts of the population of London show up to watch the Parliament burn, dressed in Guy Fawkes masks.

Guy Fawkes: British conspirator. The opening rhyme was created in the seventeenth century after Guy Fawkes failed to blow up the British parliament buildings. After Fawkes' arrest and execution, the Parliament of England enacted an annual bonfire night to celebrate the failure of the plot to kill King James I. Guy Fawkes night is still celebrated in England.

3 Today, Anonymous has taken the *V* imagery as its own. What matters is not the individual behind the mask; it is the message: "You can kill a man, but you cannot kill an idea."

4 The ideal of anonymity espoused by the movement has its benefits. The collective has managed to strike fear in the hearts of system administrators, and it has become the face of hackerdom for media outlets everywhere. Certainly, the group has caused some mischief with coordinated DoS (Denial of Service) attacks on selected targets. [During such attacks, a multitude of computers saturate a target machine with external communication requests, temporarily knocking a site offline.] For instance, the group plotted against the Church of Scientology because the church tried to remove an unflattering interview with Tom Cruise from the Internet. After a popular file-sharing service was shut down, hackers disabled the US Department of Justice website. In 2011, Anonymous became the online support arm of the Occupy Wall Street movement.

5 However, anonymity also has its setbacks. Who speaks for the hacker collective Anonymous? The problem with masks is that anyone can wear one, so making statements supposedly coming from Anonymous is rather easy. Someone can

Guy Fawkes masks

purchase a *V for Vendetta* plastic Guy Fawkes mask (licensed by Time Warner, oh the irony), find a way to distort his or her voice, make a video, and upload it to YouTube.

6 Not having a centralized structure means that, at least in appearance, any Anonymous video out there is an "official" video. This has resulted in some high-profile threats getting a lot of media attention even though they have later been decried as not representing Anonymous. Of particular note are the November 2011 threats to shut down Facebook, or the supposed plan to release information against the prominent Zetas drug gang in Mexico. Neither threat panned out. Such episodes have demonstrated that not having a unified voice can have a serious diluting effect on the cause. For how much longer will people continue to believe such threats, when so many are hollow?

relay channels: sites that feature real-time messaging and conferencing

7 The Anonymous hacker group is not entirely anarchic. As with many things in life, chaos finds a way to self-organize, and Anonymous has been building a structure based on loose meritocracy. There are semi-official Internet **relay channels** for chatting and organizing operations. There are also semi-official websites, Twitter accounts, and all sorts of ways to try to bring some sort of order to the movement. This does not stop anyone trying to talk on behalf of Anonymous, but it gives some semblance of order when the movement as a whole disparages an op [original poster], as happened with the Zetas drug gang threat.

8 Low-entry barriers to online forums have generated tension in the movement. The ease with which someone can enter the relay channels has resulted in some rather strange online macho posturing. Wannabes and hangers-on in forums around the world pretend to be part of Anonymous, or they tell their audience that they know a "high-up Anon."

9 One of the biggest problems with Anonymous is that some of the LulzSec arrests have had a real effect on the type of operations undertaken. [LulzSec—a name that roughly means "laughing at security"—is an Anonymous-associated hacker group that claimed responsibility for high-profile attacks against Sony and the CIA. In 2012, several members were arrested and charged.] Will arrests and government scrutiny change the group's focus? Could the emphasis on high-visibility attacks end, with much more effort going to political engagement?

10 In George R. R. Martin's *A Dance with Dragons*, Queen Daenerys has a group of guards called the Brazen Beasts. The beasts are freed slaves who wear bronze animal masks to hide their identity. The result is that anyone with a mask can claim to be a Brazen Beast, and a complicated system of passwords has to be established in order to make sure that any mask-wearer is a real guard. Perhaps as Anonymous evolves, it will have to resort to such tactics.

11 In a nutshell, Anonymous is being undermined by its own ideals of anonymity. Only time will tell if the members manage to overcome the faults inherent in the system. In the meantime, may the British have a safe Guy Fawkes bonfire night.

(888 words)

Source: Guadamuz, Andres. "The Problem with Anonymous." *TechnoLlama*. Cyberlog Blog, 5 Nov. 2011. Web.

COMPREHENSION: CRITICAL THINKING

Students can read the essay in class or for homework. There are additional questions in the Student Section of the Companion Website. You can verify if students have read the essay by checking their scores with the grade tracker.

1 Why does the essay open with an old British rhyme?

The rhyme refers to Guy Fawkes night, and Guy Fawkes masks have become the face of Anonymous.

2 In paragraph 2, what does *espouses* mean?

a. takes as a partner; marries

b. refutes and ignores

(c.) embraces and supports

3 According to the author, how is Anonymous organized?

There is no centralized structure. Anyone can claim to be part of the organization. But at the same time, it "is not entirely anarchic," with several semi-official Internet relay channels, websites, and Twitter accounts.

4 What are the benefits and the disadvantages of Anonymous's organizational style? See paragraphs 4 and 5.

Benefits: The group appears united and scary when the media discusses it; everyone has a voice; anybody can join; individual hackers are less likely to be discovered.

Disadvantages: There isn't a clear leader, so anyone can speak for the organization; incompetent hackers can join; people can make false threats that undermine the movement.

5 a) In paragraph 5, the author uses the word "irony." What is he referring to, and why is it ironic?

Anonymous members are anti-establishment, yet they wear a symbol produced by a large corporation.

b) Of what type of irony is that an example? See the definitions of irony on pages 76 and 77.

(a.) situational b. dramatic c. verbal

6 What empty threats have some Anonymous members made? Explain how the threats have hurt the movement.

Empty threats against Facebook and the Zetas drug gang could make the movement lose credibility.

7 According to the author, what steps does the group need to take as it evolves? Make an inference, or guess, based on information in the text.

The group needs to make membership more exclusive and perhaps have a series of passwords to ensure that only true members can enter their forums.

DISCUSSION AND WRITING

COMPANION WEB+ Answer additional questions for all the reading and listening activities. You can also access audio and video clips online.

1 How does the essay define Anonymous?

2 Security expert Joshua Corman calls Anonymous "a brand or franchise." How does this definition compare to the one in the essay? Explain your answer.

WATCHING

Hackers' World

Why do people hack? What are companies and governments doing about it? Watch and find out.

You can assign this video in class or for homework. There are additional comprehension questions in the Student Section of the Companion Website.

COMPREHENSION

1 What does Daniel Tobitt do?

He has a cyber forensic firm called Digital Wizard that investigates cybercrimes and provides security fixes for companies.

2 Who is Greg House?

An "outed" Anonymous member

3 After the Church of Scientology attack, how did the news media help or hurt Anonymous?

The media provided publicity for Anonymous. House says that it gained acceptance "as a brand" and more people got involved in the group.

4 What happened to Natasha Maksimovic? Why is she upset with Anonymous?

Her private information was compromised because she was a customer of Sony and someone hacked into Sony's customer database.

5 How much did the hack cost Sony? $150 million

6 Greg House justified the Anonymous hack of Sony. What was his defence?

Anonymous just showed that it's easy to obtain private information. They showed Sony the holes in their security.

7 According to the video, where did hacking start?

(a.) At the Massachusetts Institute of Technology (MIT)

b. At the US government CIA headquarters

c. At the University of Southern California (USC)

8 In the past, what did the term *hacker* refer to?

Someone with more knowledge of computers than others. It had no negative meaning.

9 What are "hacks of kindness"? What types of things do those hackers do?

They create software and apps that will help people and save lives.

DISCUSSION AND WRITING

What are some potential problems when young hackers go after their enemies? For example, in the video, hackers mention going after Casey Anthony, a woman who was accused of killing her daughter but who was declared "not guilty" by the courts.

READING STRATEGY

Students can visit the Companion Website to practise their reading comprehension. Questions for all readings are structured to help students do better in their reading tests, including Benchmark and TESOL tests.

Skimming and Scanning

When you **skim**, you read quickly to find the main ideas in a text. Skimming is a valuable strategy when you want to determine if an article is useful for your research. You quickly read headings, summaries, and first sentences to see if the text is of interest.

When you **scan**, you also read quickly, but you concentrate on finding specific information. For example, you scan to find particular names and dates.

PRACTICE

Before you read the next essay carefully, scan it first. You have two minutes to find as much of the following information as possible.

1. Who is Aaron Barr? A digital security executive
2. When did Barr's company get hacked? February 6, 2011
3. How much did Barr earn when he did social media training? $25,000 at a time
4. Barr contacted a reporter for which newspaper? *Financial Times*
5. What online nickname did Aaron Barr use when he went onto Anonymous chat rooms? CogAnon
6. List the nicknames of three Anonymous hackers. Sabu, Topiary, Kayla, Tflow

COMPANION WEB+ Visit the Companion Website to prepare for your reading tests. Online questions for all readings are structured to help you practise reading strategies.

READING 5.2

Parmy Olson is a journalist and a regular contributor to *Forbes* magazine. She is also the author of *We Are Anonymous: Inside the Hacker World of LulzSec, Anonymous, and the Global Cyber Insurgency*. The following excerpt is from her book.

Anonymous Strikes Back

Aaron Barr

BY PARMY OLSON

1 On February 6, 2011, millions of people were settling into their couches, splitting open bags of nachos, and spilling beer into plastic cups in preparation for the year's Super Bowl Sunday. That day, a digital security executive named Aaron Barr watched helplessly as his world turned upside down. Super Bowl Sunday was the day he came face-to-face with Anonymous. Barr, a husband and a father of twins, had made the mistake of trying to figure out who Anonymous really was.

2 The real turning point was lunchtime, with six hours to go until the Super Bowl kickoff. As Barr sat on the living room couch, he fished his iPhone out of his pocket and pressed a button to refresh his mail, when a dark blue window popped up. It showed three words that would change his life: Cannot Get Mail. Barr went into the phone's account settings and carefully typed in his password: "kibafo33." It didn't work. His e-mails weren't coming through.

3 Slowly, a tickling anxiety crawled up his back as he realized what this meant. Someone had hacked his HBGary Federal account, possibly accessing tens of thousands of internal e-mails, and then locked him out. This meant that someone, somewhere, had seen non-disclosure agreements and sensitive documents that could implicate a multinational bank, a respected US government agency, and his own company. One by one, memories of specific classified documents and messages surfaced in his mind, each heralding a new wave of sickening dread.

4 Barr dashed up the stairs to his home office and sat down in front of his laptop. He tried logging on to his Facebook account, then Twitter, then Yahoo. He'd been locked out of almost every one of his Web accounts, even the online role-playing game World of Warcraft. Barr silently kicked himself for using the same password on every account. He glanced over at his Wi-Fi router and saw frantic flashing lights. Now people were trying to overload it with traffic, trying to jam their way further into his home network.

5 He reached over and unplugged it. The flashing lights went dead.

* * * * *

6 In November 2009, a security consultant named Greg Hoglund contacted Barr. Knowing Barr's military background and expertise in cryptography, Hoglund wanted to start a company that would specialize in selling services to the United States government. It would be called HBGary Federal. Barr jumped at the chance to be his own boss, and he relished the job at first. Less than a year later, though, none of Barr's ideas was bringing in any money. Desperate for contracts, Barr was keeping the tiny company of three employees afloat by running "social media training" for executives, bringing in $25,000 at a time. These were lessons in how to use social networking sites to gather information on people—as spying tools.

7 In October 2010, salvation appeared. Barr started talking to a law firm whose clients—among them the US Chamber of Commerce and Bank of America—needed help dealing with opponents such as WikiLeaks. Barr dug out his fake Facebook profiles and showed how he might spy on the opponents. The law firm appeared interested, but there were still no contracts in January 2011, and HBGary Federal needed money.

8 Then Barr had an idea. A conference in San Francisco for security professionals was coming up. If he gave a speech revealing how his social media snooping had uncovered information on a mysterious subject, he'd get new-found credibility and maybe even those contracts. Barr decided that there was no better target than Anonymous. About a month prior, the news media had exploded with reports that a large and mysterious group of hackers had started attacking the websites of MasterCard, PayPal, and Visa in retaliation for their having cut funding to WikiLeaks. Barr was intrigued, and he believed he could do better than the Federal Bureau of Investigation—maybe help the FBI, too—with his social media snooping expertise. Going after Anonymous was risky, but he figured if the collective turned on him, the worst they could do was take down the website of HBGary Federal for a few hours—a couple of days, tops. A denial of service attack is Anonymous's most popular form of attack. It is like punching someone in the eye. It looks bad and it hurts, but it doesn't kill.

9 Barr started by lurking in the online chat rooms where Anonymous supporters congregated and creating a nickname for himself, CogAnon. He blended in, using the group's lingo and pretending to be a young new recruit. On the side, he quietly noted the nicknames of others in the chat room, paying particular attention to those who got the most attention. When these people left the chat room, he'd note the time, too. Then he'd switch to Facebook. Barr had created several fake Facebook personas and had "friended" dozens of real-world people who openly claimed to support Anonymous. If one of those friends suddenly became active on Facebook soon after a nickname had exited the Anonymous chat room, Barr figured he had a match.

10 Barr contacted a reporter for the *Financial Times*, offering an interview about how his data could lead to more arrests of "major players" in Anonymous. Barr's comments suggested, for the first time, that Anonymous was a hierarchy and not as "anonymous" as it thought. The paper ran the story on Friday, February 4, with the headline "Cyberactivists Warned of Arrest," and it quoted Barr. He got a small thrill from seeing the published article.

11 By the end of Friday, detectives from the FBI's e-crime division had contacted Barr asking if he wouldn't mind sharing his information. He agreed to meet them Monday, the day after the Super Bowl. At around the same time, a small group of hackers with Anonymous had read the story, too. They were three people, in three different parts of the world, and they had been invited into an online chat room. Their online nicknames were Topiary, Sabu, and Kayla, and at least two of them, Sabu and Topiary, were meeting for the first time. The person who had invited them went by the nickname Tflow, and he was also in the room. No one knew anyone else's real name, age, gender, or location.

12 The chat room was locked, meaning no one could enter unless invited. Conversation was stilted at first, but within a few minutes everyone was talking. Personalities started to emerge. Sabu, the heavyweight veteran of the group, was assertive and brash, and he used slang like "yo" and "my brother." None of the others in the room knew this, but he was a born-and-bred New Yorker of Puerto Rican descent. Kayla was childlike and friendly but fiercely smart. She claimed to be female and, if asked, sixteen years old. She was obsessive about her computer's privacy. She never typed her real name into her netbook in case it got key-logged, had no physical hard drive, and would boot up from a tiny microSD card that she could quickly swallow if the police ever came to her door. Rumour even had it that she'd stabbed her webcam with a knife one day, just in case someone took over her PC and filmed her without her knowledge. Topiary was the least skilled of the group when it came to hacking, but he had another talent to make up for it: his wit. Cocksure and often brimming with ideas, Topiary used his silver tongue to slowly make his way up the ladder of secret planning rooms in the Anonymous chat networks. He had become so trusted that the network operators asked him to write the official Anonymous statements for each attack on PayPal and MasterCard.

13 Tflow, the guy who'd brought everyone together, got down to business. Someone had to do something about this Aaron Barr and his "research." There was that quote from the *Financial Times* story saying Barr had "collected information on

the core leaders, including many of their real names, and that they could be arrested if law enforcement had the same data." If Barr's data was actually right, Anons could be in trouble. The group started making plans. First, they had to scan the server that ran the HBGary Federal website for any source code vulnerabilities. If they got lucky, they might find a hole they could enter, then take control and replace Barr's homepage with a giant logo of Anonymous and a written warning not to mess with their collective.

14 Sabu started scanning *HBGaryFederal.com* for a hole. It turned out Barr's site had a major bug. Though its job was to help other companies protect themselves from cyberattacks, HBGary Federal itself was vulnerable to a simple attack that targeted databases. As soon as they were in, the hackers rooted around for the names and passwords of Barr and Hoglund, who had control of the site's servers. Quickly, they found the information, but there was a stumbling block. The passwords were encrypted. Sabu picked out three hashes, long strings of random numbers. He expected them to be exceptionally tough to unlock, and when he passed them to the others on the team, he wasn't surprised to find that no one could crack them. In a last-ditch attempt, he uploaded them to a Web forum for password cracking. Within a couple of hours, all three hashes had been cracked by random Anonymous volunteers. The result for one of them looked exactly like this: 4036d5fe575fb46f48ffcd5d7aeeb5af:kibafo33.

15 Right there at the end of the string of letters and numbers was Aaron Barr's password. When they tried using kibafo33 to access his HBGary Federal e-mails, they got in. They couldn't believe their luck. By Friday night, they were watching an oblivious Barr exchange happy e-mails with his colleagues about the *Financial Times* article. On a whim, one of them decided to check to see if kibafo33 worked anywhere else. Unbelievably for a cyber security specialist, Barr had used the same easy-to-crack password on almost all his Web accounts, including Twitter, Yahoo!, Flickr, and Facebook.

16 The group decided that they would not swoop on Barr that day. They would take the weekend to spy on him and download every e-mail he'd ever sent or received during his time with HBGary Federal. But there was a sense of urgency because the team realized Barr was planning to meet the FBI the following Monday. Once they had taken what they could, they decided all hell would break loose at kickoff on Super Bowl Sunday.

* * * * *

17 Saturday started off as any other for Barr. Relaxing and spending time with his family, he had no idea that an Anonymous team was busy delving into his e-mails. The team's latest find was Barr's own research on Anonymous. It was a PDF document that started with a decent, short explanation of what Anonymous was. It listed websites, a timeline of recent cyberattacks, and lots of nicknames next to real-life names and addresses. The names Sabu, Topiary, and Kayla were nowhere to be seen. They gradually realized that Barr had been using Facebook to try to identify real people and he had no idea what he was doing. It also looked like Barr might actually point the finger at some innocent people. In the meantime, Tflow had downloaded Barr's e-mails onto his server, then waited about fifteen hours for them to compile into a **torrent**. He put the torrent file on The Pirate Bay. This meant that, soon, anyone could download and read more than forty thousand of Aaron Barr's e-mails.

torrent: type of file that can be easily shared across the Internet

18 Sunday morning, with eleven hours till kickoff, came the pleasure of telling Barr what they had just done. Of course, to play this right, the hackers wouldn't tell him everything immediately. They would toy with him first. By now they had figured out that Barr was using the nickname CogAnon to talk to people in Anonymous chat rooms and that he lived in Washington, DC. "We have everything from his Social Security number, to his career in the military, to his clearances," Sabu told the others, "to how many shits a day he takes." They decided to make Barr a little paranoid before the strike. When Barr entered the chat network as CogAnon, Topiary sent him a private message.

19 "Hello," said Topiary.

20 "Hi," CogAnon replied.

21 In another chat window, Topiary was giving a running commentary to other Anons who were laughing at his exploits. "Tell him you're recruiting for a new mission," Sabu said.

22 Topiary went back into his conversation with the security specialist. "We're recruiting for a new operation in the Washington area. Interested?"

23 Barr paused for twenty seconds. "Potentially. Depends on what it is," he said.

24 Topiary pasted the response in the other chat room. "Hahahahaha," said Sabu.

25 "I take it from your host that you're near where our target is," Topiary told Barr.

26 Back in Washington, DC, Barr held his breath. How exactly could they have figured out where he lived? Barr tried to sound helpful. "I can be in the city within a few hours ... depending on traffic LOL."

27 Topiary decided to give him another fright. "Our target is a security company," he said.

28 Barr's stomach turned. Okay, so this meant Anonymous was definitely targeting HBGary Federal. "Not sure how I can help," Barr wrote.

29 "That depends," Topiary said. "We need help gathering info on *Ligatt.com* security company."

30 Barr let out a long breath of relief. Ligatt was in the same line of work as HBGary Federal, so it looked like his company was not the target after all.

31 "Ah, O.K.; let me check them out," Barr replied almost gratefully.

32 There was no reply. "You still there?" Barr asked.

33 Soon after that, Barr was sitting in his living room and staring in dreadful fascination at his phone after realizing he'd just been locked out of his e-mails. When he saw that his Facebook and Twitter accounts were under someone else's control, it hit him how serious this was, and how potentially embarrassing. He called his IT administrators, who said they would try and regain control of *HBGaryFederal.com*.

34 On *HBGaryFederal.com*, the homepage had been replaced with the Anonymous logo of the headless suited man. At the bottom was a link that said "Download HBGary e-mails." Anyone could read all of Barr's confidential e-mails to his clients. The new homepage also had a message written by Topiary: "Greetings, HBGary. Your recent claims of 'infiltrating' Anonymous amuse us, and so do your attempts at using Anonymous as a means to garner press attention for yourself. How's this for attention?"

35 The Anonymous members had been motivated by revenge and a desire, intensified by group psychology, to bully someone who seemed to deserve it. Before their attack, his newly formed small clique of Anons had no idea that Barr's research had been so flawed or that his e-mails would be so easy to hack into. That night, Topiary felt a thrill as he posted Barr's home address. Then, he tweeted Barr's Social Security number and his cellphone number. Soon, hundreds and then thousands of people who perused Anonymous chat rooms and blogs clicked on links to Barr's website and called his number. Quite a few took his earnest corporate photo and defaced it.

36 Barr had provoked a world where taunting, lying, and stealing was how everybody got by. It was a world that brought euphoric highs with hardly any real-world consequences. Sitting in front of his laptop, Barr saw that his public Twitter feed, an important reputational tool with the public, his clients, and the press, was now an obscene mess. Topiary had posted dozens of tweets filled with swear words and homophobic and racist commentary. The graffiti was perfectly in tune with the underground culture of crude humour and cyberbullying that ran through Anonymous.

Students can read the essay in class or for homework. There are additional questions in the Student Section of the Companion Website that focus on vocabulary as well as general comprehension. You can verify if students have read the essay by checking their scores with the grade tracker. You might assign the online questions first. Then, in class, you could ask students to discuss the Written Comprehension questions in groups.

37 As Barr spent the next day fielding phone calls from journalists and trying, desperately, to pick up the pieces, Topiary, Sabu, Kayla, and Tflow met up again in their secret chat room. They celebrated their accomplishments, relived what had happened, laughed, and felt invincible. They had "owned" a security company. In the back of their minds, they knew that agents from the Federal Bureau of Investigation would start trying to find them. But the members of the small team would conclude that they had worked together so well on Barr, they had to do it all over again on other targets. No quarry would be too big: a **storied** media institution, an entertainment giant, even the FBI itself.

storied: well-known; celebrated

(2931 words)

Source: Olson, Parmy. *We Are Anonymous: Inside the Hacker World of LulzSec, Anonymous, and the Global Cyber Insurgency*. NY: Little, Brown, 2012. Print.

WRITTEN COMPREHENSION

Discuss what happened to the hackers. There is detailed information about the fates of Sabu, Topiary, Kayla, and Tflow on page 64 of *Avenues 3: English Grammar*.

Answers to questions 1 to 5 will vary but may include the following:

1. He needed money and wanted to promote his company.
2. Barr provoked Anonymous with his newspaper interview. His website had a bug and was easy to hack. He used the same password on all his Web accounts.
3. Steps included finding a hole in the site, gaining access, and deciphering the passwords.
4. It is ironic that a security expert's website is so easy to hack and that a security expert doesn't practise basic elements of IT security, such as using different passwords.
5. She seems more sympathetic to Barr. (See paragraphs 35–36.)

Answer the following questions on a separate sheet of paper. Write several complete sentences for questions 1 to 5. Answer question 6 in a paragraph of at least 100 words.

1 What motivated Aaron Barr to speak to a reporter for the *Financial Times*?

2 Why and how did Barr become a target? List some mistakes he made in public and with his website.

3 How did the hackers get into Barr's account? Using your own words, list some steps.

4 How are elements of this story ironic? (See definitions of irony on pages 76–77.)

5 What is the author's point of view? Is she neutral, or does she seem more sympathetic to the hackers or to Barr? Support your answer with evidence from the text.

6 Did Barr deserve to get hacked? Did the hackers go too far? Give your point of view and back it up with evidence from the text.

Note: Are you curious about what happened to Sabu, Topiary, Kayla, and Tflow? Do the exercise on page 64 of *Avenues 3: English Grammar* to find out.

Vocabulary **BOOST**

Words with Multiple Meanings

Sometimes, a word can have several meanings and can be different parts of speech. For instance, *fine* can be an adjective, adverb, verb, or noun.

The following words appear in "Anonymous Strikes Back." Read the words in context before you make your choice. The paragraph number is in parentheses. Beside each definition, "n" means *noun* and "v" means *verb*.

1 fish (2)
- ☐ (n) aquatic animal
- ☐ (v) search carefully
- ☑ (v) remove

2 herald (3)
- ☑ (v) announce
- ☐ (v) precede
- ☐ (n) person who gives news

3 dash (4)
- ☐ (v) strike violently
- ☑ (v) move quickly
- ☐ (n) small quantity

4 jam (4)
- ☑ (v) press or squeeze in
- ☐ (n) fruit preserve
- ☐ (v) crowd or block a road

5 target (8)
- ☐ (n) object with circles
- ☐ (v) designate
- ☑ (n) object of an attack

6 boot (12)
- ☐ (n) foot covering
- ☑ (v) start up a computer
- ☐ (v) kick with force

7 root (14)
- ☐ (v) become fixed
- ☐ (n) origin
- ☑ (v) search vigorously

8 crack (14)
- ☐ (adj) excellent
- ☑ (v) decipher
- ☐ (v) break with a sharp sound

9 toy (18)
- ☑ (v) amuse oneself
- ☐ (v) flirt amorously
- ☐ (n) child's play object

10 strike (18)
- ☐ (n) cessation of work
- ☑ (v) attack
- ☐ (v) reach a deal

White hat hackers do their job for the public good (for instance, to expose security loopholes in a website or to help protesters during a revolution). They don't rob and destroy. Black hat hackers want to benefit financially by stealing credit card information, identities, etc., or they want to destroy or create anarchy by bringing down websites or computer systems.

SPEAKING

Ethics of Hacking

Work with a partner or team and discuss the following questions. Talk non-stop until your teacher flicks the lights. You can change topics at the beginning of your turn.

- Are you worried about Internet security? Why or why not?
- What steps do you take to protect yourself online?
- What is your opinion about online shopping?
- What is your opinion about online banking?
- Are hackers seen in a positive or negative way by most young people?
- What is white hat hacking? What is black hat hacking?
- What should the punishment be for hackers?
- In the HBGary Federal case, did the hackers go too far in their attack on Aaron Barr?

LISTENING

Dark Market

Every day, individuals siphon millions of dollars through the electronic veins of the Internet, reaching right into your computer, your transactions, and your life. Listen to a discussion about the dark side of online crime.

COMPREHENSION

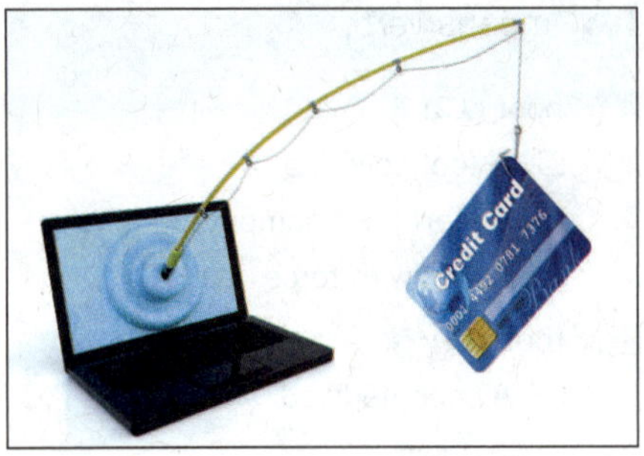

1 What does "low-impact, high-volume" fraud refer to?
Credit and debit card fraud

2 Ukrainian hackers got into the servers of two US companies. What did they do?
They got into the bookkeeping and human resources servers and created fake employees. They then provided the phantom employees with a monthly salary.

3 About how much did the Ukrainian hackers steal? $40 million

4 Which of the following are examples of malware?
a. viruses b. Trojans c. worms (d.) all of the answers

5 What is a bot-net? An army of zombie computers (computers under the control of a command-and-control computer) used by criminals to attack other network systems or particular websites

6 When was *DarkMarket.com* functional? From 2005 to 2008

7 What are three things that someone could buy or sell on DarkMarket?
Credit card information, viruses, tutorials on cybercrime

8 Briefly describe Red Brigade's lifestyle.
Living in luxury on the Upper East Side in New York and stealing more money than he can spend

9 A guy named "Drone" operated out of which city? Calgary

10 What did Drone create?
Skimming machines, or "skimmers," that read credit cards

You can assign the listening activity in class or for homework. There are additional comprehension questions in the Student Section of the Companion Website.

READING 5.3

Read about the evolution of a small Romanian town into a hub for cybercrime. After, you will define the words in green.

A Romanian Town Is Cybercrime Central

BY YUDHIJIT BHATTACHARJEE

1 Three hours outside Bucharest, Romanian National Road 7 begins a gentle ascent into the foothills of the Transylvanian Alps. Meadowlands give way to crumbling houses with chickens in the front yard and laundry flapping on clotheslines. But you know you've arrived in the town of Râmnicu Vâlcea when you see the Mercedes-Benz dealership. It's in the middle of a grassy field, shiny sedans behind gleaming glass walls. Right next door is another luxury car dealership selling a

variety of other high-end European rides. In fact, expensive cars **choke** the streets of Râmnicu Vâlcea's bustling city centre—top-of-the-line BMWs, Audis, and Mercedes driven by twenty- and thirty-something men sporting gold chains and fidgeting at red lights. I ask my cab driver if these men all have high-paying jobs, and he laughs. Then he holds up his hands, palms down, and **wiggles** his fingers as if typing on a keyboard. "They steal money on the Internet," he says.

misnomer: inaccurate name

2 Among law enforcement officials around the world, the city of 120,000 has a nickname: Hackerville. It's something of a **misnomer**; the town is indeed full of online crooks, but only a small percentage of them are actual hackers. Most specialize in e-commerce scams and malware attacks on businesses. According to authorities, these schemes have brought tens of millions of dollars into the area over the past decade, fueling the development of new apartment buildings, nightclubs, and shopping centres. Râmnicu Vâlcea is a town whose business is cybercrime, and business is booming.

Râmnicu Vâlcea, Romania

3 At a restaurant in a neighbourhood of apartment buildings and gated bungalows, I meet Bogdan Stoica and Alexandru Frunza, two of just four local cops on the digital beat. Stoica, thirty-two, is square-shouldered and stocky, with a mustache and prominent **stubble**. His expression rarely changes. Frunza, twenty-nine, is tall and clean-shaven. He's the funny one. "My English will improve after I have a few beers," he says. We sit at a table on the edge of a big courtyard, piped-in Romanian pop music blaring.

4 Stoica and Frunza grew up in Râmnicu Vâlcea. "The only cars on the streets were those made by Dacia," Stoica says, referring to the venerable Romanian carmaker. Access to information was limited, too: weekday television consisted of two hours of state-run programming, mostly devoted to covering the dictator, Nicolae Ceaușescu. "We had half an hour of cartoons on Sunday," Stoica says. Then, in 1989, a revolution that began with anti-government riots ended with the execution of Ceaușescu and his wife, and the country began the switch to a market economy. By 1998, when Stoica finished high school and went off to the police academy in Bucharest, another revolution was beginning: the Internet. Râmnicu Vâlcea was better off than many towns in this relatively poor country—it had an old chemical plant and a modest tourism industry. But many young men and women struggled to find work.

5 No one really knows how or why those kids started scamming people on the Internet. Whatever the reason, online crime was widespread by 2002. Cybercafés offered cheap Internet access, and crooks in Râmnicu Vâlcea got busy posting fake ads on eBay and other auction sites to **lure** victims into remitting payments by wire transfer. Eventually, FBI agents in the US and Bucharest started to get interested.

6 In the early days, the perpetrators weren't exactly geniuses. One crook would post ads for cellphones; his accomplice then picked up the wired money for orders that would never ship. The two men had made a few hundred dollars from victims in the US, and the guy receiving the cash hadn't even bothered to use a fake ID. "I found him sitting in an Internet café, chatting online," says Costel Ion, a Pitești cop who had been working the cybercrime beat. "He just confessed."

escrow: money, property, or a written contract held by someone until conditions are fulfilled under an agreement

7 But as in any business, the scammers innovated and adapted. One early advance was establishing fake **escrow** services: victims would be asked to send payments

to these supposedly trustworthy third parties, which had websites that made them look like legitimate companies. The scams got better over the years, too. To explain unbelievably low prices for used cars, for example, a crook would pose as a US soldier stationed abroad, with a vehicle in storage back home that he had to sell. (That **tale** also established a plausible US contact to receive the money, instead of someone in Romania.) In the early years, the thieves would simply ask for advance payment for the non-existent vehicle. As word of the scam spread, the sellers began offering to send the cars for inspection—asking for no payment except "shipping." Later, the con artists got even sneakier. "They learned to create scenarios," says Michael Eubanks, an FBI agent in Bucharest. The scammers started hiring English speakers to **craft** e-mails to US targets.

8 By 2005, Romania had become widely known as a haven for online fraud, and buyers became wary of sending money there. The swindlers adapted again, arranging for payments to be wired to other European countries, where accomplices picked up the cash. A new entry level evolved—people who'd act as couriers and money launderers for a cut of the take. Râmnicu Vâlcea was elevated to a hub of international organized crime.

9 Local police were starting to realize they needed people on the cybercrime beat full-time. Frunza, who'd studied informatics in high school before attending the police academy, was working drug cases in Bucharest when he decided to come home. He ended up joining Stoica on the hunt for online con artists. The two learned that suspects expect leniency from the police because their crimes target only foreigners. "The guys will often say, 'I am not stealing from our countrymen,'" Frunza says. "But a crime is a crime. You have to pay for it."

10 Nowadays, Stoica and Frunza occasionally find themselves investigating a childhood acquaintance. Frunza used to play on the same soccer team as a suspect who was under surveillance. At one point, Stoica **hushes** our conversation and tells me to turn around and check out a table across the courtyard, where a small group of flashily dressed young men has just arrived with two blond women who seem barely out of their teens. The men are all under investigation. "It's a small city," Stoica says.

11 "I don't know if the people of Râmnicu Vâlcea are too smart or too stupid," Stoica remarks grimly. "They talk a lot to each other. One guy learns the job from another. They ask their high school friends, 'Hey, do you want to make some money? I want to use you as a courier.' Then the friend learns to do the scams himself." It's not so different from the forces that turn a neighbourhood into, say, New York's fashion district or the aerospace hub in southern California.

12 Online thievery is a ticket to the good life. The con artists are the ones with the nice cars and fancy clothes—the local kids made good. And just as in Silicon Valley, the clustering of operations in one place made it that much easier for more to get started. "There's a high concentration of people offering the kinds of services you need to build a criminal scheme," says Gary Dickson, an FBI agent who worked in Bucharest from 2005 to 2010. "If your specialty is auction frauds, you can find a money pick-up guy. If you're a money pick-up guy, you can find a buyer for your services."

13 Class Café is an inviting coffee shop with a terrace that overlooks a quiet street. It's nearly empty when I walk in—just the owner behind the counter and a young couple at a corner table. Stoica discouraged me from attempting this meeting, but I wanted to know what an alleged **kingpin** looks like. I take a table on the terrace, waiting for Romeo Chita, a convicted cybercriminal. A green Jaguar drives up and a man in Bermuda shorts, canvas shoes, and a white T-shirt climbs out, enters the café, and approaches my table. He introduces himself as Chita's brother, Marian. He licks his lips nervously and **fidgets** with an iPhone. "Chita's coming," he says, after lighting a cigarette and making some phone calls. "But he's a little drunk."

14 A few minutes later, Chita walks around the corner and ambles into the café. Boyish, dressed in shorts, a light-blue polo shirt, and flip-flops, he looks more like a college student than a criminal mastermind. He has brought along some **muscle**—a young man in dark glasses with a big tattoo on his arm. The bodyguard slams a beer bottle down on the table and flexes his hand, as if getting ready for a boxing match.

dourly: in a gloomy, unhappy manner

15 Chita shakes my hand **dourly** and sits down next to me, looking away. "What do you say to the charges against you?" I ask.

16 "They are fake," Chita says, in English. Chita continues with his defence in Romanian, and a couple translates enthusiastically. "He doesn't even know how to speak English, so it is impossible for him to post ads or exchange e-mail with buyers," the translator says.

17 I press Chita about the wiretapped conversations, but his tattooed bodyguard interrupts loudly. "You go back to your hotel room; we send you some nice pussy," he says, raising his hand for a high five that I feel obligated to meet. The two men beside him laugh, and Chita takes a final drag from his cigarette before rising from his chair. He's in no mood to discuss the evidence. "This interview is over," Marian says.

18 They saunter out of the café and onto the sidewalk, looking surprisingly banal for guys accused of organized cybercrime, enjoying the good life with little effort or risk. I am left with the friendly couple who helped with the translating. The young man tells me he has just received a diploma in engineering from an institution in Bucharest and is now looking for a job. "I haven't found anything yet," he says. Thinking about Chita's Mercedes, I wonder if he'll consider a job in cybercrime.

19 Police constables Stoica and Frunza both complain that they're fighting an unstoppable tide with limited resources. Frunza says, "You arrest two of them and twenty new ones take their place," he said. "We are two police officers, and they are two thousand."

(1733 words)

Source: Bhattacharjee, Yudhijit. "How a Remote Town in Romania Has Become Cybercrime Central." *Wired*. Condé Nast, 31 Jan. 2011. Web.

Students can read the essay in class or for homework. There are additional questions in the Student Section of the Companion Website. You can verify if students have read the essay by checking their scores with the grade tracker.

WRITTEN COMPREHENSION

Answer the following questions on a separate piece of paper. Write several complete sentences for questions 2 to 5.

1 Define the ten words that appear in green bold in the text. Ensure that your definition matches the usage of the word in the paragraph. Write your definitions in English; do not translate.

→

Answers to questions 2 to 5 will vary but might include the following:
2. There is high unemployment and many people are involved in the trade.
3. Most people don't hack. Instead, they do e-commerce scams and malware attacks on businesses, create fake ads on eBay and other auction sites, establish fake escrow services, launder money, and act as couriers.
4. Chita lives lavishly, drinks to excess, and lies.
5. No, because police resources are limited and the money in cybercrime attracts locals.

2 What conditions in the Romanian town make it ideal to become a cybercrime centre?

3 What types of activities go on in that town? Are most criminals hackers, or do they have other duties? Provide specific examples of the types of activities that the criminals do.

4 Describe Chita. What type of person is he? Make guesses based on evidence in the text.

5 Can the Romanian police ever stop cybercrime? Explain why or why not.

DISCUSSION AND WRITING

What can ordinary people do to protect themselves from the scams that originate overseas?

Vocabulary **BOOST**

Idioms and Expressions

The following expressions appear in this chapter's readings. The page and paragraph numbers are indicated in parentheses. Match each expression with its meaning.

Expressions		Meanings
1 neither threat **panned out** (page 78, paragraph 6)	b	a. eloquent, persuasive way of speaking
2 **hollow threats** (page 78, paragraph 6)	e	b. worked; succeeded
3 **in a nutshell** (page 78, paragraph 11)	h	c. not flowing naturally
4 conversation was **stilted** (page 83, paragraph 12)	c	d. there would be chaos and confusion
5 he used his **silver tongue** (page 83, paragraph 12)	a	e. empty promises
6 **make his way up the ladder** (page 83, paragraph 12)	g	f. a quick method of attaining prosperity
7 **all hell would break loose** (page 84, paragraph 16)	d	g. advance in his career
8 **a cut of the take** (page 90, paragraph 8)	i	h. in a few words; concisely
9 **a ticket to the good life** (page 90, paragraph 12)	f	i. a part of the profits

Take Action!

WRITING TOPICS

Write about one of the following topics. For information about essay structure, see the Writing Workshops on pages 148 to 157. Before handing in your work, refer to the Writing Checklist on the inside back cover.

1 **Anonymous**

In the *Vanity Fair* article "World War 3.0," security expert Joshua Corman notes that the Web gives individuals immense power without instilling the "compassion, humility, wisdom, or restraint to wield that power responsibly." Reflect on the quotation. Then, in an essay, either defend or condemn the organization Anonymous. Describe possible benefits or problems that can occur when idealistic young hackers band together and go after their enemies. Back up your argument with information from the texts and video in this chapter.

2 **Compare Cybercriminals**

Compare and contrast the types of cybercriminals that are presented in this chapter. Are Anonymous members similar to or different from the criminals in the Romanian town? What are the motives of the two groups? In your essay, quote from this chapter's readings.

SPEAKING TOPICS

Need help with pronunciation? Visit the Companion Website and try the Pronunciation Workshops.

Prepare a presentation about one of the following topics. For details about preparing a speaking presentation, see Appendix 1 on page 174.

1 **Online Protection**

Create a video or PowerPoint presentation about the things that you can do to protect yourself from cybercrime. You can discuss passwords and safe Internet browsing. You can also discuss banking. Use your own ideas; do not simply copy information from websites. If you use online sources, credit them.

Remind students to try the Pronunciation Workshops on the Companion Website.

For topic 2, the arguments prepared can be used in debates. You could ask students to find a partner. Then each person would prepare arguments for one side of a topic.

2 **Argument**

Choose one of the following topics and prepare an argument. For your supporting ideas, survey friends and family members. Then explain your view about the topic.

- "Hacktivists" such as Anonymous are good / bad for our society.
- Computers have improved / hurt our lives.
- People should / should not do banking online.
- People should / should not use social networking sites.
- People have / don't have enough information about online safety.

MEDIA LINK

Watch a film that focuses on present or future technology or cybercrime. Examples include *MI4: Ghost Protocol*, *The Girl with the Dragon Tattoo*, *The Social Network*, *Total Recall*, *Gamer*, or *Repo Man*. (You could also do an Internet search for movies about technology or cybercrime, and then choose one.) Prepare an essay or a speaking presentation about the movie. Begin with a very brief summary (four to six sentences maximum). Then explain the message of the movie. Make a connection between the message and at least one of the readings in this chapter.

Revising and Editing

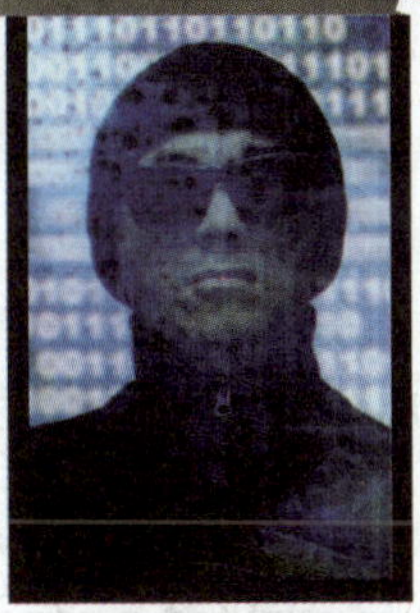

REVISE FOR A CONCLUSION
EDIT FOR MIXED ERRORS

A piece of writing should end with a concluding idea that brings the essay to a satisfactory close. (To learn more about conclusions, see page 159 in Writing Workshop 2.)

Read the short essay and follow these steps.

1 Underline and correct six errors. Look for two errors with conditionals, two errors with the passive form, and two errors with spelling.

2 Highlight the thesis statement in the introduction and the topic sentences in each body paragraph. Then write a concluding paragraph. It can be three to five sentences long. End with a prediction, suggestion, or quotation.

The Revising and Editing sections at the end of each chapter help your students prepare for writing tests, including Benchmark and TESOL tests. You can ask students to do the activities with a partner and to share ideas.

You can ask students to remove this activity and hand it in. Note that in the student books, pages are perforated.

COMPANION web+ To practise vocabulary from this chapter, visit the Companion Website.

In the film *The Girl with the Dragon Tattoo*, Lisbeth Salander is an ace computer hacker. She easily enters computers and reads private e-mails. For exemple [example], on behalf of a private investigator, she hacks into the computer of a journalist. Then, later on, while working for that journalist, she sucessfuly [successfully] hacks into some criminals' computers. *The Girl with the Dragon Tattoo* does not mention any real problems that can happen with hackers.

The movie shows no consequences for hackers, but in the world, hackers lose their freedom. For instance, if I committed cybercrime, I will [would] probably get arrested. In the movie, Lisbeth hacked a journalist's computer with no repercussions. If she would have [had] done that in real life, she would have ended up behind bars. Even excellent hackers eventually get caught. For example, in 2012, the FBI caught the LulzSec hackers, and they are in prison today.

Also, the movie makes hackers seem harmless, but they can ruin lives. In "Anonymous Strikes Back," we learned that Aaron Barr was a security consultant who was hack [hacked] by Anonymous. His e-mails were altered, his career was ruin [ruined], and his private phone number was put online. Hackers destroyed his reputation: "Quite a few took his earnest corporate photo and defaced it." (86)

ADD A CONCLUSION

____

____

____

____

____

Grammar TIP

Conditional Sentences

Make sure that your conditional sentences are properly formed. Do not use *would* in the *if* clause.

If the hacker ~~would have been~~ had been younger, he **would have avoided** a prison sentence.

To learn more about conditional forms, see Unit 7 in *Avenues 3: English Grammar*.

"When everyone has a blog, a MySpace page or Facebook entry, everyone is a publisher. When everyone has a cellphone with a camera in it, everyone is a paparazzo. When everyone can upload videos on YouTube, everyone is a filmmaker. When everyone is a publisher, paparazzo, or filmmaker, everyone else is a public figure."

– THOMAS L. FRIEDMAN, WRITER

CHAPTER 6

Viral Culture

Technological applications, social networking, and smartphones have changed our lives, causing isolation and a loss of privacy never seen before in history. This chapter examines our viral culture.

START UP

Preparing Arguments

When you write essays or do oral presentations, you are asked to present your thesis and supporting arguments. For example:

Thesis: Text messaging is causing problems in our society.

Arguments:
- Texts lead to miscommunication and less communication.
- People have accidents when they text and drive.
- The quality of the language diminishes because of texting.

Practise developing arguments. Work with a partner or a small group of students. Brainstorm to find three clear and distinct supporting arguments for the following thesis statements. Write your arguments in complete sentences.

Answers will vary.

1 Social networking sites, such as Facebook, are valuable.

Possible answers: Friends can help with a job hunt.

Everyone keeps updated on the lives of family and friends.

An artist or musician can publicize new work on the site.

2 People should stop using social networking sites such as Facebook.

Possible answers: Such sites are addictive. Stalkers can easily find someone.

Communication is not real or face-to-face. Too many online friends are not genuine.

It's easier to bully and be bullied.

READING 6.1

In this interview from *Salon.com*, Amanda Fortini asks Hal Niedzviecki about his book, *The Peep Diaries*.

Peep Culture

BY AMANDA FORTINI

1 In his new book, *The Peep Diaries*, writer Hal Niedzviecki describes "peep culture." It is reality TV, YouTube, Twitter, Flickr, MySpace, and Facebook. It is blogs, chat rooms, amateur porn sites, and cellphone photos. We have certainly learned that peep culture can escape our control. There are, for instance, the many Facebook-related firings, like that of the Swiss woman who claimed she couldn't look at a computer screen because of her migraine, and then checked Facebook from home, or the British teenager who posted a status update calling her job "boring." And then there is arguably the most inspiring example: the social network cyber-chatter that eluded the Iranian regime's attempts to stop the free flow of information. Niedzviecki spoke to me from his home in Toronto.

2 **How did you come up with the term "peep"?**

3 When I came up with this idea of "peep culture," I was thinking of peep shows, and the poor unfortunate character of Peeping Tom [who was punished for peeping at Lady Godiva as she rode naked through the streets]. Basically, we're moving from pop culture to peep culture. In pop culture, we spent a lot of time observing and enjoying the exploits of celebrities, but in peep culture, we're spending a lot of time getting entertainment from our life and from the lives of family, friends, and anonymous people around the world.

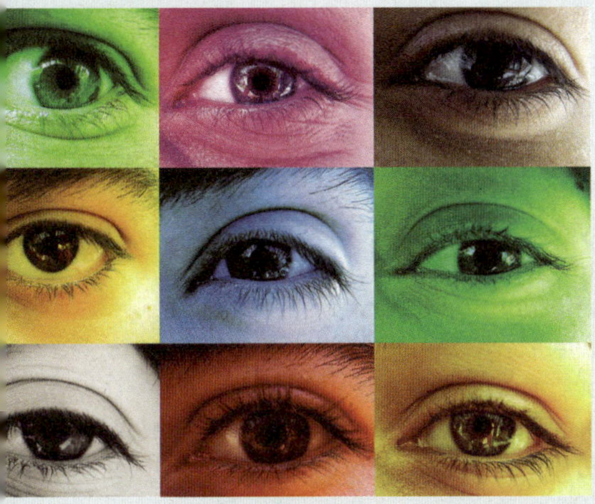

4 **Date the beginning of peep culture, and outline a little history for us.**

5 What really created peep culture is the rise of television. In the 1950s, there was a little box in every single house that showed a family, and that family could be anybody's family. *Father Knows Best* and *I Love Lucy* were real families pretending to be fake families for the public's viewing pleasure. It started to seep into people's minds that, well, if that family's interesting, then my family is interesting.

6 The mainstreaming of peep culture began around 2000 with the reality television shows *Big Brother* and *Survivor*. This fulfilled the promise that began in the '50s—that everyone should be on TV.

7 **There have always been people who seek fame or recognition, but lately it seems as though it's become an epidemic.**

8 We are extremely communal creatures. Before, we lived in small communities where everyone knew who we were. But now we have these big cities, and we have everyone sitting at home watching television, and we don't have those little communities anymore, but we are hardwired to want that. The urge to reveal ourselves is so powerful. We want to be noticed in our anonymous age and feel like we have some kind of community, even if it's just a pseudo-cyber-community. We desire to have relationships with people in which they know a lot about us, but we don't have to know anything about them, which is sort of the quintessential celebrity relationship. We start to think, "Maybe I'm a celebrity now."

9 **A lot of people don't get the appeal of Twitter. They wonder, "What's the point?"**

10 I put that exact question to the people of Twitter. And they said people like Twitter because it's connection with low expectations. That phrase has stuck with me, and has become almost an overarching explanation for the whole peep culture phenomenon. We want the feeling of connection without the weight of being expected to do something.

11 **You invited people to a Facebook party. What happened?**

curmudgeonly: grouchy; easily angry

12 I decided to hold a Facebook party because I realized at one point that I had eight hundred Facebook friends, but in real life, I really didn't have any friends in my city, Toronto. Part of that could be because I'm a **curmudgeonly** workaholic, and part of that could be because I've been in new-father mode, and I sort of lost touch with people. So, to my eight hundred Facebook friends, I said, "Come to the bar near my house in downtown Toronto. I'm buying the first round." Thirty people said, "Yes, for sure we will come." Some sixty said, "Maybe." Several hundred said "No" or didn't answer. So I really felt like I was going to have forty people at this event. But unfortunately, only one person showed up. And I was shocked; I really was shocked.

13 No one wants to hold a party and have no one come. At the same time, such a decisive result was really revealing about the truth behind social networks. We want to connect, but we don't want to have to have face-to-face interactions that could lead to demands being put on us.

14 **Can you tell us how nanny cams, GPS devices, and all these surveillance devices are examples of peep culture?**

15 These are the consequences of peep culture. Once we open the portal—if we say it's entertaining to watch other people's lives, well, then, a lot of the classic arguments against surveillance are difficult to keep going. People enjoy this, volunteer for it, and want it. Why wouldn't they want to be watched on the street if they're willing to be watched in their own houses?

16 **Do people actually think that getting on a surveillance camera is a way of being a celebrity?**

17 I think that's a pretty minor line of thinking. But take the case of the Columbine shooting: there were surveillance cameras in the school, and footage got leaked out and can be found on the Internet. It's part of their mythology now. So if someone has a twisted mentality already and is going to do certain things, it could be an extra bonus to be caught on a surveillance camera. I read an article about the twentieth anniversary of ***Cops***. The producer said, "Well you know, it used to be really hard to get people to sign the release forms. Now, as soon as they see the camera, they get very excited. They start yelling, 'I'm on *Cops*! This is awesome.'"

Cops: a reality program showing real people who get arrested by the police

18 **Can you talk about the happy benefits of peep culture—the good parts?**

19 People will find best friends that they would never have met otherwise. There are legitimate communities formed where people really do care about each other.

20 **At the very end of the book, you say you've come to the conclusion that there's value in "not knowing."**

21 Yeah. If you were born and lived and died, and nobody ever took your picture or clicked on your Facebook profile, or if you had zero Twitter followers, your life would be just the same, just as good. The amount of attention you receive through exposing yourself is ultimately not a signifier of your success as a human being.

(998 words)

Source: Fortini, Amanda. "Why We Can't Stop Looking: Have We Moved from Pop Culture to 'Peep Culture'?" *Salon*. Salon Media Group, 24 July 2009. Web.

Students can read the interview in class or for homework. There are additional questions in the Student Section of the Companion Website. You can verify if students have read the text by checking their scores with the grade tracker.

VOCABULARY AND COMPREHENSION: CRITICAL THINKING

1 In paragraph 1, what is the meaning of *eluded*?

a. opened b. freely chose (c.) evaded

2 In this essay, what does *peep* mean? spy

3 What is the main difference between pop culture and peep culture?

Pop culture focuses on celebrities, but peep culture is entertainment based on ordinary people's lives.

4 Find a four-letter word in paragraph 8 that means "desire." urge

5 In paragraph 12, what is the meaning of the term *round*?

a. having a circular shape

(b.) single serving of a drink given to everyone present

c. around or approximately

6 In paragraphs 12 and 13, what point is Niedzviecki making about social networks?

The friends people have on Facebook are often not real friends; they want a connection without demands.

7 In paragraph 15, what is Niedzviecki suggesting?

a. Surveillance devices are dangerous, and people should stop using them.

b. People enjoy watching videos of themselves.

(c.) If people are prepared to spy on others, then perhaps they should expect others to spy on them.

8 In paragraph 17, the writer says that people are excited and happy to appear on the television show *Cops*. Why is that fact strange?

Presumably, people on *Cops* are being arrested or are in trouble with the police, so the fact that they are excited and happy to be publicly exposed is strange.

9 What are some possible problems with peep culture? Give examples from the text.

People have connections that are not real. (The writer's social networking party failed.)

Surveillance and a lack of privacy will become a problem.

COMPANION WEB+ Answer additional questions for all the reading and listening activities. You can also access audio and video clips online.

SPEAKING

Definitions

Every year, new words are invented in English. Hal Niedzviecki invented the term *peep culture*. Other recent words include *overshare*, *Twittersphere*, and *unfriend*.

Work with a partner or a small team. Brainstorm to create a list of words that describe people from your generation or culture. Think about key features of the world today. Invent a new term by combining two words from your list, such as *easy* and *chat*, or create a word that has parts of different words.

WRITING

Write a paragraph explaining the new term you created. Provide examples to support your definition.

READING STRATEGY

Students can visit the Companion Website to practise their reading comprehension. Questions for all readings are structured to help students do better in their reading tests, including Benchmark and TESOL tests.

Understanding Literary Genres

Non-fiction deals with real events, people, and places. **Fiction** is imaginative and does not present reality. Nonetheless, fiction can reveal deeper truths about human nature and our world. When you read a work of fiction, such as a short story or novel, consider the plot, setting, characters, and theme. For more information about these literary elements, see Writing Workshop 4, pages 169 to 173.

There are many types of **literary genres**, including comedy, horror, romance, mystery, and the adventure story. Here are other common genres:

- **Pulp fiction:** a work that deals with lurid or sensational topics, such as murders and scandals
- **Thriller:** an exciting story with a lot of action and continuous suspense
- **Utopian fiction:** the creation of an ideal world, or utopia, as the setting
- **Dystopian fiction:** the creation of a nightmare world, or dystopia
- **Tragedy:** the story of a character who has a disastrous fate, perhaps brought about because of a tragic flaw

COMPANION WEB+ Visit the Companion Website to prepare for your reading tests. Online questions for all readings are structured to help you practise reading strategies.

READING 6.2 George Orwell was an English author and journalist who had a strong social conscience. Read this excerpt from his novel *1984*, which was published in 1949. His novel warns of a future world where the state controls every aspect of citizens' lives. Later, you will act out the words in bold.

Big Brother

BY GEORGE ORWELL

1 It was a bright, cold day in April. Winston Smith, his chin **nuzzled** into his breast in an effort to escape the vile wind, **slipped** quickly through the glass doors of Victory Mansions, though not quickly enough to prevent a swirl of gritty dust from entering along with him.

2 The hallway smelt of boiled cabbage and old rag mats. At one end of it, a coloured poster, too large for indoor display, had been **tacked** to the wall. It depicted simply an enormous face, more than a metre wide: the face of a man of about forty-five, with a heavy black moustache and ruggedly handsome features. Winston made for the stairs. It was no use trying the lift. Even at the best of times, it was seldom working, and at present, the electric current was cut off during daylight hours. It was part of the economy drive in preparation for Hate Week. The flat was seven flights up, and Winston, who was thirty-nine and had a varicose ulcer above his right ankle, went slowly, resting several times on the way. On each landing, the poster with the enormous face **gazed** from the wall. It was one of those pictures which are so contrived that the eyes follow you about when you move. BIG BROTHER IS WATCHING YOU, the caption beneath it ran.

3 Inside the flat, a voice was reading out a list of numbers. The voice came from an oblong metal plaque which formed part of the surface of the right-hand wall. Winston turned a switch and the voice sank somewhat, though the words were still distinguishable. The instrument (the telescreen, it was called) could be dimmed, but there was no way of shutting it off completely.

4 He moved over to the window. Outside, the world looked cold. There seemed to be no colour in anything except the posters that were plastered everywhere. The black-moustachio'd face gazed down from every commanding corner. There was one on the house immediately opposite with the words BIG BROTHER IS WATCHING YOU, while the dark eyes looked deep into Winston's own. In the far distance, a helicopter skimmed down between the roofs, **hovered** for an instant like a **bluebottle**, and **darted** away again with a curving flight. It was the police patrol, **snooping** into people's windows. The patrols did not matter, however. Only the Thought Police mattered.

bluebottle: flying insect

5 Behind Winston's back, the voice from the telescreen was still **babbling** away about the Ninth Three-Year Plan. The telescreen received and transmitted simultaneously. Any sound that Winston made, above the level of a very low whisper, would be picked up by it. Moreover, as long as he remained within the field of vision that the metal plaque commanded, he could be seen as well as heard. There was, of course, no way of knowing whether he was being watched at any given moment.

The Thought Police **plugged** in on individuals at any time. It was even conceivable that they watched everybody all the time. People lived with the assumption that every sound made was overheard and every movement scrutinized.

6 Winston turned around abruptly. He had set his features into the expression of quiet optimism, which was advisable to wear when facing the telescreen. He crossed the room into the tiny kitchen. Winston **poured** out a teacupful of Victory Gin, nerved himself for a shock, and **gulped** it down like a dose of medicine. Then he went back to the living room and sat down at a small table that stood to the left of the telescreen. He could be heard, of course, but so long as he stayed in his present position, he could not be seen.

7 The thing that he was about to do was to open a diary. This was not illegal, but if detected, it was reasonably certain that it would be punished by death, or at least by twenty-five years in a forced-labour camp. Winston's pen was an archaic instrument, seldom used even for signatures. Actually, he was not used to writing by hand. Apart from very short notes, it was usual to dictate everything into the speak-write, which was of course impossible for his present purpose. He put the pen to paper, but then faltered for just a second. His eyelid **twitched**, and a tremor went through his bowels. To mark the paper was the decisive act.

8 For some time, he sat gazing stupidly at the paper. The telescreen had changed over to strident military music. It was curious that he seemed not merely to have lost the power of expressing himself, but even to have forgotten what it was that he had originally intended to say. All he had to do was to transfer to paper the interminable restless monologue that had been running inside his head, literally for years. At this moment, however, even the monologue had dried up. The seconds were ticking by. He was conscious of nothing except the blankness of the page in front of him, the itching of the skin above his ankle, the blaring of the music, and a slight booziness caused by the gin.

(851 words)

Source: Orwell, George. *1984*. [Originally published in 1949] *Project Gutenberg*, 2008. Web.

Ask students to discuss the comprehension questions in teams.

Students can read the story in class or for homework. There are additional questions in the Student Section of the Companion Website. You can verify if students have read the text by checking their scores with the grade tracker.

COMPREHENSION: ANALYZING FICTION

1 In the text, who or what is Big Brother?

It is a government leader or organization that spies on citizens.

2 Describe the setting. Describe the outside world and Winston's apartment building. Use your own words.

Outside: It is cold and gray. The only colour is on the giant posters that say, "BIG BROTHER IS WATCHING YOU." Helicopters spy into windows.

Apartment building: Winston lives on the seventh floor. The elevator rarely works. The hall smells badly. Winston's living room has a large telescreen that plays constantly. There is a table in the corner.

3 Briefly describe Winston. Write a few details about his appearance and character.

Winston is thirty-nine and has a varicose ulcer above his right ankle. He wants to express his true thoughts in his diary. He seems depressed. He drinks gin to get through the day.

4 How does Winston's knowledge of Big Brother affect him?

He is very nervous about what he says and does, and he keeps an expression of "quiet optimism" whenever he faces the screen in his room. He wants to express his true feelings but must write his diary in a secret spot that the screen can't detect.

5 Which literary genre is this excerpt?

a. tragedy b. utopian fiction (c.) dystopian fiction d. pulp fiction

Explain your answer.

The world seems cold and gray, and people have no freedom. They must be careful because the government spies on them. There is an evil dictator who wants to watch what everyone does. It seems like a horrible nightmare of the future.

Point out that communist countries of the 1920s to 1980s resembled Orwell's vision, with very little colour and no advertising except for posters and paintings of leaders such as Lenin and Stalin. People were closely monitored by government spies, such as the Stasi (East Germany) and the KGB (Soviet Union). Also, today in China and other countries, certain keywords are carefully monitored by the government. According to *The New York Times*, the US Department of Homeland Security tracks hundreds of keywords used online and in tweets, such as *airport*, *subway*, and *infection*. According to the *Financial Post*, the airport in Ottawa, Ontario, contains hidden microphones to monitor travellers' conversations.

DISCUSSION

1 What do you know about communist countries of the past? What was Orwell mocking when he wrote about Big Brother?

2 This story was published in 1949. Which elements of the story were prescient and seem true today? Or was Orwell completely wrong in his predictions? Explain your answer.

Vocabulary BOOST

Act It Out

The verbs listed below appear in the story, "Big Brother." Half of the class will define the words in column A, and the other half will define the words in column B.

- Working with a small team, define the words in your column using context clues and a dictionary. (The paragraph numbers are indicated in parentheses.)
- Then, taking turns, various students from the "A" teams will act out their words. The "B" teams must guess which word is being mimed. Then the "B" teams will act out their words and the "A" teams will make guesses.

A		B	
nuzzle (1):	______	snoop (4):	______
slip (1):	______	babble (5):	______
tack (2):	______	plug (5):	______
gaze (2):	______	pour (6):	______
hover (4):	______	gulp (6):	______
dart (4):	______	twitch (7):	______

READING 6.3 These days, online shaming is becoming an issue. Read about viral vigilantes. After you finish reading, you will define the words in green.

Viral Vigilantes

BY MATTHEW FRASER

1 In August 2010, a dowdy middle-aged English woman called Mary Bale committed a baffling and senseless act that not even she could explain. Walking down a residential street in Coventry, England, she came across a local cat in front of a row house. After gently caressing the friendly tabby, she **coaxed** it toward a large garbage bin, picked it up by the scruff of the neck, and **flung** the cat inside the container. Then she closed the lid and coldly walked away. The unfortunate cat, called Lola, was rescued fifteen hours later by its owner Darryl Mann, who, searching for his lost pet, heard its distressed meows.

2 In a pre-Internet age, this puzzling act of animal cruelty would have had no consequences for Mary Bale. But Darryl Mann had purchased and placed two closed-circuit cameras in front of his house for security purposes. Mann was determined to track down the cruel woman who had flung his cat Lola into the rubbish bin. He turned to social media, posting a short video on YouTube and setting up a Facebook page called "Help Find the Woman Who Put My Cat in the Bin."

3 The feedback was explosive. The video instantly went viral, and almost immediately, Mary Bale was recognized and named. Forty-five-year-old Bale was leading a quiet life as an unmarried bank clerk living with her widowed mother. Yet, on the Web, she was **dubbed** "the most evil woman in Britain." An anti-Bale page on Facebook rapidly attracted 20,000 fans. Spoof videos began popping up on YouTube, mocking Bale's thoughtless act. In one such video, someone dressed in a "Sylvester the Cat" suit walks past a woman sitting on a ledge. The cat dumps the woman into a garbage bin.

4 The surveillance video was played on TV newscasts around the world. A media frenzy descended on Coventry as scrums of reporters followed Bale's every movement, **badgering** her with questions about her disturbing act. Questioned by a TV reporter as she was fleeing the media, Bale made the mistake of retorting, "It's just a cat." She refused to explain her **puzzling** gesture, except to say that she "thought it might be funny." The Royal Society for the Prevention of Cruelty to Animals became involved, and a spokesman told the BBC, "People assume animal cruelty might be carried out by people wearing a hoodie, and it is not always the case. You can have people from all walks of life." Mary Bale, meanwhile, went into hiding, hated and ostracized and fearing that she would lose her job. The police eventually charged her for causing unnecessary suffering to an animal.

5 Bale's story provides an alarming illustration of how the dynamics of surveillance have been radically transformed by social media. For centuries, we have associated surveillance with institutional power, especially states monitoring their populations. Most of us have seen television news footage from a **CCTV** video of a traffic accident or a bank robbery. These traditional forms of surveillance are top-down. In the past, only states, corporations, and large Kafkaesque bureaucracies were able to **marshal** the resources needed to monitor the actions of individuals. While these surveillance techniques could raise troubling questions, we passively accepted that they were in place.

CCTV: closed-circuit television

6 Today, states and institutions no longer possess a monopoly on surveillance as a form of coercion. As the WikiLeaks controversy illustrated—the diffused power dynamics of the Web are difficult for states to control. Now people can participate in everything from Wikipedia and citizen journalism to viral marketing and political protest. Social media played a pivotal role during the Arab uprisings of early 2011. Citizen journalists have captured police misconduct on cellphones. Thanks to the Web, citizens can now monitor and hold to account the states that govern their lives.

7 Digitally-mediated "Little Brother" surveillance puts everyone on a level playing field. Make no mistake there can be disturbing consequences to **ubiquitous** visibility. However odious her gesture, Mary Bale was unquestionably the victim of Web-based snooping and snitching—not much different from the pernicious ambience of neighbourhood spying that can quickly poison social relations in any small town. While the tabby cat's ordeal lasted only fifteen hours, Mary Bale isn't likely to recover from the explosive reaction to the YouTube video that turned her into one of the most hated people in Britain.

8 Beyond the Cat-Bin Lady, there are many documented examples of people whose lives have been destroyed because of digital surveillance. In South Korea, a teenage girl was shamed before the entire country. On a train with her tiny dog, her pet pooped, and the **mishap** was filmed by another passenger using a cellphone camera. In a country where shame is a culturally devastating stigma, the so-called "Dog Poop Girl" was so haunted by the online video campaign against her that she **dropped out** of university.

9 We will never know why Mary Bale flung Lola into the rubbish bin. But the Cat-Bin Lady saga has given us fascinating insights into the coercive power of "Little Brother," its role in the enforcement of social norms, and how digital vigilantism can degenerate into public shaming. Today we must accept that everything we do, including our smallest gestures, risks being exposed by some form of intrusive surveillance. As Mary Bale discovered, nobody can hide; someone is watching.

(891 words)

Source: Adapted from Fraser, Matthew. "Viral Vigilantes: The Unblinking Panopticon and the Wheelie-Bin Cat Lady." *Digitally Mediated Surveillance.* Research Papers. Apr. 2011. Web.

Students can read the text in class or for homework. There are additional questions in the Student Section of the Companion Website. You could use the online questions as a practice reading test. You can verify if students have read the essay by checking their scores with the grade tracker.

VOCABULARY AND COMPREHENSION: CRITICAL THINKING

1 Write a definition for each word. Use context clues, and only use a dictionary if necessary. The paragraph numbers are indicated in parentheses.

a) coax (1): persuade
b) fling (1): throw violently
c) dub (3): call; label
d) badger (4): harass; nag persistently
e) puzzling (4): odd and confusing
f) marshal (5): assemble and organize
g) ubiquitous (7): widespread
h) mishap (8): unfortunate accident
i) drop out (8) quit school

2 What happened to Mary Bale after she was outed as the Cat-Bin Lady?

She was mocked, followed by reporters, and ostracized. She was also charged by the police.

3 Why was the reaction to Mary Bale's act so intense? Make inferences or guesses.

People love animals. Her act was senseless. She did not seem apologetic, saying, "It's just a cat."

4 Is the writer objective (neutral) or subjective (biased)? In other words, does he express his opinion of Mary Bale's situation? Explain your answer.

He is subjective. In paragraph 7, he suggests that Bale is a victim who likely won't recover quickly from her experience.

5 What is the main idea, or thesis, of the essay? Use your own words to sum up the main point.

It is worrisome when ordinary people engage in digital vigilantism, leading to public shaming.

The Discussion and Writing topic could be used as a writing test.

DISCUSSION AND WRITING

What is the difference between Orwell's "Big Brother" and the "Little Brother" snooping that is mentioned in this essay? Compare and contrast the types of surveillance. Which type is worse?

Grammar TIP

Making Comparisons

Be careful when you use comparative and superlative forms. Generally, when adjectives and adverbs have one syllable, add the endings *–er* or *–est*. When they have two or more syllables, add *more* or *most* before the word.

Cameras are small**er** today than they were in the past.
CCTV cameras are **more** prevalent on city streets than they were in the past.
We are living in the **most** exciting time in history.

To learn more about adjectives and adverbs, see Unit 5 in *Avenues 3: English Grammar.*

Vocabulary BOOST

Canadian, American, and British English

Not all English nations spell words the same way. Canada, which has British roots but proximity to the United States, is a hybrid nation regarding spelling. Canada retains some British rules, but has also adopted certain American spelling practices.

Canada	Great Britain	United States
colour	colour	color
metre	metre	meter
realize	realise	realize

British English also includes vocabulary that is quite different from Canadian and American English.

Canada and the United States	Great Britain
cookie	biscuit
truck	lorry
potato chips	crisps
to snitch	to grass

PRACTICE

The readings "Big Brother" and "Viral Vigilantes" contain British vocabulary. Find the British terms for the following Canadian and American words. The text and paragraph numbers are indicated in parentheses.

1 From "Big Brother" a) elevator (2): lift

b) apartment (2, 3): flat

2 From "Viral Vigilantes" a) garbage can (2): rubbish bin

WATCHING Geotagging

There is new technology installed in your smartphones and cameras. Watch and find out about geotagging.

COMPREHENSION

1 Paris Hilton posted an image to Twitter. What did the photo depict?

It was a picture of a man who had tried to enter her house. He was being handcuffed by police.

2 Why was it a mistake for Hilton to post the photo online?

She used her smartphone to take the picture. People can identify her exact location with the photo.

You can assign the video in class or for homework. There are additional comprehension questions in the Student Section of the Companion Website.

3 What is geotagging?

It is a GPS chip embedded in a camera or smartphone. Photos contain coded information about someone's exact location within fifteen feet.

4 What does Larry Pesce's website do?

It tracks Twitter feeds and posts the location of people based on their photos.

5 Monica Rooney wasn't worried about the photos of her twins online. Why doesn't she worry about the availability of her address?

She says that people can also find where she lives with a phone book.

6 Larry's website appears unethical. How does he justify what he does?

He argues that people have already posted the information online, so it's already in the public domain.

7 How can you stop others from tracing the location of your photos?

You can turn off the geotagging feature in your phone.

Do a quick poll to see if students have turned off geotagging on their phones or if any of them know how to do it.

8 If you've already posted a photo online that has a geotag, can you go online and remove the geotag address? ☐ Yes ☑ No

Possible answers for discussion question 2: Runaways could be found; people could track down someone they love. Possible answers for question 3: Spousal abusers could use geotagging to find a partner who has left; governments could use it to spy on people.

DISCUSSION AND WRITING

1 Have you turned off the geotagging on your phone? Would you bother doing it?

2 How could geotagging potentially help people?

3 How could geotagging potentially hurt people?

READING 6.4

After Ada Calhoun got a job tracking down information about people on the Web, she learned just how vulnerable people really are. Read about her experiences.

I Can Find Out So Much about You

BY ADA CALHOUN

Gabrielle Giffords: American politician who was shot by a deranged gunman in 2011

1 When I first heard about the shooting of **Gabrielle Giffords**, I jumped on a computer. Within minutes, I had the link to Jared Loughner's MySpace page. I had a probable photo of Loughner at a rally from a local newspaper. And I had a YouTube manifesto. Then I forced myself to shut down the computer. I was, after all, at a family party.

2 I'd left my job at a tabloid newsroom just days earlier, and I was still suffering withdrawals from the adrenaline rush of news reporting. I had learned that it takes less than a minute to find twenty people in Brooklyn, NY, talking in real time about a tornado going past their windows. I had a savant-like instinct for what people of interest might be writing online at any given moment, which allowed me to find them via Twitter or Facebook's "Posts by Everyone" search option. It let me essentially read walls set to private, just because I was able to guess what's on them.

3 Sometimes, I found useful things hiding in plain sight: the wedding photo of the Times Square Bomber[1] on his brother-in-law's abandoned MySpace page. Any original trace of information, I learned, could be a place to start tracking down someone's bitter ex-girlfriend or paranoid, self-published novel. Particularly in the case of Internet-addicted twenty-somethings, I often wound up with way too much information. Sifting through some young people's mountains of blog posts and photos taken with their iPhones has taken me a full workday of non-stop reading. At the end of those days, I almost felt like I knew them.

4 It scared me how much someone like me—with no private-investigation experience or training—could discover. Freaked out by this epiphany, I adjusted all my social media settings and tried to ensure there was at least one relatively flattering photo of me publicly available, just in case. I almost tagged it, "please-use-this-photo-if-I-am-hit-by-a-bus.jpeg." Then I would reconsider my online

Students can read the text in class or for homework. There are additional questions in the Student Section of the Companion Website. You can verify if students have read the text by checking their scores with the grade tracker.

1 On May 1, 2010, Faisal Shahzad placed an explosive device in a Nissan Pathfinder in New York's Times Square. Street vendors noticed the smoking vehicle and alerted police. The bombs didn't detonate. Shahzad admitted to the crime.

lockdown, wondering if it was better to have more information than less. I began posting on Facebook more than once a week and even putting up the occasional picture. But then I would swing back to the other side and delete the pictures, worried that they might fall into unfriendly hands. I became the social-media equivalent of bipolar.

5 One manic day, I posted on my Facebook wall about a cover story I was proud of. It was lame and self-congratulatory in retrospect. In any case, a Facebook "friend" of mine mocked me. I responded. She got more aggressive. Suddenly, embarrassingly, I was having a fight with a practical stranger on my own Facebook wall, right in front of nearly everyone I knew. In a depressive episode, I unfriended her, then went through and deleted everyone else I didn't really know. (Sorry, real friends mistakenly swept up in this **purge**.)

purge: cleansing

6 Even for people who don't live their lives largely online, what happens on the Internet can feel realer than what happens in person. A friend of mine who's a shrink tells me more than half of every session with a young person involves things that happened on Facebook. "My ex-boyfriend changed his status to single," a distraught young woman told her, "and all his friends 'liked' it."

7 The problem with investing so much of our ego into our online presences isn't just that our "friends" aren't necessarily our real friends. It's also that it's incredibly easy to inflict pain on other people because here's the weird thing about online bullying: it is easier to humiliate someone online than it is to do it face-to-face. Often, it feels like nothing at all. But being humiliated online can feel worse than being mortified in real life because it can stay in public view for years. It can go viral, and anyone with a laptop can see the person's embarrassment and comment on it—or, god forbid, "like" it.

8 No story brought the issue of online humiliation into relief for me more than the case of Tyler Clementi, a gifted teenage violinist, who killed himself after roommates live-streamed a private moment he shared in his dorm room with another man. I was assigned to the Clementi story, too. Shortly after the police released his name, I was online looking at his profile picture. It broke my heart.

9 From conversations with his real-life friends, I learned that the chatty online figure I'd found was shy and private in person. In a way, Clementi's story is a reminder that we all maintain a wall between what we want people to know and what we don't want them to know. Many of us depend on that wall more than we think we do.

10 Maybe that's the moral for those of us who have Facebook pages and other online profiles. The creations we build up around our user names and profile pictures are shadows of the real world, not the real world itself. What is real: our bodies, our families, our friends, our co-workers, the thoughts and feelings that have never been posted on a computer screen.

11 In October, I was put on a story about porn star Capri Anderson, who was found in **Charlie Sheen**'s Plaza hotel room. She has the online profile you'd expect: making out with other girls on Twitter, covering herself with whipped cream on her club site, leering on MySpace. But then I found public photos posted years ago by a relative, and there she was in photo after photo, smiling and without makeup. She was at a relative's wedding. She was at a restaurant, smiling on her sister's shoulder. Maybe those photos aren't any more "her" than the vixen ones. But to me, they felt more real. Maybe it's because she'd tried to keep them secret.

Charlie Sheen: former star of *Two and a Half Men*, known for his addictions and outrageous behaviour

(957 words)

Source: Calhoun, Ada. "I Can Find Out So Much about You." *Salon*. Salon Media Group, 18 Jan. 2011. Web.

The Teacher Section of the Companion Website includes a reading test entitled "Cultural Renaissance or Cultural Divide."

WRITTEN COMPREHENSION

On a separate piece of paper, write ten questions about this text. Then, on the back of the paper, write the answers. Later, you will exchange sheets with a partner and answer your partner's questions.

SPEAKING

Reflections on Peep Culture

In his book, *The Peep Diaries*, Hal Niedzviecki says, "Peep, like the sudden stunning rise of television in the 1950s, seems relatively innocent. But look at what happened with television: such virtuous fare as *Rin Tin Tin* and *Father Knows Best* somehow led us to TV dinners and childhood obesity. In less than a decade, television changed how we ate, socialized, and maybe even thought. Television changed society forever, but while it was happening, it was hard to notice."

With a team of students, define peep culture. Then brainstorm at least five ways that our world has changed with peep culture. List your ideas on a separate sheet of paper.

WRITING

Write an essay about how peep culture has changed us. In your supporting arguments, refer to readings and the video from this chapter.

Take Action!

WRITING TOPICS

Write about one of the following topics. For information about essay structure, see the Writing Workshops on pages 148 to 157. Before handing in your work, refer to the Writing Checklist on the inside back cover.

1 Social Media

What are two or three advantages or disadvantages of online social media such as Facebook? Introduce your topic, and provide at least two supporting ideas. You can provide examples from your life, from the media, but also from the readings and the video in this chapter.

2 Surveillance Society

These days, we live in a "Little Brother" surveillance society. We peep on the private lives of others. People can be publicly shamed because they made a mistake and someone else filmed it and posted the video online. Police can use images from cellphone cameras to catch lawbreakers.

Write an essay about our surveillance society. You can explain the problems with widespread surveillance, or you can explain how it benefits us. Support your thesis with examples from this chapter's readings and video.

3 The Value of Computers

Chapter 5 deals with computer hacking, and this chapter examines the lack of privacy and viral shaming. Have computers been good or bad for our society? Provide three supporting arguments. Back up your argument with information from the texts and videos in chapters 5 and 6.

COMPANION Web+ Need help with pronunciation? Visit the Companion Website and try the Pronunciation Workshops.

Remind students to try the Pronunciation Workshops.

SPEAKING TOPICS

Prepare a presentation about one of the following topics. For details about preparing a speaking presentation, see Appendix 1 on page 174.

1 Addictions in the Technological Age

What addictions have people developed in this technological age? Think about addictions related to cellphone applications, videogames, and particular computer sites. In your supporting arguments, discuss various types of addictions and provide specific examples to back up your arguments.

2 Tech Review

With a group of students, discuss some popular websites and tech products. Then present a review of a new technological product or website. (Each student must choose a different topic.) In your evaluation, discuss the following:

- Who created the item or website?
- What human need does the item or website fulfill?
- How complicated is the item to use? How is the site organized? Is it difficult to navigate?
- What are a few positive and negative points about the item or website?
- Make a prediction about the durability of this item or website.

MEDIA LINK

Utopian fiction is the creation of an ideal world, or utopia, as the setting for a novel or film script. **Dystopian fiction** is the opposite: the creation of a nightmare world, or dystopia. Read a novel or watch a film that presents a dystopian vision of the world, such as *The Hunger Games, District 9, Planet of the Apes,* or *Blade Runner.* You could prepare an essay or a speaking presentation about the novel or movie. Begin with a very brief summary (four to six sentences maximum). Then explain the message of the novel or movie. Make a connection between the message and at least one of the readings in this chapter.

Revising and Editing

The Revising and Editing sections at the end of each chapter help your students prepare for writing tests, including Benchmark and TESOL tests. You can ask students to do the activities with a partner and to share ideas.

REVISE FOR SENTENCE VARIETY
EDIT FOR REPETITIVE WORDS

When a piece of writing only has short, simple sentences, it can seem stilted. Good writing should have sentence variety—in other words, sentences should be long, short, simple, compound, and complex. (To learn more about essay structure and combining ideas, see Writing Workshops 2 and 3 on pages 158 to 168.)

Read the essay and follow these steps:

1 Combine six of the sentences by using the words below. You might have to make changes in punctuation and capitalization. The first one has been done for you.

although	~~since~~	whereas	yet
because	so that	whenever	

2 In the essay, the word *people* is repeated ten times, not including the example. Underline all of them. Then replace five usages of "people" with other words. Do not use "we" or "they." The first one has been done for you.

Answers will vary.

In this technological age, people [citizens] offer up a lot of private information. People [Men and women] love social networking sites~~. They~~ [, since they] can share vacation photos and personal thoughts. While walking in the rain, driving, or having a coffee, people [members of the public] tweet, send a text, or check their Facebook account. People [Tech users] are losing their privacy~~. Technology~~ [, yet technology] also makes people's [everyone's] lives more private, insular, and lonely.

First, it is very rare to have a spontaneous connection with a stranger. In the past, people [commuters] would chat with others while riding a bus~~. These~~ [, whereas these] days, on the subway, people [passengers] listen to music or send text messages. Lara Sinclair, a college student, says that her train ride every morning is quite lonely. Other people [riders] concentrate on their smartphones or iPads. Random chats with bank tellers or receptionists are also rare~~. Most~~ [because most] businesses have voice mail services.

With technology, even real conversations among friends are shorter and less frequent than they were in the past. Instead of speaking in person, young people [the younger generation] will text or use online status updates~~. They~~ [so that they] don't have to talk. When I was a child, I chatted with my friends constantly. These days, I rarely see certain friends. [Whenever] I try to contact them~~. They~~ [, they] respond with a text or Facebook comment. As Hal Niedzviecki explained in the text "Peep Culture," "We want the feeling of connection without the weight of being expected to do something."

People [Although social media users] expose their private thoughts online~~. They~~ [, they] also have fewer spontaneous connections with others. Young people [Youths] are retreating into their own restricted technological worlds. Perhaps the best solution is to stop texting and start talking.

COMPANION WEB+ To practise vocabulary from this chapter, visit the Companion Website.

Grammar TIP

Using Subordinators

Subordinators are words such as *although*, *whenever*, *because*, and *even though*. Never put a comma after a subordinator.

Although~~,~~ it was expensive, the cellphone did not work well.

To learn more about combining sentences, see Unit 8 in *Avenues 3: English Grammar*.

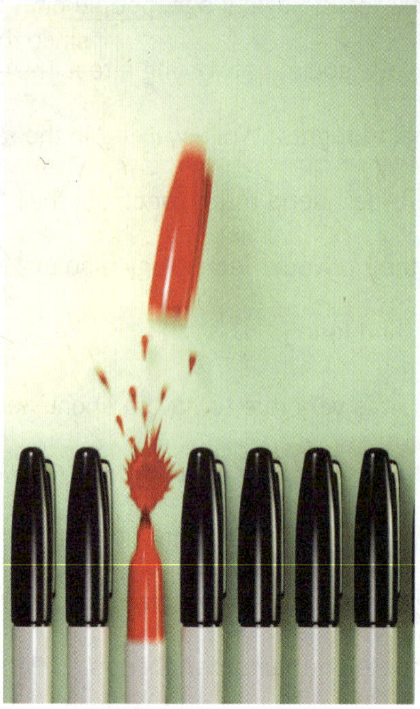

"Follow the path of the unsafe, independent thinker. Expose your ideas to the danger of controversy."

– THOMAS J. WATSON, FORMER CEO OF IBM

CHAPTER 7

Social Pressure

Throughout our lives, we are confronted with situations that test our values. In this chapter, you will read about conformity and group-think.

START UP

Revolutionary Events in History

Work with a team of students. Identify these revolutionary events in history.

1 **Sixteenth century.** In China, powdered smallpox scabs were used to inoculate people. In 1796, British physician Edward Jenner refined the technique. Today, people have longer lifespans because of this invention. vaccination

2 **1687.** After observing an apple fall from a tree, Sir Isaac Newton published this theory. gravity

3 **1848.** German philosopher Karl Marx published a manifesto that changed history. What political system did he propose? Communism

4 **1859.** Charles Darwin's book *On the Origin of Species* developed this theory. evolution

5 **1885.** Gottlieb Daimler attached one of these to a bike, creating the first motorcycle. combustion engine

6 **1916.** Albert Einstein became internationally famous for this theory. relativity

7 **1918.** The federal government awarded this right to women over twenty-one. Certain provinces only granted this right to women at a later date, including Newfoundland (in 1925) and Quebec (in 1940). the vote

8 **1927.** *The Jazz Singer* was the first full-length movie that incorporated this feature. talking (full sound)

9 **1947.** Tommy Douglas, the Saskatchewan Premier, launched this system for the first time in Canada. He faced stiff opposition from other politicians and from doctors' groups. Medicare

10 **1961.** A Yale University psychologist developed this experiment to test if people would obey authority and give electric shocks to a stranger. It led to new insights about our human capacity to commit evil acts. Milgram experiment

11 **1967.** Dr. Christiaan Barnard performed this surgical procedure on a human being. It was the first time it had been done. heart transplant

12 **1969.** Neil Armstrong made a "giant step for mankind." This action was broadcast to the world. first moon walk

13 **1975.** IBM 5100 was introduced and sold. At over $10,000, most people could not afford to buy this object. portable computer (PC)

14 **1989.** Tim Berners-Lee introduced a global information (management) system that would allow computers to communicate. His idea changed the world. World Wide Web

15 **2010–2011.** Using Facebook and Twitter, protestors toppled dictatorships in Tunisia and then in Egypt. This period of uprisings has a special name. Arab Spring

READING 7.1

Mark Tyrrell is the creative director of Uncommon Knowledge. In this essay, he discusses bystander apathy.

Bystander Apathy

BY MARK TYRRELL

1 In the Monty Python film *Life of Brian*, Brian, the reluctant messiah, shouts exasperatedly down to his throngs of followers, "You must think for yourselves!"

2 To which they all slavishly respond (in unison!), "We must think for ourselves!"

3 He then shouts out, "You are all individuals!"

4 And again the masses collectively and robotically echo his words: "We are all individuals!"

5 A tiny voice pipes up from the crowd: "I'm not!"

6 Absurd as this may seem, it neatly matches what psychologists have discovered about much human group nature. We like to think of ourselves as individuals, but a surprising amount of what we do and think is really prompted by group-action and group-think.

7 When I was thirteen, I saw a boy having an epileptic fit at school. He writhed and rolled around on the floor, and I just watched. I wanted to help, but no one else was helping, so I didn't either. Eventually, he came out of the fit and a teacher arrived. I had experienced "bystander apathy" first hand, and I'm not proud of it.

8 The concept of bystander apathy—which refers to witnesses of a problematic event who do nothing when they could or should—has horrific origins. In March 1964, twenty-eight-year-old Catherine "Kitty" Genovese was arriving home from a late night shift as a bar manager in Queens, New York. She was suddenly attacked with a knife by a man named Winston Moseley. She screamed for help. Moseley saw lights come on in the apartments nearby, and he knew people could be watching. He ran off, leaving Kitty to drag herself into a doorway where she lay bleeding. She might have survived at that point, but her attacker decided to return to finish off what he'd started because, as he later said in court, "It didn't seem like anyone was going to stop me."

9 Although badly weakened by now, Kitty Genovese again screamed for help. Many witnesses heard or saw some part of the attack—which took place over about half an hour in total—but no one took action to help her. By the time the police were eventually called, she was dead.

10 The tragedy wasn't given that much coverage at first. But when *The New York Times* ran a piece on the astonishingly apathetic behaviour of thirty-eight witnesses, moral outrage ensued. Newspapers threatened to print the names and addresses of the witnesses. Readers wrote in saying the vicious bystanders should be punished for their "crime" of not helping when they had the power. [We now know that the media exaggerated some of the details about the case. A 2007 *American Psychologist* article mentions that there were fewer eyewitnesses than reported and that at least one call was made to police during the attack. Still, nobody intervened in time, and Genovese died.]

11 Many other instances have occurred showing that bystanders can be callously indifferent to the suffering of others. For instance, in *Cities and Urban Life*, sociologist John Macionis recounts a 1983 case in St. Louis in which three men attacked a woman in a crowded baseball stadium. She screamed, but nobody helped. In an interview quoted by *The New York Times*, she said, "I was shocked more than hurt. I just sat there and screamed, and not one soul stopped. I saw all these legs going by, and I thought about reaching out and grabbing somebody." More recently, in October 2011, a two-year-old girl walked into a busy street in China. She was run over—first by a van and then a few minutes later by a truck. Pedestrians walked past the child. Finally, ten minutes later, an old woman carried the small girl to the side of the road.

12 Such incidents also happen in Canada. In May 2001, employees in a Montreal office building looked out the windows and noticed a woman lying in the parking lot, naked from the waist down. As it rained on the unconscious woman, nobody called the police or an ambulance. The office supervisor advised employees to ignore the woman. Three hours later, an employee finally decided to disobey his boss and call for help. Police discovered that the woman had been raped and beaten and left in the parking lot, comatose. The supervisor was subsequently fired, but the story invites the question, "Why did nobody defy his orders and immediately make that phone call to the police?"

13 When events like that happen, it's comfortable to assume that only other people ignore the suffering of strangers. Yet research has shown that bystander apathy is actually quite normal. Two young experimental psychology researchers, John Darley and Bibb Latané of Columbia University, wanted to discover if inaction during a crisis was common. For instance, if a fire alarm goes off in a building and no one else seems concerned, most people will continue to do nothing *because other people are doing nothing*.

14 Concealing their real objective, Darley and Latané recruited a group of student volunteers and told them they were to take part in a study about adapting to student life. Each student had to sit alone in a room and talk into a microphone for two minutes about his or her experiences of university life. In the neighbouring rooms, tape recorders played other students' stories. However, the subject was not aware that these "student" accounts were pre-recorded.

15 The first voice was a pre-recorded account from a supposedly "epileptic" student. He confessed to the rest of the "group" (remember there was only *one* actual student present) that he was prone to life-threatening seizures. He said exams were tough for him and that New York was tough to live in. He spoke with halting embarrassment about his "condition." His voice then muted, and another pre-recorded voice spoke. The real live students listened to what they thought were other students speaking in real time.

16 This carried on—"student" after "student" speaking for two minutes at a time—until something happened. A seizure started. The real student subject could not, of course, *see* the seizure, but he or she could *hear* it. The epileptic actor's voice became more panicky and insistent: "I'm ... I'm having a fit ... I ... I think I'm ... help me ... I ... I can't ... Oh my God ... err ... if someone can just help me out here ... I ... I ... can't breathe p-p-properly ... I'm feeling ... I'm going to d-d-die if ..." Then there was a final choke, then silence. The "seizure" lasted a full six minutes.

17 Now the real student listener believed that several other listeners could also hear what was going on. At any point, the student could get up, leave the

room, go down the hall, and ask the experimenter for help. The real student *thought* it was impossible to communicate with the students in the other rooms (because the microphones would be off if it wasn't the student's turn). The real students had six minutes to reflect on what to do. They became scared and anxious. But very few tried to help—just 31 percent, to be exact. That means that *most* people didn't help, even though they believed someone might be dying.

18 The researchers found that if the subjects believed they were in a group with four or more others, they were actually *far less* likely to go for help. If, however, the subjects believed they were alone with the epileptic student, then 85 percent would seek help. The bigger the group, the less likely the individual was to act. This research has been replicated among other sectors of the population, and the helping rates remain constant. Statistically, it's safer for a person to collapse in front of one or two people than in a crowd of onlookers.

19 Darley and Latané conducted further research. They wanted to see if we would still be influenced into inaction by group-think if the person "in need" was *us* instead of *someone else*. They constructed an office with an air vent. In this office sat one student (again ignorant of the real object of the study) and two actors. They were to sit together filling in psychological questionnaires. Several minutes into the experiment, the researchers released non-hazardous but convincing-looking smoke into the room via the air vent.

20 The actors were under instructions to ignore the smoke and keep filling in their questionnaires. The smoke made them all cough, and it got so thick it was hard to see. Still, the two actors just went on calmly filling out their forms. The real students looked concerned, and a few actually got up and went to the vent, then looked back at their calm fellow questionnaire-fillers. Then they went back to their own forms! Because they were in a minority of one, they ignored their own logic and instincts. Some ventured to ask the other two whether the smoke was strange, but the actors just shrugged such questions off. In the whole experiment, only one student actually left the room and reported the smoke.

21 The subjects based their action, or inaction, on the social cues of those around them rather than on the evidence before them. They had smoke in their eyes and they coughed, but they continued to do nothing about it—because the others were doing nothing—until the experimenter arrived and stopped the experiment. It seems people would rather risk their lives than go against the grain and "break rank."

22 In contrast, when the subjects were alone in a smoke-filled room, they nearly always decided the situation was an emergency and went to raise the alarm. So when we *have* to take responsibility because no one else is there, we do so. When other people are present, many of us look to others to signal to us what we should do. This may seem depressing at first sight, but remember that there is a minority of people who *will* try to act, regardless of the group consensus.

23 It seems that knowing about the phenomenon of bystander apathy may protect people from actually becoming that apathetic bystander. Social scientist Arthur Beaman took a group of college students and showed them footage of the smoke experiment. He also spoke about the seizure research study. He found that after

exposure to this information, the students were twice as likely to offer help "in the street" as compared with people who had not been educated about this. Thus, try to remember this study the next time you encounter a stranger in need.

(1733 words)

Source: Tyrrell, Mark. "Bystander Apathy—It's None of My Business." *Uncommon Knowledge*. Uncommon Knowledge LLP, 2011. Web.

Students can read the essay in class or for homework. There are additional questions in the Student Section of the Companion Website. You can verify if students have read the essay by checking their scores with the grade tracker.

VOCABULARY AND COMPREHENSION

1 Choose the letter of the appropriate definition. The paragraph numbers are in parentheses. Read the words in context before you make your guess.

Expressions		Definitions
1. pipe up (5)	c	a. knock down with a moving vehicle
2. run over (11)	a	b. not be influenced by others
3. shrug off (20)	d	c. speak up and say something
4. go against the grain (21)	b	d. brush aside; ignore

2 Highlight the thesis statement in the text. The thesis sums up the main idea of the essay. Look in the introductory section.

3 What is bystander apathy?

It is when witnesses do nothing during a problematic event.

4 Briefly describe four examples from the text of real-life bystander apathy. Mention where each event took place.

In Queens, New York, Kitty Genovese was murdered, and bystanders did nothing to help her.

In St. Louis, a girl was attacked by three men in a baseball stadium, but nobody helped.

In China, bystanders ignored a little girl who had been run over by a van and then a truck.

In Montreal, office workers ignored a comatose woman lying half-naked in a parking lot.

5 At the end of paragraph 16, why is the word "seizure" in quotation marks?

To indicate that the seizure wasn't real, it was fake

6 What does the "fake epileptic student" experiment by Darley and Latané demonstrate about people?

During a crisis, when people think others are also present, they are less likely to take action than when they are alone.

7 What does the "smoke in the room" experiment demonstrate?

Even when people's own lives are in danger, most will follow the crowd and not take action to save themselves. If they are alone, they will take action.

COMPANION WEB+ Answer additional questions for all the reading and listening activities. You can also access audio and video clips online.

DISCUSSION AND WRITING

1 Based on information in the text, why don't people help others who are in distress? Why does bystander apathy exist?

2 Have you ever witnessed a school peer being bullied? Explain why you did or did not intervene.

SPEAKING

You can assign students a topic and have them debate each other.

Debate

Work with a partner and develop arguments for or against one of the following topics, or come up with your own topic.

- Strikes are an effective bargaining method.
- To make a political point, violent action is sometimes necessary.
- The government should shorten the number of years of high school.
- During a strike, an effective strategy is to disrupt the lives of citizens (block roads, put smoke bombs in subways, block entrances to buildings, etc.).
- Police officers should be more appreciated and respected.
- College tuition fees should increase.
- There should be a compulsory voting law in this country.
- Your own topic:

____

READING STRATEGY

Students can visit the Companion Website to practise their reading comprehension. Questions for all readings are structured to help students do better in their reading tests, including Benchmark and TESOL tests.

Visit the Companion Website to prepare for your reading tests. Online questions for all readings are structured to help you practise reading strategies.

Considering the Context

Each essay, story, or novel is written within a specific context. The context is the social, political, and cultural milieu in which the author lived and worked. We, as readers, may approach a reading with a completely different context. For instance, a twenty-first-century woman may feel appalled at the views about females expressed in an essay written a hundred years ago. A person who grew up in a middle-class Canadian suburb might not understand why certain traditions were followed in the 1970s in China.

When you read essays that were written in another time or cultural milieu, be aware of the context. Question your own reactions to the reading. For example, if you feel uncomfortable with the language used or the ideas expressed, consider what was going on at the time and place the text was written.

READING 7.2

In 1832, Susanna Moodie left England with her husband and child and came to Canada. In 1852, she published *Roughing It in the Bush* about her experiences. In this excerpt from Chapter 3, she describes her arrival in Quebec.

My Visit to Montreal

BY SUSANNA MOODIE

1 Of Montreal I can say but little. The cholera was at its height, and the fear of infection, which increased the nearer we approached its shores, cast a gloom over the scene and prevented us from exploring its infected streets. That the feelings of all on board very nearly resembled our own might be read in the anxious faces of both passengers and crew. Our captain, who had never before hinted that he entertained any apprehensions on the subject, now confided to us his conviction that he would never leave the city alive: "This cursed cholera!

Left it in Russia—it meets me again in Canada. No escape the third time." If the captain's prediction proved true in his case, it was not so in ours. We left the cholera in England, we met it again in Scotland, and we managed to escape its fatal visitation in Canada.

2 Yet the fear and the dread of it on that first day caused me to throw many anxious glances at my husband and my child. I had been very ill during the three weeks that our vessel was in Newfoundland. I was weak and nervous when the vessel arrived in Quebec, but during the voyage up the St. Lawrence, the fresh air and beautiful scenery were rapidly restoring me to health.

The Port of Montreal in 1830

3 From the river, Montreal has a pleasing aspect. However, it lacks the grandeur and stern sublimity of Quebec. The fine mountain that forms the background to the city, the Island of St. Helens in front, and the junction of the St. Lawrence and the Ottawa rivers constitute the most remarkable features in the landscape. The town itself was dirty and badly paved. The opening of all the sewers, in order to purify the place and stop the ravages of the pestilence, rendered the public thoroughfares almost impassable. The air was loaded with intolerable vapours.

4 The dismal stories told to us by the excise officer who came to inspect the unloading of the vessel, about the frightful ravages of the cholera, by no means increased our desire to go on shore. "It will be a miracle if you escape," he said. "Hundreds of emigrants die daily, and if Stephen Ayres had not providentially come among us, not a soul would have been alive at this moment in Montreal."

5 "And who is Stephen Ayres?" I asked.

6 "God only knows," was the grave reply. "It's certain that he is not of the earth. Flesh and blood could never do what he has done—the hand of God is in it. No one knows who he is or where he comes from. When the cholera was at the worst, and the hearts of all men stood still with fear, and our doctors could do nothing to stop its progress, this man, or angel, suddenly made his appearance in our streets. He came in great humility, seated in an ox-cart. Only think of that! He made no parade about what he could do, but only fixed up a plain notice on a board informing the public that he possessed an infallible remedy for the cholera and would endeavor to cure all who sent for him."

7 "And was he successful?"

8 "Successful! It beats all belief, and his remedy so simple! For some days, we all took him for a quack and would have no faith in him at all, although he performed some wonderful cures upon poor folks who could not afford to send for the doctor. The Indian villagers were attacked by the disease, and he went out to them and restored upward of a hundred of the Indians to perfect health. This established him at once, and in a few days' time he made a fortune. Doctors asked him to cure them, and it is hoped that in a few days he will banish the cholera from the city."

9 "Do you know his famous remedy?"

10 "Did he not cure me when I was at the last gasp? Why, he makes no secret of it. It is all drawn from the maple tree. First, he rubs the patient all over with an ointment, made of hog's lard and maple sugar and ashes, from the maple tree. Then he gives him a hot dose of maple sugar and **ley**, which throws him into a violent perspiration. In about an hour, the cramps subside. He falls into a quiet sleep, and when he awakes he is perfectly restored to health." Such were our first tidings of Stephen Ayres, the cholera doctor, who is universally believed to have discovered some wonderful cures. He obtained a wide celebrity throughout the colony.

ley: metallic compound

11 The day of our arrival in the port of Montreal was spent in packing and preparing for our long journey up the country. At sunset, I went up on deck to enjoy the refreshing breeze that swept from the river. The evening was delightful. The white tents of the soldiers on the Island of St. Helens glittered in the beams of the sun, and the bugle-call wafted over the water. It sounded so cheery and inspiring that it banished all fears of the cholera, and, with fear, the heavy gloom that had clouded my mind since we left Quebec. I could once more enjoy the harmonious scene.

beheld: noticed; saw

bowsprit: beam that extends out from a ship

12 A loud cry from one of the crew startled me; I turned to the river and **beheld** a man struggling in the water a short distance from our vessel. He was a young sailor who had fallen from the **bowsprit** of a ship near us.

13 There is something terribly exciting in beholding a fellow creature in imminent peril, without having the power to help him. It is a horrible thing to witness his death-struggles—to feel all the dreadful alternations of hope and fear—and, finally, to see him die, with scarcely an effort made for his preservation.

yard: one yard is about 91 centimetres, or slightly shorter than a metre.

14 At the moment he fell into the water, a boat with three men was within a few **yards** of the spot. It actually sailed over the spot where he sank. Cries of "Shame!" from the crowd collected upon the bank of the river had no effect in rousing these people to attempt the rescue of a perishing fellow creature. The boat passed on. The drowning man again rose to the surface, the convulsive motion of his hands and feet visible above the water. It was evident that the struggle would be his last.

15 "Is it possible that they will let a human being perish, and so near the shore, when an oar held out would save his life?" was the agonizing question at my heart, as I gazed on the fearful spectacle. The eyes of a multitude were fixed upon the same object—but not a hand stirred. Everyone seemed to expect someone else to make an effort which he was incapable of attempting himself.

16 At that moment—splash! A sailor plunged into the water from the deck of a neighbouring vessel and dived after the drowning man. A deep "Thank God!" burst from my heart. I drew a freer breath as the brave fellow's head appeared above the water. He called to the man in the boat to throw him an oar, or the drowning man would be the death of them both. Slowly they rowed the boat back. One of the men handed out an oar, but it came too late! The sailor, whose name was Cook, had been obliged to shake off the hold of the dying man to save his own life. He dived again to the bottom and succeeded in bringing to shore the body of the unfortunate being he had vainly endeavoured to save. Shortly afterwards, he came on board our vessel. He was foaming with passion at the barbarous indifference manifested by the men in the boat.

17 "If they had given me the oar in time, I could have saved him. I knew him well—he was an excellent fellow and a good seaman. He has left a wife and three children in Liverpool. Poor Jane! How can I tell her that I could not save her husband?" He wept bitterly, and it was impossible for any of us to witness his emotion without joining in his grief. From the mate, I learned that this same young man had saved the lives of three women and a child when the boat was swamped at Grosse Isle.

18 Such acts of heroism are common in the lower walks of life. Thus, the purest gems are often encased in the rudest crust, and the finest feelings of the human heart are fostered in the chilling atmosphere of poverty.

(1430 words)

Source: Moodie, Susanna. *Roughing It in the Bush.* Ch. III. [Originally published in 1852]. Digital Library U. Penn, n.d. Web.

Students can read the essay in class or for homework. There are additional questions in the Student Section of the Companion Website. You can verify if students have read the essay by checking their scores with the grade tracker.

WRITTEN COMPREHENSION

Answer each question in a paragraph of about 150–200 words. Do not plagiarize; use your own words to answer the questions. Include at least one quotation in each answer.

1. How was the context that Moodie lived in different from your life? Using your own words, describe the time, place, and culture that the story depicts, and compare it to your own location and era.
2. What happened to the sailor who fell overboard? Relate the essay to the reading "Bystander Apathy."

Grammar TIP

Quoting from a Source

When you introduce a quotation with a phrase (incomplete idea), put a comma after the phrase. Indicate the page number in parentheses.* Put the final period after the parentheses.

> She said**,** "I had been very ill during the three weeks that our vessel was in Newfoundland" (119).

When you introduce a quotation with a complete idea, put a colon after the introductory sentence.

> Nobody helped the man**:** "The boat passed on" (120).

* When you quote from readings in this book, your teacher may ask you to put the paragraph number or line number in parentheses instead of the page number.

To learn more about using quotations, see Unit 11 in *Avenues 3: English Grammar*.

WATCHING

The Power of Social Roles

You can assign the video in class or for homework. There are more detailed comprehension questions in the Student Section of the Companion Website. You might ask students to do the online questions, and then they could discuss these comprehension questions in teams.

Why do seemingly normal people sometimes do evil actions? For instance, during the Iraq War, why did ordinary soldiers torture and humiliate prisoners under their care? Watch and find out about the power of social roles.

WRITTEN COMPREHENSION

Answer the following questions on a separate piece of paper. Your answers should be written in complete sentences.

1. Describe the Milgram experiment. Explain how the updated experiment is different from the original.
2. Who is Lynnie England? Explain what she did and describe what happened to her.
3. Explain what happened in the McDonald's case. Describe the situation that occurred between Donna Summers and high school student Louise Ogborn.
4. Describe Zimbardo's experiment. What did he do? What happened?
5. According to the video, what causes ordinary people to do evil actions?

READING 7.3

Jan Wong was born and raised in Montreal. In 1972, she was one of two foreigners invited to study at Beijing University in China during the height of the Cultural Revolution. In this excerpt from her book *Red China Blues*, Wong reflects on her youthful idealism.

Snitch

BY JAN WONG

1 In July 1973, I prepared to leave China. For more than a year, I had been subjected to a relentless barrage of propaganda and had absorbed many of the values. Maoism suited the absoluteness of youth. I was so self-absorbed. I knew so little about human suffering. And I was always being judged myself. I wanted to prove that despite my "bad" background, I could be as "good" as the next person.

2 I had also studied Mao's famous essay *On the Correct Handling of Contradictions among the People,* in which he promised that only the worst class enemies would be treated harshly. Ordinary people who made mistakes would be encouraged to reform and clasped to the bosom of the motherland. Only class enemies would be sent off to the **gulag**. I did not know that the reason I enjoyed biking down the empty streets of Beijing was because so many of its seven million residents had been sent down to farms and communes for **thought reform**.

gulag: system of forced labour camps used during the communist era of the Soviet Union

thought reform: movement that asked intellectuals to throw away the vulgar perspectives of individualism and liberalism

3 During one school break, I visited an aunt who had been so frightened of losing touch with her brother in Canada that she secretly jotted his address down in a textbook. Aunt Yuying was a chemistry professor in Tianjin, a two-hour train ride from Beijing. She welcomed me to stay in her campus apartment even though it meant hassling with the university bureaucracy. Every morning, she made me omelets for breakfast, an unheard-of luxury that also used up her monthly ration of eggs. For lunch, she made spring rolls, which wiped out her meagre cache of cooking oil. When I left, she gave me her vast collection of Mao buttons, including a hand-painted porcelain one and another made from the tip of a toothbrush.

4 But Aunt Yuying never talked frankly to me. More than twenty years later, when I was forty and she was seventy, I asked why she had never hinted at the problems in China back then. "You were so radical," she said gently. "You believed everything. We didn't dare tell you. It was too dangerous."

5 I am not blaming anyone but myself for what I did next. Just a few weeks before I was scheduled to leave Beijing University, a student I knew only slightly approached **Erica** and me. Yin Luoyi was in the year ahead of us, in the very first history class of worker-peasant-soldier students. She was pretty, with large, expressive eyes. "Let's go for a walk around No Name Lake," Yin suggested. Since most people avoided us, Erica and I were pleased and readily agreed. Yin seemed nervous. As we strolled around the lake, she peppered us with questions about the West.

Erica: Erica Jen, an American foreign exchange student and the only other Westerner invited to study at Beijing University in 1972

6 "Do you have refrigerators?" she asked. "What kind of class background do you need to attend university?" Erica and I were annoyed. Why was she so fixated on the West? Didn't she understand it was capitalist? She did. Yin paused and took a deep breath. "I want to go to the United States," she said. "Can you help me?"

7 We decided Yin did need help. The Communist Party would save her from herself. She would be reprimanded, and that would be the end of it. And this way she would be rescued from the dangers of the USA. After all, Mao had said, "Persuasion, not compulsion, is the only way to convince people."

8 Although Erica and I still had misgivings about the ethics of snitching on people, we suppressed them. We were just twenty years old, with a quite undeveloped moral sense. Like millions of Red Guards our age, we were trying to do the right thing for the revolution. After talking it over, we reported Yin to the Foreign Students Office. "I remember ratting. I really hate myself for that," said Erica, when I asked her two decades later what she recalled. "We actually thought we were doing the right thing. It was for her sake. We weren't trying to get points for ourselves."

Chairman Mao's Red Guards during the Cultural Revolution in China in 1971

9 Unlike Aunt Yuying, who knew me better, Yin Luoyi never dreamed Erica and I were True Believers. Two decades later, I mentioned the incident to my classmate Forest. She said, "We were all reporting on each other and meddling in each other's affairs under the guise of being revolutionary and patriotic." Forest confessed that in 1966, when she was fourteen, she had denounced her own father, then the deputy minister of propaganda. "The Communist Party taught us, 'Love your dad and love your mom, but not as much as Chairman Mao.'"

10 Chen Kaige, whose evocative *Farewell My Concubine* won the 1993 Palme d'Or at the Cannes Film Festival, also betrayed his father, a successful movie director. At a mass rally during the Cultural Revolution, Chen denounced his father and shoved him around, then stood by as his Red Guard classmates ransacked the family home and burned their books. Chen's three-hour epic, about the tragic fate of three actors during the Cultural Revolution, was partly intended as a tribute—and an apology—to his father.

11 Luckily for *my* father, he was safe in Montreal because Yin wasn't the only person I betrayed. During my last week at Beijing University, a woman named Liu Yimei showed up at my dormitory. Granny, our normally pleasant housekeeper-guard, brought her to my room, then walked out, slamming the door behind her. Liu giggled nervously. Her eyes darted around my room, taking in the precious armoire, the bookcase, the desks. She was short and thin, with old-fashioned rimless glasses and hair prematurely streaked with gray. She explained that her husband, Zhao Lihai, a law professor at Beijing University, was a friend of my McGill professor Paul Lin. She insisted I dine out with her family that night.

12 They took me to the Moscow Restaurant, which had real tablecloths, thirty-foot-high ceilings and a Western menu that offered borscht, bread and jam, and Chicken Kiev. Their shy fifteen-year-old daughter never said a word and could scarcely bring herself to look at me all evening. Professor Zhao seemed neurotically insecure. He ordered shrimp and duck, the two most expensive dishes. When the waiter brought the food, Zhao clucked his tongue and apologized for the poor quality. I bristled; it was far better than most ordinary people ever ate.

13 During dinner, he and his wife kept their voices pitched at a conspiratorial whisper. They both talked a steady stream of counter-revolutionary thoughts. Nothing in China was as good as in the West; the education system was in a shambles; people didn't have enough to eat or wear. I was shocked and disgusted. In an entire year of living in China, they were the first people I met who disagreed with almost everything the government was doing.

14 "Why on earth does the Foreign Students Office make you take part in physical labour?" Professor Zhao asked sympathetically.

15 "I want to," I replied stiffly.

16 "What does your father do?" said his wife, changing the subject. When I told her he owned several restaurants, she uttered a small cry of approval, the first person in China to admire my blood-sucking background. She asked how much money he had. I was deeply offended, but she didn't seem to notice.

17 "I was an accountant at the Beijing Library," she said. "But I don't work now because of my health." She laughed unnaturally. "Why don't I go to Canada and work in your father's restaurant as an accountant?"

18 I was stunned. I couldn't believe that a person who lived in paradise would forsake it all to be exploited by a capitalist. "How long has it been since you worked?" I asked her coldly.

19 "Since my daughter was born," she said.

20 *A parasite for fifteen years,* I thought with self-righteous revulsion. Had I had any brains, I would have figured out that she had stopped working around 1957, the time of the Anti-Rightist Campaign, when 55,000 people, mostly intellectuals, were labelled rightists and fired. But even if I had, it wouldn't have changed my low opinion of her. At that point, I had no inkling that China's rightists were almost all honourable men and women.

21 Professor Zhao got to the point. "We want to send our daughter abroad to study. She has zero chance here. Can you help us?" His wife began to beg me to help, flattering me and grovelling. So that was why they had spent a month's wages on dinner. I felt sick. I muttered something non-committal. Back in the dormitory, I told Erica all of my doubts and suspicions. The next morning, I asked my teacher about the Zhaos.

Kuomintang: political party that ruled before the Communists

22 "They're evil people," Fu said instantly. "Zhao Lihai sold secrets to the **Kuomintang** and the Americans. He's famous for his crime." She added that he hadn't dared contact me directly because he was on lifelong parole and had to report all his actions to the Communist Party Committee. So he sent his wife. She had come over many times in the past year, and the Foreign Students Office had always turned her away. No one had ever told me. Now that I was leaving, Fu said, they agreed to let the couple see me once, but only because they knew my professor at McGill. Without another moment's hesitation, I reported to Fu the Enforcer that Professor Zhao and his wife had asked me to get their daughter out.

23 Many years later, I learned that Yin Luoyi was hauled before her classmates and denounced for her "traitorous" thoughts. Scarlet, a classmate who had introduced Yin to us, was asked to make a speech attacking Yin. To her credit, she refused. Yin was expelled from Beijing University and sent in disgrace back to her home in northeast China. I have no idea what happened to her. Nor do I know what befell Professor Zhao and his family. I only hope that, eventually, they were all able to join the exodus to the West. May God forgive me; I don't think they ever will.

(1656 words)

Source: Wong, Jan. *Red China Blues*. Toronto: Doubleday, 1996. 106–110. Print.

Students can read the essay in class or for homework. There are additional questions in the Student Section of the Companion Website. You can verify if students have read the essay by checking their scores with the grade tracker. Note that "Snitch" can be used as a practice reading test.

COMPREHENSION: CRITICAL THINKING

1 When was Wong in China, and why was she there? In 1972-1973

2 Why was Wong in China?

She was a guest student at Beijing University.

3 Today, many parts of China are prosperous and there is a growing middle class. What was China like at the time of Wong's visit?

Streets were empty. Many people had been sent to farms and communes for thought reform.
Most people were poor and could not afford to eat in nice restaurants.

4 Whom did Wong snitch on? Name the two people and explain why she snitched.

Yin Luoyi, a classmate, wanted to go to the US.
Professor Zhao, a friend of her McGill professor, wanted to send his daughter to the West.

5 What was Wong's attitude during her dinner with professor Zhao?

She was very cold, uncomfortable, and judgmental.

6 Wong lists three other people who snitched on someone. Who were they, and whom did they snitch on?

Her classmate Erica also snitched on Yin.
Her classmate Forest snitched on her father.
Filmmaker Chen Kaige betrayed his father.

7 Wong appears to justify her snitching. Underline her excuses in the text, and list at least five of them here.

She was young and idealistic and knew so little about human suffering; she had been subjected to a relentless barrage of propaganda and had absorbed the values; she was always being judged and wanted to prove that she was good; she had an undeveloped moral sense; she was trying to do the right thing for the revolution. Also, she thought she was helping Yin and the country, and lots of other people also snitched.

8 Who is Scarlet, and how was her reaction unusual at that time in China?

Scarlet, Wong's classmate, was asked to attack Yin, but she refused. She resisted authority.

Answers will vary.

COMPANION WEB+ Why do people riot? Read Andrew Potter's views in his text, "Rioting Is Fun," on the Companion Website.

9 Why did Wong write about this event in her life? Make an inference or guess.

Perhaps she felt very guilty about what she had done. Maybe she wants to warn others about over-zealousness.

DISCUSSION AND WRITING

1 What does this essay suggest about the political idealism of youths?

2 What should Wong have done when Yin Luoyi and Professor Zhao asked for help?

3 How was the context that Wong lived in different from your life? Using your own words, describe the time, place, and culture that the story depicts, and compare it to your own location and era.

Grammar TIP

Should have + Past Participle

When you write the past forms of modals, remember to use *have* + the past participle.

She **should have refused** the dinner invitation.

To learn more about modals, see Unit 6 in *Avenues 3: English Grammar*.

Vocabulary BOOST

Vivid Verbs

The following vivid verbs appear in "Snitch," and the paragraph numbers are in parentheses. Match the verb with the appropriate meaning. Write the letter of the appropriate answer in the space. **Read the word in context before you make each guess.**

Verbs		Definitions
1 hassling (3)	e	a. showed visible anger
2 wiped out (3)	h	b. moved quickly
3 ratting (8)	j	c. lightly laughed
4 meddling (9)	i	d. abasing oneself and begging
5 ransacked (10)	f	e. dealing with
6 giggled (11)	c	f. searched thoroughly, leaving a mess behind
7 darted (11)	b	g. spoke in a low voice
8 bristled (12)	a	h. exhausted; used up
9 grovelling (21)	d	i. interfering
10 muttered (21)	g	j. snitching

SPEAKING

The Faust and Cayo Cases

The Faust and Cayo cases are fictional and loosely based on real-life events, including the Ludwig Wiebo and FLQ cases. You might have a class debate, with two large teams arguing that the defendants should be released or punished.

Faust and Cayo's genders are purposely not expressed. View how the class discusses the activists. Ask if they would judge Faust and Cayo differently if they were females.

Read about the following case. Then work with a team of students to answer the questions. Explain the reasons for your opinions.

In 1994, Alex Faust lived on a farm in northern Alberta. Faust believed that oil and gas facilities were killing local wildlife and damaging the water supply. Faust formed an activism group called "Stop Oil." By 1996, thirty-year-old Faust had attracted ten members to the group, including Riley Cayo, twenty-five, a bright engineering student. At first, members distributed pamphlets, but then they became more radical. They attacked oil extraction facilities, occasionally disrupting supplies.

In early 1997, Faust decided that the group was not getting enough media attention, and people didn't seem to care about the environment. The group made more prominent attacks. They attacked an oil company office building near the Alberta Tar Sands project. Cayo, who was extremely good with electronics and explosives, built a bomb. Then another member dropped a backpack containing the bomb beside the oil company office building, next to a propane tank. The group wanted to send a severe

Alberta Tar Sands

message, but they did not want anyone to get hurt, so a member phoned in a bomb warning.

Police immediately evacuated the building. Twenty minutes later, the bomb exploded. That started a chain reaction, which caused the propane tank to explode. Shattered glass injured police officers at the scene. Glass flew into the eye of Officer Celine Day. Dwayne Shepherd, an office worker who had been in the bathroom and had not heard the evacuation order, was killed.

Since the bombing

- Three members of "Stop Oil" were arrested and spent some time in prison. They have testified that Faust controlled the group and made the decision to plant the bomb.
- Alex Faust and Riley Cayo have hidden from the authorities. In 1998, Faust moved to Denver, Colorado, and raised a family. Faust worked in an advertising company under a false name and never had any problems with the law. According to neighbours, Faust was very kind and charitable, donating money and time to various social causes.
- Riley Cayo moved to Brazil and worked in a construction company. Six months ago, Cayo was arrested when trying to visit family in Canada. In a deal with police, Cayo divulged Faust's location. Faust has been deported to Canada. Both activists face murder and terrorism charges.
- Riley Cayo's family say that Cayo was easily manipulated and naive. However, Cayo's friends in Brazil say that Cayo is self-confident and often quite arrogant.
- In Alberta, Dwayne Shepherd's four children want justice for their father's death. His daughter, Anna, says, "My dad was a good man. He was just an accountant. He should not have been murdered! My family misses him terribly. My mother was so depressed after his murder that she died shortly afterward."
- Officer Celine Day says that the accident has changed her life. She is blind in one eye and has constant ringing in her ears because she was so near the explosion.
- Riley Cayo has apologized: "I'm sorry for what I have done. I was an idealistic but gullible youth. I was just following the orders of Faust, who was the mastermind."
- Faust expresses sincere regret: "I was profoundly upset to learn about the death of Mr. Shepherd. It was never our group's intention to hurt anyone." However, Faust still believes in violent political actions: "Oil companies are destroying the environment. Oil extraction in the tar sands uses almost 350 million cubic metres of water per year. Local communities have seen increases in cancer deaths. We had to do something."

Questions

1 What punishment should Alex Faust receive? Explain why.

2 What should happen to Riley Cayo? Explain why.

3 Is "political activism" ever a justifiable reason for murdering someone? Why or why not?

Question 3 of the speaking activity can be an essay-writing topic.

Take Action!

WRITING TOPICS

Write a composition about one of the following topics. Remember to include a thesis statement and to provide supporting examples. Include at least one direct quotation in your essay. Before handing in your work, refer to the Writing Checklist on the inside back cover.

1 Peer Pressure

Think about peer pressure in high schools. What types of pressures do students face? In which ways do they conform? Do many students exhibit "bystander apathy" when they witness bullying, for instance? In an essay, discuss peer pressure. Ensure that your thesis statement makes a point about the topic. In your body paragraphs, include specific examples from your life, events in the news, and readings from this chapter.

2 Reasons for Bad Behaviour

Why do ordinary people sometimes do very bad things? For instance, why would a normally decent person hurt a stranger or ignore someone who is in distress? Think of three reasons. Consult this chapter's readings and video. Refer to the Milgram experiment and the Stanford Prison experiment, which are described in the video *The Power of Social Roles.* Also refer to the text, "Bystander Apathy."

3 War Crimes

When soldiers commit war crimes, is the defence of "I was following orders" legitimate? Why or why not? In your body paragraphs, refer to the video and the readings in this chapter and to events in the news.

Need help with your pronunciation? Visit the Companion Website and try the Pronunciation Workshops.

SPEAKING TOPICS

Prepare a presentation about one of the following topics. For details about preparing a speaking presentation, see Appendix 1 on page 174.

1 Political Movement and Strikes

Sometimes union members strike to get higher pay or better working conditions. In 2012, Quebec students went on strike to protest a tuition fee increase. Are strikes effective bargaining tools? Why or why not? What are better alternatives? Support your opinions with specific examples.

Remind students to try the Pronunciation Workshops on the Companion Website.

2 An Effective Protest Movement

What are the elements of a successful protest movement? Should protestors block streets or close down subway systems? Is there any place for violence or rioting? Describe how to have an effective protest movement. Explain clearly what people should and should not do.

3 A Past Political or Social Movement

Brainstorm about a social or political movement from the past. What types of actions did the members of the movement take? Did they march in streets, clang pots, or disrupt the daily lives of citizens? Did they resort to violence, murder, kidnapping, or bombing? Were such actions useful and justified? Then explain what should have happened or describe what people should have done.

MEDIA LINK

Watch a movie or documentary about politics or political idealism, such as *Inside Job*, *The Ides of March*, *A Separation*, *Good Night, and Good Luck*, *The Trotsky*, or *The Constant Gardener.* You could also do an Internet search for movies about politics and then choose one. Prepare an essay or a speaking presentation about the movie. Begin with a very brief summary. Then explain the message of the movie. Make a connection between the message and at least one of the readings in this chapter.

Revising and Editing

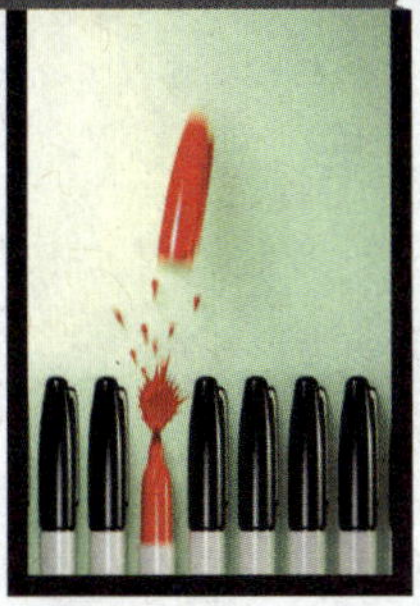

The Revising and Editing sections at the end of each chapter help your students prepare for writing tests, including Benchmark and TESOL tests. You can ask students to do the activities with a partner and to share ideas.

Answers will vary.

The circled words should be made consistent. There are many possible choices, but ideally, students will make the general sentences focus on "we" or "they."

REVISE FOR POINT OF VIEW
EDIT FOR PUNCTUATION

A well-constructed paragraph or essay should present a consistent point of view. For example, do not switch unnecessarily from "they" to "you." (To learn more about consistent point of view, see Writing Workshop 2, page 164.)

Read the following paragraph and follow these steps.

1 Modify, add, or remove words to make the point of view consistent.

2 Correct nine errors with punctuation and capitalization. Underline any titles that should normally appear in italics.

Everyone wants to change the world. We all wish that we could contribute something positive during our short time on earth. Probably you worry, about issues in the news, you feel angry that politicians aren't fixing major problems. When we are young, we tend to be especially hopeful and strong-minded about politics. But sometimes, political idealism can cause people to make reckless and dangerous decisions. In her essay Snitch, which was taken from her book Red China blues, Jan Wong presents political idealism at its worst. In 1972, Wong studied in China, and she believed Communist propaganda. Wong says: "Maoism suited the absoluteness of youth". Wongs self-righteousness affected the lives of others. For instance, she denounced two people: Yin Luoyi and Professor Zhao. Later in life, Wong regretted her decision, "May God forgive me; I don't think they ever will.

To practise vocabulary from this chapter, visit the Companion Website.

Grammar TIP

Writing Titles

Capitalize the major words in titles. Use quotation marks around the titles of short works such as articles, short stories, and songs. Italicize (or underline in the text above) titles of longer works such as magazines, novels, movies, and albums.

Susanna Moodie's story "My Visit to Montreal" is from her book *Roughing It in the Bush*.

To learn more about writing titles, see Unit 11 in *Avenues 3: English Grammar*.

CHAPTER 8

"On the whole, human beings want to be good, but not too good, and not quite all the time."

– GEORGE ORWELL, WRITER

The Good Life

What contributes to a good life? How can we become better people? This chapter examines our need to connect and feel good about ourselves.

START UP

Trivia Quiz

Work with a team of students to answer the following questions.

You can do the Trivia Quiz as a competition. Give teams a time period (about five minutes) to answer as many questions as possible. The team that has the most correct answers wins. Ensure that students do not use their smartphones to search for the answers.

1 What school did Harry Potter go to? Hogwarts

2 What is a topic sentence? a sentence that expresses the main idea of a paragraph

3 What is Brazil's official language? Portuguese

4 Who wrote *Hamlet*? Shakespeare

5 Underline and correct the mistake in this sentence.

Susanna Moodie's story shows us how did people live (how people lived) in the past.

6 Name three famous Canadian actors. Ryan Gossling, Ryan Reynolds, Rachel McAdams, etc.

7 Underline and correct three mistakes in this sentence.

My school has less (fewer) problems than yours, (;) for exemple (example), nobody drops out.

8 Name three sports that don't use balls. hockey, swimming, skiing, wrestling, etc.

9 In a quotation, should the final punctuation be inside or outside the quotation marks? inside

10 What two countries occupy the largest territories? Russia, Canada

11 Underline the word that has a spelling mistake, and correct it. responsible

a. future b. responsable c. exaggerate

12 What is a thesis statement? a sentence that expresses the main idea of an essay

13 How many provinces and territories does Canada have? ten provinces and three territories

14 Underline and correct three errors in this sentence.

In the past, my uncle was teaching (taught) my brother and I (me) to speak english (English).

15 Name four countries that start with the letter C, not including Canada.

Chile, Cuba, China, Cambodia, Costa Rica, Congo, etc.

16 Underline and correct two mistakes in this sentence.

The governement (government) must continue his (its) actions to stop global warming.

17 What is the next number in this series? 1, 3, 6, 10 15

18 What do the letters RCMP stand for? Royal Canadian Mounted Police

19 Which title should be written in italics: a book title or an article title? a book title

20 Which planet is closest to the sun? Mercury

READING STRATEGY

Students can visit the Companion Website to practise their reading comprehension. Questions for all readings are structured to help students do better in their reading tests, including Benchmark and TESOL tests.

Visit the Companion Website to prepare for your reading tests. Online questions for all readings are structured to help you practise reading strategies.

Identifying Figurative Devices

Some writers use figurative devices such as similes or metaphors to make their writing more descriptive.

- A **simile** is a comparison using *like* or *as*.

  She drops names like autumn trees drop leaves.
  His hands were as rough as tree bark.
  "The kiss was like spinach to Popeye."
  Heather O'Neill, *Riff-Raff*

- A **metaphor** is a comparison that does not use *like* or *as*.

  The drunk's legs were rubber.
  My little office was a prison cell.
  "All the world's a stage, and all the men and women merely players."
  William Shakespeare, *As You Like It*

- **Personification** is the act of attributing human qualities to an inanimate object, idea, or animal.

  The grass was dancing in the breeze.
  The walls begged for a new coat of paint.
  "The wipers … scraped and squeaked in protest."
  Douglas Adams, *The Long Dark Tea-Time of the Soul*

Answers will vary.

PRACTICE

Alone or with a partner or team, write original examples of the following figurative devices. As George Orwell said, "Never use a metaphor, simile, or other figure of speech which you are used to seeing in print."

1 Simile

a) It is as red as ______________________

____

b) After working in the hot sun all day, Devon felt like ______________________

____

c) (Your choice) ______________________

____

2 Metaphor

a) The tree is ______________________

b) The city is ______________________

c) (Your choice) ______________________

3 Personification

a) The airplane ______________________

____

b) The water ______________________

____

c) (Your choice) ______________________

____

Students can practise identifying these figurative devices by looking at "Cyclops" on page 49. It contains personification in paragraphs 2, 8, and 19, a metaphor in paragraph 5, and similes in paragraphs 8 and 14.

READING 8.1 Ani DiFranco is a successful folksinger, guitarist, and writer, and she runs her own record company, Righteous Babe Records. As you read the lyrics to one of her songs, try to appreciate the imagery and figurative devices.

what if no one's watching

BY ANI DIFRANCO

1 if my life were a movie
there would be a sunset
and the camera would pan away
but the sky is just a little sister
tagging along behind the buildings
trying to imitate their gray
the little boys are breaking bottles
against the sidewalk
the big boys, too
the girls are hanging out at the
candy store
pumping quarters into the phone
because they don't want to go home

2 and i think
what if no one's watching
what if when we're dead
we are just dead
I mean what if god ain't looking down
what if he's looking up instead

3 if my life were a movie
i would light a cigarette
and the smoke would curl
around my face
everything i do would be interesting
i'd play the good guy
in every scene
but i always feel i have to
take a stand
and there's always someone on hand
to hate me for standing there
i always feel i have to open my mouth
and every time i do
i offend someone somewhere

4 but what
what if no one's watching
what if when we're dead
we are just dead
what if there's no time to lose
what if there's things we gotta do
things that need to be said

5 you know i can't apologize
for everything i know
i mean you don't have to agree
with me
but once you get me going
you better just let me go
we have to be able to criticize
what we love
say what we have to say
'cause if you're not trying
to make something better
as far as I'm concerned
you are just in the way

6 I mean what
what if no one's watching
what if when we're dead
we are just dead
what if it's just us down here
what if god is just an idea
someone put in our head

(315 words)

Source: DiFranco, Ani. "what if no one's watching." *Righteous Babe Music*. Righteous Babe Records, 1992. Web.

COMPREHENSION: ANALYZING A LYRIC

1 a) Identify a metaphor in the first verse of the lyric.

the sky is just a little sister tagging along behind the buildings

b) Explain how the metaphor is also an example of personification.

The sky cannot tag along consciously like a human being.

2 In the first verse, DiFranco paints a picture with words. What point is she making about the boys and girls?

They are bored and are finding ways to pass the time with friends.

Answers will vary.

3 Use your own words to explain the message in verse 3. What does DiFranco desire?

She wants to be good, important, and respected. She understands that she might offend others with her views.

4 What is DiFranco's view of spirituality? Does she believe in God? Explain your answer.

She questions the existence of a higher power when she asks, "what if no one's watching." She says, "what if god is just an idea."

Answers will vary.

5 What is the entire song about? In two or three sentences, explain the song's general message.

Imagine that there is no afterlife, and live as if this is your only life. Be yourself and don't apologize or worry if others disagree with you. Have faith in your ideals because they just might be your mission in this life on earth.

COMPANION WEB+ Answer additional questions for all the reading and listening activities. You can also access audio and video clips online.

WRITING

You can make the freewriting activity a competition. Students should write in class, and then they should choose the writing that would make the best lyrics.

Try freewriting, or writing without stopping, about a person or place. You can also write about larger ideas such as the meaning of your life. Then look again at your freewriting, and turn them into lyrics. Try to include a simile, metaphor, or personification. Also use images that appeal to the senses. (For examples of imagery, see page 2 in Chapter 1.)

Vocabulary **BOOST**

Literary Versus Academic English

Writers of stories, poems, and lyrics often break English language rules and conventions. They may use spoken English instead of academic English. They might incorporate dialect (the language of a particular district or social class) to make dialogue seem more authentic. For example, the next excerpt is from *Half-Blood Blues* by Esi Edugyan.

> We **come** round the corner, onto the wide square, when **all a sudden** my stomach lurched. I **been** expecting it—**you need guts of iron to ride out what all we drunk** last night. **Iron guts I ain't got**, but don't let that fool you **bout** other parts of my anatomy.

Now notice the changes when the excerpt contains academic English.

> We **came around** the corner, onto the wide square, when **suddenly** my stomach lurched. I **had been** expecting it. **We needed strong stomachs to endure what we had drunk** last night. **I don't have a strong stomach**, but don't let that fool you **about** other parts of my anatomy.

PRACTICE

Make the lyrics of "what if no one's watching" into academic writing. Directly on Ani DiFranco's lyrics, on page 133, add punctuation and capitalization. Also fix any words that are grammatically incorrect.

WATCHING

Good News

Never lose faith in humanity. At least that's what two Canadian businessmen are trying to promote with their People for Good movement. But how easy is it to get strangers to commit random acts of kindness?

You can assign the video in class or for homework. There are additional comprehension questions in the Student Section of the Companion Website. You might assign the online questions, and then discuss these comprehension questions with the class.

COMPREHENSION

Answer each question in complete sentences.

1 What are the jobs of Zak Mroueh and Mark Sherman?

Zak Mroueh is the president of a Toronto-based advertising agency. Mark Sherman is the founder of a media-buying firm in Montreal.

2 Describe two of the People for Good advertisements.

There are ads in grocery stores suggesting that shoppers let someone with fewer items go ahead in line. There is another ad advising people to act more like dogs and be friendly.

3 How much does the People for Good app cost? It's free.

4 Do the ads seem to be working? What do the statistics demonstrate?

The statistics show that 30 percent of Canadians heard the message. People who saw the ads were 50 percent more likely to give up their seat on transit and twice as likely to let someone in line.

5 What did York University's Myriam Mongrain do with a control group?

She asked a control group to do one nice thing a day for six months.

6 What were the results of Dr. Mongrain's study?

The results showed that it helped boost immune functioning and increase creativity.

DISCUSSION AND WRITING

What is your opinion of advertisements that promote acts of kindness? Are such ads a good idea, or would people find them preachy and annoying? Explain your answer.

READING 8.2 Why do people show compassion and self-sacrifice? Read some theories about altruism.

We're Not All Bad

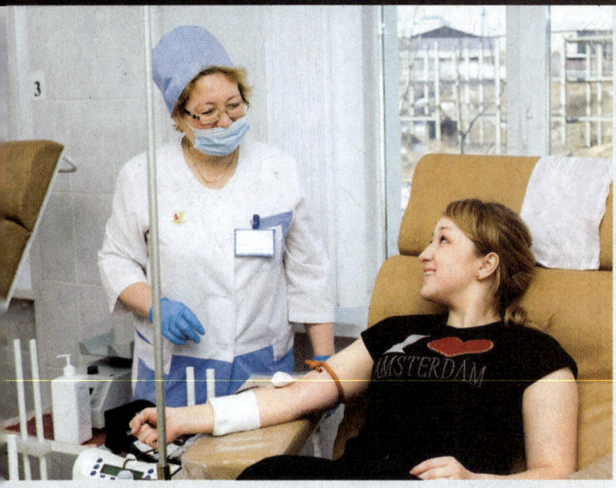

BY DIEGO PELAEZ

1 Daily headlines about war, genocide, and murderous shooting sprees paint a bleak image of humanity. It's sometimes difficult to remember that millions of people try to do good every day. Of course, parents would lay down their lives for their offspring, but such biological altruism has a clear—albeit subconscious—goal: the proliferation of family genes. What about those who help strangers, with no hope of a reward? Every day, families snowed under with bills give money to the homeless; men and women pull off highways to help accident victims. Social scientists and psychologists have attempted to determine why humans display empathy and what motivates them to be charitable.

2 Altruism may actually be an inborn human trait. Felix Warneken, a German psychologist, created a study involving eighteen-month-old babies. The toddlers, still in diapers and able to say only a few words, showed a surprising eagerness to help a stranger. In front of each child, Warneken performed a series of actions, such as stacking books or hanging clothes on a line. When he dropped a clothespin or knocked over his books, nearly all of the toddlers immediately crawled over and attempted to help him gather his things. To avoid influencing each toddler's actions, he never asked for help and never thanked the child afterward—which is sort of how most empathetic adults are treated. Curiously, when it was evident that he had deliberately dropped or thrown something, the toddler would not help. Apparently, small children possess the capacity for empathy, but they can also detect purposeful foolishness.

3 So if humans are born with a helping gene, why are so many willing to overlook or ignore large-scale tragedies? Famines and genocide may elicit a great deal of sympathy, but they rarely spur the average person into action. Some pundits suggest that an overwhelming onslaught of depressing media images from places such as Syria, Sudan, and Darfur have numbed people. Perhaps citizens in our celebrity-obsessed, superficial society have become too self-absorbed to help, or even pay attention to, millions of suffering people abroad.

4 Often, the causes that people *are* interested in only exacerbate this view. In his article, "What Moves Us," *The New York Times* columnist Nicholas Kristof describes his bewilderment after his 2004 visit to Darfur. The genocide resulted in a tepid public response, whereas back home in New York, local citizens were galvanized to save a hawk that had made a home on a high-rise. Shortly before that, a dog that had been stranded on a ship "aroused so much pity that $48,000 was spent trying to rescue it," according to Kristof. Why were people so generous to a dog and bird, and so unfeeling toward millions of suffering humans?

5 The answer is not as disheartening as one might expect. In 2006, Deborah Small, a Wharton marketing professor, published a study about donations to charitable causes. Citizens were asked to give $5 to combat hunger. Some of the subjects were shown a photo of a hungry young girl named Rokia from Mali. The others were asked to donate to a fund for 21 million starving Africans. The Rokia group

donated much more than the second group. Curiously, if Rokia was presented as just one of the millions in need, donations also dropped off. Thus, people aren't simply unfeeling, self-absorbed monsters who care more about pets than people. They are physiologically more likely to feel a spontaneous emotional connection with an individual human or animal than with faceless millions, regardless of their tragic circumstances.

6 Confusingly, the more information someone is given, the less likely he is to donate. "It's easy to override people's feelings by giving them statistical information," according to Small. Thus, charitable organizations should try appealing to people's feelings, not their logic. Major tragedies have trouble capturing the public's imagination. Although it's clear that events like genocide and mass displacement are horrible and wrong, the average person cannot really fathom the machinations involved and feels helpless when faced with such massive problems. It's much easier to understand the plight of a single starving child; one can conceive of a possible solution to the child's problems.

7 Humans can also be inspired to do better when they hear about the altruism of others. Karl Aquino, an anthropology professor at the University of British Columbia, says, "When we witness other people do these really virtuous things, it makes us take stock of our own lives." He devised an experiment in which two groups were shown positive images and then asked to donate to a charity. The first group was shown a short video about a couple who witnessed a beautiful sunset. The second group watched a video about some Amish families who had lost their children in a schoolhouse shooting. (A deranged neighbour had opened fire, killing several children and then himself. Instead of expressing outrage, the families banded together and offered help to the murderer's widow and children.)

8 After watching the videos, both groups were given $10 and asked to donate as much as they wanted to a charity. The subjects who had seen the Amish community's inspiring act of forgiveness donated 32 percent more than those who had seen the sunset. In an interview with *The Vancouver Sun*, Aquino said, "When we observe others in extraordinary acts of virtue, we can have a very visceral and emotional response, coupled with thoughts of wanting to do better ourselves."

9 Most people aren't malicious. Almost everyone has the capacity for empathy and longs to do good in the world. Perhaps the media can help foster compassion. Video clips showing forgiveness, benevolence, and heroism could replace a few of those clips showing looting, death, and destruction. If a toddler can understand how to be altruistic, the rest of us should be able to manage it, too.

(976 words)

Sources: Briggs, Helen. "Altruism 'Inbuilt' in Humans." *BBC News*. British Broadcasting Corporation, 3 Mar. 2006. Web.
Kristof, Nicholas D. "What Moves Us." *The New York Times*. The New York Times Company, 14 May 2007. Web.
Ryan, Denise. "Virtuous Actions Can Inspire." *The Vancouver Sun*. Canada.com, 30 Mar. 2011. Web.
"To Increase Charitable Donations, Appeal to the Heart, Not the Head." *Knowledge@Wharton*. U. of Pennsylvania, 27 June 2007. Web.

Students can read the essay in class or for homework. There are additional questions in the Student Section of the Companion Website. You can verify if students have read the essay by checking their scores with the grade tracker. Note that "We're Not All Bad" can be used as a practice reading test.

WRITTEN COMPREHENSION

Using your own words, summarize this text. Write a paragraph of about 180–200 words. For rules about summary writing, see page 23 in Chapter 2.

SPEAKING Kindness Week

Create your own "Act of Kindness" project. First, with a partner, brainstorm at least ten different random acts of kindness that you might do to help a total stranger. Then think of at least ten actions that you could do to help people who you know, including family members, friends, co-workers, and classmates. Brainstorm some actions that you do not normally do. For instance, if you do not normally wash the dishes or open doors for people, then you can put those actions on your list. Do not repeat the same action twice.

For the next week, do ten acts of kindness. Do at least five random acts of kindness for a stranger and five acts of kindness for people you know. Vary the types of actions that you do. Keep a notebook or computer log detailing your acts of kindness. Then, with a partner or in small groups, present your experiences to your classmates. Describe what you did, explain how others reacted, and discuss what you learned from the experience.

You might give students two weeks to complete the activity. If you have a computer lab, students can send progress reports to you or to each other.

WRITING

In an essay, write about your "Act of Kindness" experience.

LISTENING Voluntourism

You can assign the listening activity in class or for homework. There are additional comprehension questions in the Student Section of the Companion Website.

Should students include volunteer work in their travel adventures? Jian Ghomeshi spoke to Daniela Papi, founder of PEPY, an education and development organization based in Phnom Penh, Cambodia. Listen as Papi describes some of the problems with volunteer work abroad.

COMPREHENSION

School in Ko Chang, Thailand

1 In the UK, what is a gap year? a year spent travelling or volunteering abroad before going to college or university.

2 a) Where did Papi paint a school? Thailand

b) What was her impression of the school painting project?

It was badly planned. The volunteers were tired and they painted badly by the end of the day. It would have been preferable to give the school money to hire teachers.

3 According to Papi, why do many aid organizations like to build schools instead of giving money for teachers?

It's easier to see the results of the donations. People like having a building with their name on it.

4 According to Papi, what is the main benefit of volunteering? What should students hope to gain from the experience?

They learn leadership skills and learn about development.

5 A Unicef report says that ___ percent of kids in Cambodian orphanages have at least one living parent.

a. 15 b. 30 c. 60 (d.) 75

6 Why is Papi concerned about orphanages in Cambodia?

They have become a business. Many people make money from them. Perhaps desperate parents sell their children to such orphanages.

7 What is Papi's overall tone about volunteering abroad?

a. positive (b.) cynical c. frightened d. serious

8 What is Papi's main message to students who are thinking of volunteering abroad?

They should do it, but they should not expect to change the world. They need to learn before they can help.

DISCUSSION AND WRITING

1 Would you like to volunteer overseas? Why or why not?

2 Have you already done volunteer work in another country? Describe what happened.

READING 8.3

The following excerpt is from best-selling author Nick Hornby's book, *How to Be Good*. Before you read the story, review the following background information.

- **Katie Carr**, a doctor, has been married to David for nearly two decades. Katie is deeply unhappy and has recently become involved with another man.
- **David**, Katie's husband, writes a column called *The Angriest Man in Holloway*. Previously, David's back pain was unbearable, so he decided to see a faith healer by the name of DJ GoodNews. Not only did David's pain heal, but he has become a new man. David has become good—piously, righteously, save-the-world good.
- **Tom and Molly** are the children of David and Katie.
- **GoodNews** is David's faith healer. When GoodNews becomes homeless, David invites him to stay with his family.

Now read and discover what happens.

How to Be Good

BY NICK HORNBY

hence: therefore

He's a funny little man, GoodNews. Thirtyish, small, and astonishingly skinny. He has huge, bright-blue, frightened-looking eyes, and lots of curly, dirty-blonde hair, although I suspect that personal hygiene might not necessarily be a priority for him at the moment, and perhaps I should reserve judgment on the hair colour until he has been persuaded to shower. There has been an unwise and spectacularly unsuccessful attempt to grow a goatee. **Hence**, there's a fluffy little tuft of something or other, just underneath the centre of his lower lip, that any mother would want to rub off with a bit of spit. What you notice first of all, however, is that both his eyebrows have been pierced, and he is wearing what appear to be brooches over each eye. The children are particularly and perhaps forgivably fascinated by this.

"Are those tortoises?" Tom asks, even before he's said hello. I hadn't wanted to stare at the eyebrow jewellery before, but now I see that my son is right: this man is wearing representations of domestic pets on his face.

"Nah," says GoodNews dismissively, as if Tom's error was ignorant in the extreme, and he's about to expand when Molly steps in.

"They're turtles," she says. I am momentarily impressed by her authority until I remember that she has met GoodNews before.

"What's the difference?" asks Tom.

"Turtles can swim, can't they?" says David overcheerfully, as if trying to enter into the spirit of a completely different occasion—an occasion where we're sitting around eating pizza and watching a nature program, rather than an occasion where we're welcoming a spiritual healer with animals dangling from his eyebrows into our home.

"Why did you want turtles and not tortoises?" Tom asks. It's not the first question that came to my mind, but DJ GoodNews is such a curious creature that any information he cares to give us is endlessly fascinating.

"You won't laugh if I tell you?"

I laugh even before he tells us. I can't help it. GoodNews looks hurt. "I'm sorry," I say.

"That was quite rude," says GoodNews. "I'm surprised at you."

"Do you know me?"

"I feel like I do. David's talked a lot about you. He loves you very much, but you've been going through some bad times, yeah?"

For a moment I think he's asking me for confirmation—but then I realize that the "yeah" is just one of those annoying verbal tics that this generation pick up like head lice. I have never met anyone like GoodNews. He talks like a **dodgy geezer vicar**, all cockiness and glottal stops and suspect **solicitude**.

dodgy geezer vicar: corrupt old religious man

solicitude: concern

"Anyway," he says, "The turtles. I've always had this thing about turtles. I've always thought that they could see stuff that we can't, yeah?"

The children stare at their father, clearly baffled.

"What can they see?" asks Molly.

"Good question, Molly." He points at her. "You're good. You're sharp. I'm going to have to watch you." Molly looks pleased, but there is no attempt to answer the question.

"He doesn't know," says Tom with a snort.

"Oh, I know all right. But maybe now's not the time."

"When's the time, then?"

"Do you want to show GoodNews to his room?" says David to the children, clearly with the intention of bringing the subject of turtles and their psychic powers to a close, and as GoodNews doesn't want to expand on his theories anyway, he picks up his bags and goes upstairs.

David turns to me. "I know what you're thinking."

"What am I supposed to think?"

"I know he talks nonsense some of the time. Try not to get bogged down in the superficial stuff."

"What else is there?" I reply.

"You don't pick up a vibe?"

"No."

"Oh. Oh well," he says, somewhat smugly.

In other words: some people—the intuitive, soulful, and spiritual among us—can pick up a vibe, and others—the flat, dull literalists, like me—can't. I resent this. "What vibe should I be picking up, then, according to you?"

"It's not according to me. It's there. It's interesting that Molly and I can feel it, and you and Tom can't."

"How do you know Tom can't? How do you know Molly can?"

"Did you notice that Tom was rude to him? If you pick up the vibe, you wouldn't be rude. Molly isn't rude. She got it the first time she saw him."

"And me? Was I rude?" I ask.

"Not rude. But skeptical."

"And that's wrong?"

"You can almost see it, what he has," David says, "if you know how to look."

"And you don't think I do?" I don't know why this bothers me so much, but it does. I want to know how to look—or at least, I want David to think of me as the sort of person who might know how to look.

"Calm down. It doesn't make you a bad person."

"That's not true, though, is it? According to you, that's precisely why I'm a bad person. Because all I saw was the eyebrows, not the ... the ... aura."

"We can't all be everything." And he smiles that smile and goes to join the others.

"There are a few things GoodNews has a problem with," says David when they have all come down again.

"I'm sorry to hear that," I say.

"I don't really agree with beds," says GoodNews.

"Oh," I say. "Do you mind if we sleep in them?" I want to sound dry and light, like a nice white wine, but I fear that what comes out is a lot more vinegary than that.

"What other people do is their business," says GoodNews. "I just think they make you soft. Take you further away from how things really are."

"And how are things?"

David shoots me a look. Not the old-style, I-hate-you-and-I-wish-you-were-dead look I would have got, once upon a time. This is the new-style, I'm-sooooooo-disappointed look, and for a moment I am nostalgic for the days when hatred was our common currency.

"That's a big question, Katie," says GoodNews. "And I don't know if you're ready for the big answer."

"You are, aren't you, Mum?" says Tom, loyally.

"Anyway," says David. "GoodNews would like the bed taken out of the spare room because there isn't really room for him to sleep on the floor if it stays there."

"Right. And where shall we put it?"

"I'll put it in my office," says David.

"Can I take my bed out?" Molly asks. "I don't like it."

"What's wrong with your bed?" I address this to David rather than Molly, just so that he can see what a mess of the world his friend is making.

"I don't agree with it," says Molly.

"What, precisely, don't you agree with?" I enquire.

"I just don't. They're wrong."

flat: British term for *apartment*

"When you have your own **flat**, you can sleep on nails for all I care. While you're here, you'll sleep in a bed."

"I'm sorry," says GoodNews. "I'm causing trouble, aren't I? Please, forget it. It's cool."

"Are you sure?" David says.

"No, really. I can cope on a bed." There is a pause, and he looks at David, who has clearly become GoodNews's representative on Earth.

David pauses and says, "The other thing that GoodNews was—well, we both were worried about, was where he's going to heal people."

"He was intending to heal them here?" I ask.

"Yes. Where else?"

"I thought he was only here for a couple of nights."

"Probably he will be. But he needs to work. And he has commitments to people. So, you know. If it does turn out to be a bit longer than a couple of days ..."

"Funnily enough, we've got an empty healing room that we never use."

"I'm afraid sarcasm is one of Katie's indulgences," David says.

"Sorry. Maybe your bedroom is the best place for now."

"Fine," GoodNews says. "I can do good work there. It has a nice atmosphere, you know?"

"And the last thing is, GoodNews is a vegetarian," David announces.

"Fine."

"A vegan, actually."

"Good. Very sensible. Enjoy your stay," I tell GoodNews, who is sure that he will be very happy here. For my part, I am sure that he will never ever leave.

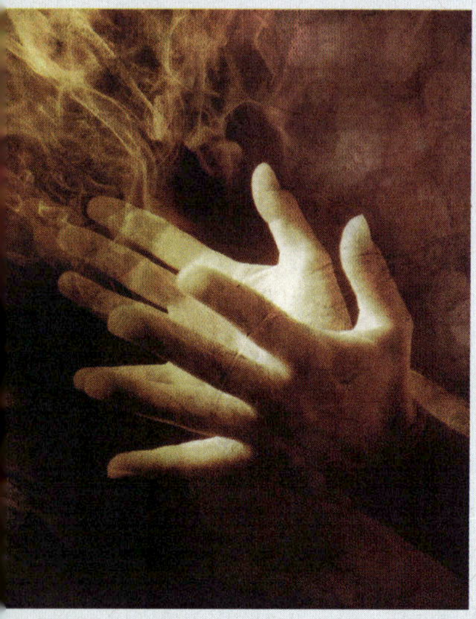

David cooks chicken pieces for us and vegetables for everyone while he and GoodNews talk in the kitchen, and then we have our first meal together. The main topic of conversation is GoodNews: GoodNews and the turtles (what they see is not really explicable in, like, words), GoodNews and how things really are ("Bad, man. But there's hope, you know?"), and GoodNews and his healing hands. Molly wants him to warm them up there and then, on the spot, but David tells her that it's not a party trick.

"Have you always been able to do it? Could you do it when you were my age?"

"No. I couldn't do it till I was, like, twenty-five?"

"How old are you now?"

"Thirty-two."

"So how did you know you could do it, then?" This from Tom, who has remained oblivious to the GoodNews charm.

"My girlfriend at the time—she had a cricked neck and she asked me to give her a massage and ... everything went all weird."

"What sort of weird?"

"Weird weird. The lightbulbs got brighter, the room got hot. It was a real scene."

"And how do you think your gift came about?" There is, I am pleased to note, less vinegar in my voice. I'm learning.

"I know," he says, "but I can't tell you in front of the kids. Bad form." I have no idea what this means, but if GoodNews thinks that the story of how he became a healer is unsuitable for minors, I am not prepared to argue with him.

"No," says GoodNews. "I mean it. Ask me another question."

"What was your girlfriend's name?" Molly asks.

"That's a stupid question," Tom snorts. "Who wants to know that? Idiot."

"Hey Tom, man. If that information is important to someone, then who are we to judge?" says GoodNews. "There might be all sorts of reasons why Molly wanted to know what my girlfriend's name was. Probably some pretty good reasons, if I know Molly. So let's not be calling people idiots, eh? She was called Andrea, Molly."

Molly nods smugly. Tom's face becomes a picture of smouldering hate, and I know that DJ GoodNews has made himself an enemy.

For the rest of the meal, we manage to avoid flashpoints. GoodNews asks politely about our jobs and our schools and our math teachers, and we all answer politely (if, in some cases, tersely), and we pass the time in this way until the last mouthful has been eaten and it is time to clear away.

"I'll wash up," says GoodNews.

"We have a dishwasher," I tell him, and GoodNews looks anxiously at David. It is not difficult to anticipate what is coming, and so I do.

"You don't hold with dishwashers," I say, with a weariness exaggerated to convey the idea that GoodNews's various antipathies might at some point become grating.

"No," says GoodNews.

"You don't hold with a lot of things that a lot of people don't have a problem with," I observe.

"No," he agrees. "But just because a lot of people don't have a problem with something, it doesn't mean they're right, does it? I mean, a lot of people used to think that ... I don't know ... slavery was OK, but, you know. They were wrong, weren't they? They were so wrong it was unreal. Because it wasn't OK, was it? It was really bad, man. Slaves. No way."

"Do you think that slavery and dishwashers are the same thing, GoodNews?" I ask.

"Maybe to me they're the same thing," he replies.

"Maybe to you all sorts of things are the same thing. Maybe pedophilia is the same thing as ... as ... soap. Maybe fascism is the same thing as toilets. But that doesn't mean I'm going to make my children pee in the garden, just because your peculiar moral code would prefer it." I really said that fascism is the same as toilets. I suddenly inhabit a world where this might pass for a coherent line of argument.

"You're being silly. And sarcastic," David says.

Sarcasm—my terrible indulgence. "Oh, so it's me being silly, is it? Not the man who won't sleep on a bed because it's not, like, real?" I feel bad. I should be able to handle the slavery-versus-dishwashers argument without recourse to childish insult.

"I try to survive without things that not everybody has," says GoodNews. "I'm not joining in until everyone's got everything. When, like, the last peasant in the Brazilian rain forest has a dishwasher, or a, you know, like a cappuccino maker, or, or one of those TVs that's the size of a house, then count me in, yeah? But until then, I'm making a stand."

"That's very noble of you," I say. Nutter, I think, with an enormous sense of relief. There is, after all, nothing to learn from this person, no way that he can make me feel small or wrong or ignoble or self-indulgent. He is simply a crank, and I can ignore him with impunity.

"Everybody in the world's got a dishwasher," Molly says, clearly puzzled, and all the times I felt I have failed as a mother are nothing compared to this one, humiliating moment.

"That's not true, Molly," I say quickly and sharply. "And you know it."

cheeky: impertinent and bold

"Who hasn't, then?" She's not being **cheeky**. She just can't think of anyone.

"Don't be silly," I say, but I'm just buying myself time while I dredge up someone in her universe who does their own washing up. "What about Danny and Charlotte?" Danny and Charlotte go to Molly's school and live in a **council flat** down the road, and even as I speak, I realize I am guilty of the most ludicrous form of class stereotyping.

council flat: subsidized apartment for people with low incomes

"They've got everything," says Molly.

"They've got DVD and OnDigital," says Tom.

"OK, OK. What about the children Daddy gave Tom's computer to?"

"They don't count," says Molly. "They've got nothing. They haven't even got homes. And I don't know any of them. I wouldn't want to know them, thank you very much, because they sound a bit too rough for my liking, even though I feel sorry for them and I'm happy they've got Tom's computer."

This is my daughter? The moral education of my children has always been important to me. I have talked to them about the Health Service and about the importance of Nelson Mandela. We've discussed the homeless, of course, and racism, and sexism, and poverty, and fairness. David and I have explained, as best we can, why anyone who votes Conservative will never be entirely welcome in our house, although we have to make special arrangements for Granny and Grandpa. There was a part of me that thought, yes, she's coming along, she gets it. All those conversations and questions have not been in vain. Now I see that she's a stinking patrician Lady Bountiful who in twenty years time will be sitting on the committee of some revolting charity ball in Warwickshire, moaning about the refugees and giving her unwanted pashminas to her cleaning lady.

"You see," says GoodNews. "This is why I don't want to play the possessions game, because I think people become lazy and spoiled and uncaring."

I look at my lazy and uncaring and spoiled daughter, and then I tell GoodNews that my children would love to help him with the dishes.

(2634 words)

Source: Hornby, Nick. *How to Be Good*. NY: Riverhead Books, 2001. 116–127. Print.

Students can read the excerpt in class or for homework. There are additional questions in the Student Section of the Companion Website. You can verify if students have read the essay by checking their scores with the grade tracker.

VOCABULARY AND COMPREHENSION

1 Explain the meaning of each expression. The line numbers are in parentheses.

a) You're sharp (43) You're bright or intelligent

b) Try not to get bogged down in (55) Try not to focus on

c) shoots me a look (91) looks at me quickly

d) nutter (200) crazy person

2 What is the meaning of "It's cool" (line 111)?

a. It's fantastic. b. It's trendy. (c.) It's fine.

3 Underline two similes, or comparisons using *like* or *as*. Look in lines 30 to 90.

4 In line 229, the narrator describes her daughter as a *stinking patrician Lady Bountiful*. What is her point?

Her daughter does not understand or have compassion for the poor.

Answers will vary.

5 Describe the narrator, Katie. What is her attitude toward her visitor, GoodNews? Give examples.

She's suspicious and cynical. For instance, her tone is "vinegary" when GoodNews says he doesn't like beds, asking, "Do you mind if we sleep in them?" Also, she is sarcastic when GoodNews explains that he doesn't like dishwashers.

6 How is David portrayed in the story? Describe his attitude toward his wife and GoodNews.

He seems to be searching for some spirituality. He thinks GoodNews has a special vibe. He feels superior to his wife, responding "somewhat smugly" when she says that she can't feel GoodNews's vibe.

You could ask students to remove this page and hand it in. In the student books, pages are perforated.

7 Compare the children, Molly and Tom. How are they similar or different?

Molly accepts GoodNews and is interested in what he has to say. When he refuses to sleep in a bed, Molly also decides to stop using a bed. Tom seems to dislike GoodNews and is rude with him. After GoodNews refuses to answer a question about turtles, Tom's response is cold. "'He doesn't know,' says Tom with a snort."

8 Is GoodNews a good person? If not, what type of person does he seem to be? Describe GoodNews.

He is eccentric, with his turtle brooches eyebrow piercings and odd beliefs. He acts a bit superior to others, believing that he has healing hands, for example. He has strong views about living a simple life and says that he doesn't "want to play the possessions game." He doesn't want luxuries when so many other people don't have them.

9 Near the end of the story, Katie becomes defensive and embarrassed. What happened, and why is she embarrassed?

After GoodNews and Katie argue about dishwashers, Molly mentions that everyone has a dishwasher. Katie tries to remind her daughter that some people don't have them, but Molly honestly doesn't believe it. Then when Molly remembers a poor family, she says that "they sound a bit too rough for my liking." Katie is mortified, thinking that her daughter is spoiled and uncaring.

10 Why is the story called "How to Be Good"? Make some guesses.

Perhaps the title is cynical because all of the characters have flaws (pride, conceit, etc.). The guest, GoodNews, makes the family members sensitive about their own levels of goodness. GoodNews believes he has the answers to many of life's questions. David wants to be good by following GoodNews. Molly wants to copy the decisions of GoodNews. Katie tries to be good by accepting the new visitor, but she can't hold back her cynicism and sarcasm.

The Teacher Section of the Companion Website includes a reading test about robots and their connections with humans.

Take Action!

WRITING TOPICS

Write about one of the following topics. For information about essay structure, see the Writing Workshops on pages 148 to 157. Before handing in your work, refer to the Writing Checklist on the inside back cover.

1 **The Good Life**

In an essay, define a good life. What ingredients would it have? You can reflect on George Orwell's quotation on the opening page of this chapter. Give examples from your life. Also refer to at least one of the readings in this chapter.

2 **Is Someone Watching?**

At the beginning of this chapter, Ani DiFranco ponders the existence of a higher power when she asks, "what if no one's watching." In an essay, discuss why people believe in gods and spirits. Provide three reasons, and refer to at least one of the readings in this chapter.

3 **The Benefits of Reading**

What is the value of literature (essays, stories, poems, and lyrics)? Write an essay about the benefits of reading. Provide three supporting ideas. In your body paragraphs, refer to specific readings in this book.

COMPANION WEB+ Need help with pronunciation? Visit the Companion Website and try the Pronunciation Workshops.

Remind students to try the Pronunciation Workshops on the Companion Website.

SPEAKING TOPICS

Prepare a presentation about one of the following topics. For details about preparing a speaking presentation, see Appendix 1 on page 174.

1 **Gratitude Video**

Create a video or PowerPoint presentation about the things in life for which you are grateful. To plan your presentation, create a gratitude journal. Take time to consider what is really worthwhile in your life. Explain why each person, place, moment, privilege, or item is important to you.

2 **Religious or Moral Education**

Should religious or moral education have a role in schools? Why or why not? Back up your views with specific examples and anecdotes.

3 **Compare Two Works**

Speak about one of the following topics.

- Compare two readings that are in this book. Clarify how the themes or main messages are similar. Discuss which text you prefer.
- Choose one reading from this book, and compare it to another piece of art that has a similar theme. You can choose another story, song lyrics, a painting, a photograph, or a film. In an oral presentation, discuss how the two works develop a similar theme.

MEDIA LINK

Choose a classic English-language movie about characters who struggle to make morally correct choices. You could watch a movie about infidelity, crime, or any moral issue. For example, you could watch *Quiz Show*, *Changing Lanes*, *The Godfather*, or *Doubt*. Then, in an essay or speaking presentation, explain the message of the movie. Begin by briefly summarizing the plot. Describe what the movie demonstrates about that time, place, and culture. End by linking the movie's message to a reading from this book.

The Revising and Editing sections at the end of each chapter help your students prepare for writing tests, including Benchmark and TESOL tests. You can ask students to do the activities with a partner and to share ideas.

Revising and Editing

REVISE FOR THE THESIS STATEMENT
EDIT FOR MIXED ERRORS

A well-constructed introduction should have a clear thesis statement. The thesis expresses the main idea of the essay and makes a point. (To learn more about introductions, see Writing Workshop 2, page 158.)

Read the introductory paragraph and follow these steps.

1. Underline and correct ten grammatical errors.
2. Revise the thesis statement, which is in bold.

Point out that a thesis statement must not be in the form of a question. Possible thesis: People should read literature because it is informative and entertaining.

A lot of people think that reading is boring and useless. Today, with [the] Internet and television, [it] is so easy to be entertain [entertained]. Most ~~of~~ teenagers don't like to read books, essays, and short stories. Many of them wonder why should they [they should] read. There is [are] two way [ways] to view literature: in [on] one hand, literature develops your [people's] imagination with descriptive paragraphs. On another [the other] hand, it educates readers about different times and places. **So how is literature informative and entertaining?**

Grammar TIP

Embedded Questions

When a question is embedded inside another sentence or question, the embedded question does not require the special question word order nor the auxiliary.

Question	Embedded Question
Why do people commit crimes?	He asked <u>why people commit crimes</u>.

For more information about embedded questions, see Unit 10 in *Avenues 3: English Grammar*.

To practise vocabulary from this chapter, visit the Companion Website.

WRITING WORKSHOP 1

Writing an Academic Essay

Essay Format

An **essay** is divided into three parts: an **introduction**, a **body**, and a **conclusion**. Look at the following example to see how different types of paragraphs form an essay. Also notice how the essay is formatted. **Note:** Do not include title pages for your essays unless your teacher specifically asks for one. Instead, put your identification information in the top left corner of your essay.

Your name
Teacher
Course
Date

Kim Gagne
Dan Rowen
English 102
12 Nov. 2013

Centre title and capitalize main words.

The Importance of Voting

The **introduction** generates interest in the topic.

Most people get involved in politics for the right reasons. For instance, those who knew Canadian politician Jack Layton said that he simply wanted to make a difference. Each person in the country can also make a difference. Every time there is an election, there is an action that everyone should take. **Everyone should vote for three reasons.**

The **thesis statement** tells the reader what the essay is about.

Each **body paragraph** begins with a **topic sentence**.

First, it is easy to vote. During each election, students and workers are given enough hours to present themselves to polling stations. There are a lot of volunteers who ensure that the voting process is smooth. Those with limited mobility can get a ride to the polling station, usually with a team from the party that they are supporting. College student Luc Robitaille says, "It only took fifteen minutes of my time to vote."

Furthermore, every single vote can have an impact. Many people protest that their single vote doesn't matter, but each vote can make a difference. For instance, in Quebec's 2012 provincial election, one candidate won by just twelve votes. And in 2003, there was a tie between PQ candidate Noëlla Champagne and Liberal Pierre Brouillette, so one vote would have determined the result. Also, large enough groups of like-minded people can change policies and laws, so voting can lead to concrete results.

Each **body paragraph** contains details that support the thesis statement.

Double space and use a 12-point font. **Indent** each paragraph or leave an extra row between paragraphs.

Finally, in many countries, people have given up their lives to make voting a right. In our nation, nobody should take the right to vote for granted. In recent years, Egyptians, Libyans, and Tunisians have died because they wanted their nations to have free and open elections. When people live in a nation that has a thriving democracy, they should support it.

Unfortunately, many people are cynical about politics. But each vote is important, and the right to vote is a right that everyone should respect. As critic and editor George Jean Nathan said, "Bad officials are elected by good citizens who do not vote."

The **conclusion** briefly restates the main points and ends with a suggestion, prediction, or quotation.

Generating Ideas

There are various strategies that you can use to develop a topic. The three most common strategies are **freewriting**, **brainstorming**, and **clustering**.

FREEWRITING

When you **freewrite**, you write without stopping for a limited period of time. You record whatever thoughts come into your mind without worrying about spelling, grammar, or punctuation.

EXAMPLE: I have to write about sports. What interests me? Sports and health? Professional athletes earn too much. They shouldn't be paid as much as they are. They earn more than police, teachers. Also, what about injuries? Some sports are dangerous. Maybe the cost of going to sporting events. It's too high. And fans riot after the final games. That's crazy.

BRAINSTORMING

When you **brainstorm**, you create a list of ideas. If necessary, you can stop and think while you are creating your list. Once again, don't worry about grammar or spelling—the point is to generate ideas.

EXAMPLE: Topic: War

- Why do nations continue to engage in war?
- When is war justified?
- What is the best way to prevent war?
- The impacts that war has on civilians
- Post-traumatic stress syndrome

CLUSTERING

When you **cluster**, you draw a word map. You might write a topic in the centre of the page and then link ideas to the central topic with lines. When you finish, you will have a visual image of your ideas.

EXAMPLE:

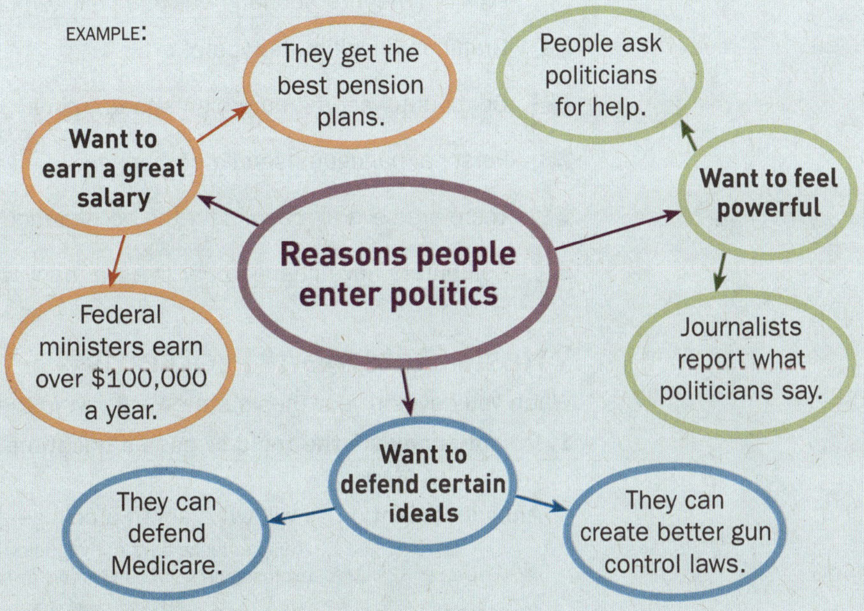

Compose It | **Generate Ideas**

Use freewriting, brainstorming, or clustering to generate ideas about one of the following topics.

Survival   Tolerance   Technology   Your own topic

The Introduction

The **introductory paragraph** introduces the subject of your essay. It helps your reader understand why you are writing the text. The thesis statement is the last sentence in your introduction.

SAMPLE INTRODUCTION

General information → In our neighbourhood, there are very few public parks. The landscape is full of large red brick apartment blocks. There are almost no trees, so it is depressingly barren. The main street has a boarded-up restaurant, and beside it is an empty lot filled with chunks of concrete and garbage.

Thesis statement → **More green spaces would provide several clear benefits for our community.**

The Thesis Statement

A **thesis statement** expresses the main idea of the essay. It includes a **controlling idea** that expresses the writer's opinion, attitude, or feeling about the topic. The controlling idea can appear at the beginning or end of the thesis statement.

topic + controlling idea

Art courses should be compulsory in all high schools.

controlling idea + topic

School districts should stop funding **art courses.**

WRITING EXERCISE 1

All types of academic essays require thesis statements. Circle the topic and underline the controlling idea in the following thesis statements. (To find the topic, ask yourself what the essay is essentially about.)

EXAMPLE: The intersection near this college is dangerous.

Ask students to brainstorm supporting ideas for one of the thesis statements in Writing Exercise 1.

1. Graffiti is a legitimate type of art.
2. Our country needs more high speed trains.
3. Personal handguns should be banned.
4. There are several reasons for the acceleration of climate change.
5. Computers have changed our lives in many ways.

Thesis Statement Problems

When you develop your thesis statement, avoid the following problems.

1. **Do not announce the topic or pose a question.** Your thesis must present a clear point of view.

   Announcement: I will write about a college education.
   (This sentence says nothing relevant about the topic. Do not use expressions such as *My topic is*, *I think*, or *I will write about.*)

   Question: Why do people decide to go to college?
   (This question does not express a point of view about the topic.)

2. **Do not write a statement that is too broad, vague, or narrow.** Your thesis must be easily supported.

   Too broad / vague: Education is important.
   (Important to whom? What type of education? This topic needs a more specific and narrow focus.)

Too narrow: The tuition fee at the University of Toronto is almost $6,000 a year.
(This needs a stronger and broader focus.)

3. **Do not make an obvious or invalid comment.** Ensure that the thesis presents a valid point.

Obvious: There are many public colleges in our province
(So what? This idea is boring and obvious.)

Invalid: Everybody needs a college education
(This statement is difficult to support. Some people don't want or need to go to college.)

Ask students to brainstorm possible benefits of a college education.

An effective thesis statement has the following qualities:

- It expresses an attitude or point of view about the topic.
- It can be supported with several points.
- It is a valid and complete statement that interests the reader.

Good thesis statement: A college education provides several clear benefits.

TIP

Guided Thesis Statement

You can also guide the reader through your main points. To do this, mention both your main and supporting ideas in your thesis statement. It is not necessary to prolong the introduction with extra sentences that provide details about your main points.

Weak: Part-time jobs teach students many things. I will explain how they learn about responsibility. I will also discuss how they learn to organize their time and develop an appreciation for the importance of teamwork.

Better: Part-time jobs teach students about responsibility, organization, and teamwork.

WRITING EXERCISE 2

Examine each statement. If it is a good thesis statement, write **TS** on the line. If it is weak, identify the type of problem(s).

Q – question **A** – announcement **V** – vague **I** – invalid

EXAMPLE: This essay is about cybercrime. A

Ask students to work in pairs. They should choose three of the weak statements and create better thesis statements.

1 Why is the price of oil so high? Q

2 In this paper, I will discuss the causes of riots. A

3 Susanna Moodie effectively portrays bystander apathy in her text, "My Visit to Montreal." TS

4 Some problems are serious. V

5 My subject is the problems in our healthcare system. A

6 Student job seekers should consider their attitude, appearance, and adaptability. TS

7 Canadians are less patriotic. V, I

8 I am going to write about the reasons good people do bad things. A

Revising Your Thesis

When you plan your thesis, ask yourself if you can support it with at least three ideas. If not, you have to modify your thesis statement. Sometimes, just by adding a few words, a dead-end statement becomes a supportable thesis.

Poor thesis: Many students drop out of college.
(How could you develop this fact into an essay? It is a dead-end statement.)

Better thesis: Students drop out of college **for several reasons**.
or Students drop out of college **due to emotional, financial, or health issues**.
(You could support this thesis with at least three ideas.)

OVERVIEW: WRITING A THESIS STATEMENT

To create a forceful thesis statement, you can follow these steps.

Step 1

Find your topic. Explore the topic to give you ideas.

General topic: Education

Brainstorming:
- Public spending on education
- Classroom size
- Time students spend in school each year
- Benefits of having more teachers
- Ways to make school more entertaining

Step 2

Narrow your topic. Decide what point you want to make.

Narrowed topic: Important role of teachers

Point I want to make:
Many young people can be either inspired by good teachers or crushed by bad ones. The influence of teachers on young people is significant and important.

Step 3

Develop a thesis statement that you can support with specific evidence. You may need to revise your statement several times.

Initial thesis statement:
Teachers serve a valuable function in our society.

Revised thesis statement:
Teachers can have a profound impact—both positive and negative—on students' lives.

Compose It

You can assign your own topics for the Compose It section. More detailed writing topics appear at the end of Chapters 1 to 8.

Write Thesis Statements

Choose from the following topics and write three thesis statements. First, narrow your topic. Then, ensure that your statements present a point of view.

Survival Tolerance Technology Your own topic

Your topics: ______________________

EXAMPLE: *Topic:* Survival *Narrowed topic:* Surviving a breakup
Thesis statement: There are several ways to get over a broken romance.

1. Topic: ____________ Narrowed topic: ____________
   Thesis statement: ______________________
2. Topic: ____________ Narrowed topic: ____________
   Thesis statement: ______________________
3. Topic: ____________ Narrowed topic: ____________
   Thesis statement: ______________________

The Body Paragraphs

The next step in essay writing is to plan your supporting ideas for your thesis. Support is not simply a restatement of the thesis. The body paragraphs must develop and prove the validity of the thesis statement.

Each body paragraph has a **topic sentence** that expresses the main idea of the paragraph. Like a thesis statement, a topic sentence must have a **controlling idea**. Details and examples support the topic sentence. In the following illustration, you can see how the ideas flow in an essay. Topic sentences support the thesis statement, and details bolster the topic sentences. Every idea in the essay is unified and helps to strengthen the essay's thesis.

Introduction

The **thesis statement** identifies the main idea of the essay.

↓

Body paragraphs

The **topic sentence** identifies the main idea of each supporting paragraph.

Facts | Examples | Anecdotes | Relevant quotations

Creating Topic Sentences

What is the difference between a thesis statement and a topic sentence?
An essay has one thesis statement and several topic sentences.

- The **thesis statement** is in the introduction, and it explains what the essay is about.
- **Topic sentences** are in the body paragraphs. Each topic sentence explains what the body paragraph is about.

Thesis statement Ordinary people become thieves for many reasons.

Topic sentence 1
They may steal to feed themselves and their children.

Topic sentence 2
Many people steal because they are greedy and never have enough.

Topic sentence 3
Kleptomaniacs have a compulsion to steel.

WRITING EXERCISE 3

Answers will vary.

Generate three topic sentences that support the thesis statement.

Thesis statement: First-year college students make some serious mistakes.

Topic sentence 1: ______________________________

____

Topic sentence 2: ______________________________

____

Topic sentence 3: ______________________________

____

Suggest that students read the entire essay before trying to insert the missing thesis statement and topic sentences. You can have students do this exercise in pairs or groups.

WRITING EXERCISE 4

Read the following essay and then complete the tasks below.

1 Create an effective thesis statement. The thesis statement sums up the point of the entire essay.

2 At the beginning of each body paragraph, write a topic sentence. The topic sentence should sum up the main point of the paragraph in an interesting way.

Social Networking Issues

Introduction

When the Internet became popular in the 1990s, some people realized the potential for social networking. Friendster, which began in 2002, was one of the first social media sites. In 2003, LinkedIn and MySpace began, and Mark Zuckerberg launched Facebook in 2004. Such sites are appealing and are used by over a billion people around the globe.

Answers will vary.

Thesis statement: Social networking sites can cause three serious problems for users.

Body paragraph 1

Topic sentence: A phone number or address in a social media profile can lead to identity theft.

According to an article by Harriette Halepis, identity theft has been on the rise for several years. A study from McMaster University found that nearly 1.7 million Canadians were victims of identity theft in 2007. This represents roughly 6.5 percent of the population. Often, all a criminal needs is someone's name and birthdate to steal his or her identity. Of course, those are two very common pieces of information available on social networking profiles.

Body paragraph 2

Topic sentence: Photos of illegal or inappropriate activities can cause problems for job hunters and employees.

Of course, many people use social media to post photos of themselves at bars or parties. According to PCWorld, over 20 percent of employers admit checking Facebook before hiring someone. Karine Woo was fired from her teaching job at a private school because she had posted photos of herself partying at a "Girls Gone Wild" party. A student saw the photos and told his parents, and the school fired the teacher. Thus, information online can impact a person's career prospects.

Body paragraph 3

Topic sentence: People can be nasty online.

According to Ada Calhoun, in a *Salon* article, her psychologist friend spends a lot of time with patients discussing Facebook: "'My ex-boyfriend changed his status to single,' a distraught young woman told the psychologist, 'and all his friends 'liked' it.'" Furthermore, in schools, unpopular kids may be targeted and ridiculed on other students' Facebook pages. According to a study by polling company Ipsos Reid, 8 percent of children aged seven to seventeen have been bullied online.

Conclusion

Like any new technology, social networking can present a set of problems. If people post their name and birthdate on a site such as Facebook, the information might be used in identity theft. Social networkers should be careful about the types of photos they post online. They also need to realize the importance of respecting others. Brian Solis, of FutureWorks, says, "Social Media is about sociology and psychology more than technology."

WRITING EXERCISE 5

Brainstorm three supporting ideas for each thesis statement.

EXAMPLE: High school students should learn water-based survival skills for three reasons.

1. They can save themselves if caught in a rip tide.
2. They can safely save others who are drowning.
3. They can be knowledgeable about tsunami and flood survival.

Answers will vary. Possible answers are given.

1 Many people in our culture hurt their bodies and their wallets in the pursuit of beauty.

1. They get plastic surgery to change their appearance.
2. They exercise too much.
3. They develop eating disorders.

2 In this technological era, there are several new types of addictions that people have developed.

1. People use Facebook every day.
2. People text even when with friends or while driving.
3. Gamers play video games or do online gambling obsessively.

The Essay Plan

An **essay plan** or an **outline** is a visual map that shows the essay's main and supporting ideas. Read the essay plan below. Notice that each topic sentence provides evidence for the thesis statement. Supporting examples and details back up each topic sentence.

Point out that the body paragraphs in the essay plan contain supporting details and examples. Remind students to include details that back up their supporting ideas.

Thesis statement: Our political leaders should never promote intolerance for several reasons.

1. **Topic sentence:** North American nations have multicultural populations.

Support: In Canada, citizens are from many different ethnic groups.
Detail: According to Statistics Canada, there are thirty-four different ethnic groups in Canada.
Support: The US and Mexico also have multi-ethnic populations.
Detail: They have indigenous populations as well as groups with European, Asian, and African ancestries.

2. **Topic sentence:** Speeches that promote intolerance can divide citizens and marginalize specific groups.

   Support: Workplace discrimination can increase when intolerance is promoted.

   Detail: Studies show that people with certain ethnically different names are less likely to be hired by many local companies.

   Support: Sometimes the basic civil rights of religious or ethnic groups are suspended.

   Detail: Some nations are making laws that prohibit certain religious or cultural attire.

3. **Topic sentence:** Intolerant leaders can inflame supporters, leading to violent acts.

   Support: Since 2001, some American politicians have promoted stereotypes, which can lead to violent actions.

   Detail: US politician Michele Bachmann's complaints about Muslims have coincided with the firebombing of mosques.

   Support: Hateful speech can inflame crowds and lead to massacres.

   Detail: In "Small Differences, Large Conflicts," Paul K. Kim mentions the genocide in Rwanda.

Concluding prediction: Political leaders must have the integrity to condemn discrimination of all types.

WRITING EXERCISE 6

Generate three topic sentences and supporting details for the following thesis statement.

Thesis statement: People who follow these suggestions can have a fulfilling and healthy life.

Topic sentence 1: ______________________________

____

Support: ______________________________

____

____

Topic sentence 2: ______________________________

____

Support: ______________________________

____

____

Topic sentence 3: ______________________________

____

Support: ______________________________

____

____

Compose It

Create an Essay Plan

Develop an essay plan for one of the ideas that you have developed in this workshop, or choose a topic from the Take Action! sections at the end of Chapters 1 to 8.

Topic: ______________________________

Introduction

Thesis statement: ______________________________

____

Body paragraph 1

Topic sentence: ______________________________

____

Support: ______________________________

____

Details: ______________________________

____

____

Support: ______________________________

____

Details: ______________________________

____

____

Body paragraph 2

Topic sentence: ______________________________

____

Support: ______________________________

____

Details: ______________________________

____

____

Support: ______________________________

____

Details: ______________________________

____

____

Conclusion

(Think of a final suggestion, prediction, or quotation.) ______________________________

____

____

Enhancing Your Essay

Write an Effective Introduction

After students have written their first essay, you might assign this workshop. Students can work on revising the parts of their essays.

Write your **introduction** after you have already planned the main points of your essay. A strong introduction will capture the reader's attention and make him or her want to continue reading. Introductions may have a lead-in, and they can be developed using many different styles.

The Lead-In

You can begin the introduction with a lead-in, which is an attention-grabbing opening sentence. There are four common types of lead-ins.

Quotation   Question   Surprising/Controversial statement   Definition

Introduction Styles

You can develop the introduction in several different ways. Experiment with any of the following introduction strategies.

- Give **general background information**. Explain the **significance** of the topic.
- Present **historical background information**.
- Tell an **interesting anecdote** or give a **vivid description**.
- Develop a **definition** of a concept.
- Present a **contrasting position** or idea that is the opposite of the one you will develop. You could challenge a common opinion.

Lead-in

Anecdotal information

Thesis statement

"I can accept failure. Everyone fails at something," said Michael Jordan. Despite being one of the most successful professional athletes of all time, Jordan was not given a free pass to the NBA. Jordan was crushed when he was cut from his high school's varsity team. His coach said that Jordan was too short to play at that level. Instead of feeling sorry for himself, Jordan persevered and eventually got on the senior team. Mistakes provide people with valuable life lessons.

TIP

Thesis Statement Placement

Most introductions lead the reader to the main point of the essay. Generally, the thesis statement is the last sentence in the introduction.

WRITING EXERCISE 1

Read the following introductions. Underline each thesis statement, and then identify the type of lead-in and introduction style used.

1 "Somebody help! Call 911," I shouted. I was babysitting three children, and the smallest child had fallen into the swimming pool. I pulled him out as quickly as I could. Then I tried to give him mouth-to-mouth resuscitation. The problem was that I had never been trained and didn't really know how

to do it. Luckily, the child was fine. Schools should teach common life-saving and survival strategies.

a) Lead-in: ☑ Quotation ☐ Question ☐ Controversial statement

b) Introduction style: (Indicate the best answer.)

☐ General ☐ Historical ☑ Anecdote ☐ Contrasting position

2 Nobody should ever be a billionaire. If the CEO of a company is super rich, it means that the company is not paying the workers enough. These days, many companies have stopped providing pensions to workers, but they give the directors obscene bonuses. Higher taxes on the wealthy can lead to the following benefits.

a) Lead-in: ☐ Quotation ☐ Definition ☑ Controversial statement

b) Introduction style:

☐ Definition ☑ General ☐ Historical ☐ Contrasting position

3 Patriotism is excessive love of one's country. It can be expressed when people cheer for national sports teams. During events such as the Olympics, people carry flags and cheer for their nation. Citizens also show their patriotism when they fight for their countries. Patriotism has both advantages and disadvantages.

a) Lead-in: ☐ Quotation ☑ Definition ☐ Controversial statement

b) Introduction style:

☐ Anecdote ☐ Historical ☑ Definition ☐ Contrasting position

4 "Canada is hockey," says golfer Mike Weir. Playing in the NHL seems so exciting! It would be fun to play a sport every day and get paid for it. It must be thrilling to travel to different cities for games. Also, the money is fantastic. Top hockey players can earn millions of dollars. However, playing professional hockey is not as great as it sounds. Hockey players can receive severe and life-threatening physical injuries.

a) Lead-in: ☑ Quotation ☐ Question ☐ Controversial statement

b) Introduction style:

☐ Anecdote ☐ Historical ☐ Definition ☑ Contrasting position

5 How do you communicate with your friends? In past centuries, people simply visited their friends to converse. The invention of the telephone helped people stay connected even when they lived far apart. In the 1990s, e-mailing became popular. Today, almost everyone has a cellphone and does texting and online chatting. The newest communication technologies provide three clear benefits.

a) Lead-in: ☐ Quotation ☑ Question ☐ Definition

b) Introduction style:

☐ Anecdote ☐ General ☑ Historical ☐ Contrasting position

REVISING AND EDITING LINK

For more practice writing introductions, see the Revising and Editing section of Chapter 3, on page 54.

Write an Effective Conclusion

Your concluding paragraph should do three things.

- It should restate the thesis.
- It should summarize your main points.
- It should make an interesting closing statement. You can end with a suggestion, a prediction, or a quotation. (You can quote from one of the readings in this book, or you can go to a quotations website such as *quotationspage.com*.)

For example, here is a conclusion for an essay about online addictions.

Remind the reader of your main points.

End with a prediction or suggestion.

In conclusion, during this computer age, people have developed a new variety of addictions. Online gambling sites have proliferated, causing an increase in gambling addicts. Large numbers of young adults are obsessed with online fantasy games. Furthermore, YouTube has too many devoted followers who spend hours watching silly videos. As technology becomes more sophisticated, it's certain that online addictions will only increase.

TIP

Avoiding Conclusion Problems

To make an effective conclusion, avoid the following:

- Do not contradict your main point or introduce new or irrelevant information.
- Do not apologize or back down from your main points.
- Do not end with a rhetorical question. (A rhetorical question is a question that won't be answered, such as "When will people stop texting while driving?")

WRITING EXERCISE 2

Do the following activity on a separate piece of paper.

1 Determine what the essay is about. Underline or highlight the topic sentence in each body paragraph.

2 Write three possible introductions. Label each introduction to indicate the style you used (anecdote, general, historical, definition, or contrasting position). Ensure that you end your introduction with a clear thesis statement.

3 Write a conclusion. End with a prediction, suggestion, or quotation.

Write three possible introductions.

Body paragraph 1: First, travel teaches people about cultural differences. Nations often have their own unique cuisine that is a pleasure to discover. The lifestyles and music can also be inspiring. For instance, Chambrie Yates travelled to Nicaragua with some classmates when she was sixteen, and she lived with a host family in a small village. She says, "I learned that I take my luxuries for granted, such as having a lot of hot water. I also discovered that the local people are more open and friendly to each other than my neighbours are back home." Thus, travel opens our minds to other ways of living.

Body paragraph 2: Furthermore, travellers become educated about the common qualities that all humans share. In every nation, ordinary people want decent work and loving relationships. They want their children to have an education and to be happy, and they want to live in peace. In his essay, "How Travel Changed My Life," Arthur Frommer describes his experience in the hut of a Maasai family in Africa. The daughter complained about her mean teacher, just as small children do all over the world. Frommer writes, "Travel has taught me that despite all the exotic differences of dress and language, of political and religious beliefs, all the world's people are essentially alike."

Write a conclusion.

REVISING AND EDITING LINK

For more practice writing conclusions, see the Revising and Editing section of Chapter 5, on page 94.

Revise for Coherence

Your writing should have coherence. Connections between ideas should be logical. You can use different words and expressions to help the reader follow the logic of a text.

- **Coordinators** connect ideas inside sentences. Common coordinators are *and*, *but*, *or*, *yet*, and *so*.

    Texting while driving is dangerous, **but** many people do it anyway.

- **Subordinators** join a secondary idea to a main idea inside a sentence. Some common subordinators are *although*, *after*, *because*, *before*, *if*, *unless*, and *until*.

    Although there were many bystanders, nobody offered to help the drowning man.

- **Transitional words and expressions** connect sentences and paragraphs. Common transitional words are *first*, *then*, *however*, *therefore*, *of course*, and *in conclusion*. For a complete list of transitional words and expressions, see Appendix 4 on page 178.

    Generally put a comma after transitional words and expressions. A sentence can begin with a transitional expression. You can also combine sentences with a transitional expression, but put a semicolon before it.

    Yirga was not guilty. **Nevertheless,** he was convicted.

    Yirga was not guilty**; nevertheless,** he was convicted.

Answers will vary.

WRITING EXERCISE 3

Write definitions or translations for the following connecting words and expressions.

1 although ____________

2 even though ____________

3 furthermore ____________

4 hence ____________

5 however ____________

6 in short ____________

7 meanwhile ____________

8 moreover ____________

9 nevertheless ____________

10 on the other hand ____________

11 subsequently ____________

12 therefore ____________

13 thus ____________

14 undoubtedly ____________

15 until ____________

16 whereas ____________

REVISING AND EDITING LINK

For practice adding transitional words and expressions to an essay, see the Revising and Editing section of Chapter 4, on page 73.

Answers will vary.

WRITING EXERCISE 4

Add appropriate linking words or expressions to the following paragraph. Use the subordinators and transitional expressions from Writing Exercise 3, and do not use the same expression more than once.

In Australia, all adults must vote in national elections, ___whereas___ in Canada, voting is not compulsory. Is forced voting a good idea? On the one hand, perhaps those who are not informed about politics should stay home. ___On the other hand___, strong voting laws would help our nation have a more robust democracy. Canada should follow Australia's example and institute compulsory voting. ___Undoubtedly___, optional voting isn't working in Canada. In the most recent election, just 31 percent of eligible voters visited their polling stations. ___There fore / Thus___, the majority of citizens stayed home ___even though___ they knew that their votes were important. For example, Dominique Jones complains about the lack of funding for health care. ___However___, she thinks it is too much trouble to line up at a polling station. Jared Marcotte, a student, says, "During the last election, I had a lot of homework, so I didn't have time to vote." ___Nevertheless___, he found the time to go to a movie that day. ___Although___ people have good intentions, they often fail to follow through with actions. ___In short___, a strong voting law, with penalties for those who don't vote, would be great for our nation.

Students sometimes confuse *although* and *however*. Point out that *although* is never followed by a comma. Students can practise using *however* and *although* in Unit 10 of *Avenues 3: English Grammar.*

Revise for Unity

A paragraph has unity when every idea in the paragraph supports the topic sentence. Check for the following common errors when you revise your body paragraphs.

- **Lack of unity**

  Some ideas in the paragraph do not relate to the topic sentence.

- **Rambling**

  The paragraph rambles on about different ideas. It has several topics and lacks a clearly identifiable topic sentence.

- **Artificial breaks**

  The paragraph is divided into smaller paragraphs, and each smaller paragraph lacks a central focus.

To correct this essay, students should break Body paragraph 1 into two paragraphs. They can join Body paragraph 2 and Body paragraph 3. The sentences about Tyler's mother being in the hospital don't support the main idea of that paragraph, so they should be removed.

WRITING EXERCISE 5

Read the body paragraphs below and edit them. Follow these steps.

1 Highlight three possible topic sentences.

2 If a paragraph rambles on, suggest a paragraph break.

3 If two paragraphs could be joined, indicate it.

4 If a sentence is unnecessary and not linked to the main idea, remove it.

Thesis: To have a well-adjusted generation of adults, parents and schools should remember three points.

Body paragraph 1: First, parents and schools should teach children to embrace new experiences and not fear them. Often, schools overprotect students and teach them to avoid risks. My high school, for example, would not permit sixteen-year-old students on a field trip to spend a day in New York without supervision. Parents also overprotect children. For example, in the essay "Cyclops," David Sedaris describes his father's parenting style: "Danger was everywhere, and it was our father's lifelong duty to warn us" (50).

Furthermore, schools and parents should teach children about compassion and helping others. Schools can make a difference. For instance, students in Ottawa, Ontario, receive high school credits for doing volunteer work. In colleges, students learn about altruism. In the essay, "Bystander Apathy,"

Mark Tyrrell describes instances when people didn't act to help others. The essay suggests that after learning about bystander apathy, "students were twice as likely to offer help 'in the street' as compared with people who had not been educated about this" (114). Parents also play a role in teaching children about compassion. Generous and helpful parents provide clear role models for their children.

Body paragraph 2: Most importantly, parents and schools should remember to act as proper authority figures. Some new "open-concept" schools give students too much liberty. Students end up skipping classes because they don't feel like anyone is in charge. Some parents also fail to act as authority figures. When we were ten years old, my friend Tyler sometimes texted me at 1 a.m. while I was sleeping.

Body paragraph 3: Tyler's mom was nice, but she was too relaxed. When Tyler began to smoke, his mother sometimes smoked with him. She was not a good example to her son. ~~She's in the hospital right now. She has lung cancer, and we're all worried about her.~~ Tyler wishes that his mom had acted more like a parent. So it's important for parents and schools to act with authority.

Concluding suggestion: Parents and schools play important roles in every child's life.

Revise for Adequate Support

An essay has **adequate support** when there are enough details and examples to make it strong, convincing, and interesting. When you write your body paragraphs, do not offer vague generalizations and do not simply repeat your ideas. Provide evidence for each topic sentence by inserting specific details. You might include examples, facts, statistics, anecdotes, or quotations.

TIP

Essay without Research

You have not done any research, and yet you must write a well-developed essay. What can you do? Provide specific examples from one or more of the following sources:

- Your life
- The lives of people you know
- Events in history
- Events in the media
- The lives of well-known people
- Information from readings and videos in this course

Notice how an unconvincing paragraph becomes stronger with specific examples.

Weak: Insufficient details

First, people should be very careful when they buy items online. It's important to do an Internet search for reviews of the online store. Moreover, if a deal on eBay seems too good to be true, it's probably fraudulent. Cybercriminals are becoming more sophisticated, so everyone has to take more precautions.

When the paragraph is expanded with specific examples, it becomes more convincing.

Better: With specific examples

First, people should be very careful when they buy items online. It's important to do an Internet search for reviews of the online store. **For example, after my friend bought shoes on an online shoe-selling site, strange deductions started to appear on his credit card bill. When he did a Google search for information about that shoe retailer, he saw that many customers gave warnings.** Moreover, if a deal on eBay seems too good to be true, it's probably fraudulent. **In the text, "A Romanian Town Is Cybercrime Central," Yudhijit Bhattacharjee says, "Cybercafés offered cheap Internet access, and crooks in Râmnicu Vâlcea got busy posting fake ads on eBay and other auction sites to lure victims into remitting payments by wire transfer" (89).** Cybercriminals are becoming more sophisticated, so everyone has to take more precautions.

WRITING EXERCISE 6

Revise this paragraph by adding specific examples.

These days, people can meet potential partners online. There are many dating sites. Also, people can meet using social networking sites.

____

____

____

____

REVISING AND EDITING LINK

For more practice revising for adequate support, see the Revising and Editing section of Chapter 2, on page 35.

Revise for Consistent Point of View and Varied Vocabulary

In your writing, maintain a **consistent point of view**. If your essay is about "people" or "students," then use pronouns such as *they*. Do not shift unnecessarily to *you* or *we*. Your writing should also contain **varied vocabulary**. Avoid repeating the same words over and over.

Weak: Inconsistent point of view
Club fires are dangerous. **You** can be having fun and, suddenly, there is a fire. Most **people** don't know what to do. **We** freeze or run to the main entrance. In such situations, **you** should look for alternative exits.

Boring: Repeated words
Club fires are dangerous. **People** can be having fun and, suddenly, there is a fire. Most **people** don't know what to do. **People** freeze or run to the main entrance. In such situations, **people** should look for alternative exits.

Better: Consistent point of view and varied vocabulary
Club fires are dangerous. **Customers** can be having fun and, suddenly, there is a fire. **Most people** don't know what to do. **They** freeze or run to the main entrance. In such situations, **club patrons** should look for alternative exits.

REVISING AND EDITING LINK

To practise revising for a consistent point of view, see the Revising and Editing section of Chapter 7, on page 129. To practise editing for repetitive words, see the Revising and Editing section of Chapter 6, on page 110.

Compose It | **Revise Your Essay**

Choose a previous essay that you have written, and write a new introduction using one of the introduction styles on page 158. Revise the body paragraphs to ensure that they have unity and adequate support. Ensure that your conclusion ends with a prediction, suggestion, or quotation.

WRITING WORKSHOP 3

Developing an Argument Essay

The ability to argue effectively is important in both your personal and professional life. When you debate which university to attend, which career to choose, or which movie to watch, you communicate your choice based on a logical analysis of the alternatives.

Take a Position

In argument writing, you take a position on an issue and then defend it. In other words, you try to convince somebody that your point of view is the best one. The thesis statement of an argument essay should express a clear point of view.

topic — controlling idea

College students should become more politically active.

Your thesis statement should be a debatable statement. It should not be a fact or a statement of opinion.

Fact: Many people believe in gods and spirits.
(This is a fact. It cannot be debated.)

Opinion: I think that all religious courses should be banned in schools.
(This is a statement of opinion. Nobody can deny that you feel this way. Therefore, do not use phrases such as *In my opinion*, *I think*, or *I believe* in your thesis statement.)

Argument: Religious courses should be banned in schools.
(This is a debatable statement.)

WRITING EXERCISE 1

Evaluate the following statements. In each blank, write *F* if the statement is a fact, *O* if it is an opinion, or *A* if it is a debatable argument.

1. In our province, many youths drop out of school. F
2. I think that high schools should have more practical courses. O
3. Oil companies should never be permitted to drill in oceans. A
4. In my opinion, the government should ban handgun sales. O
5. Private citizens should not be permitted to own handguns. A
6. After the hockey game, thousands of rioters broke store windows. F
7. People who get involved in riots should consider the consequences. A
8. Many Internet sites have pop-up advertising. F

Instead of asking students to write about the suggested topics, you could give students topics that you plan to use on your next writing test. Argument writing topics appear at the end of Chapters 1 to 8.

WRITING EXERCISE 2

Write an argument thesis statement for the following topics.

1. Crime: ______________________________

____

2. Survival skills: ______________________________

____

Develop Strong Supporting Ideas

In the body of your essay, give convincing supporting arguments. Find support for your views from reliable sources. You could use the following types of evidence:

- **Tell a true story.** Find stories from the news or include personal anecdotes to support your point of view.
- **Quote from readings or videos that were used in this course.** Find material that backs up your main points.
- **Quote respected sources.** An expert's opinion can give added weight to your argument. For example, if you want to argue that the courts treat youths who commit crimes too harshly or too leniently, you might quote a judge who deals with juvenile criminals.
- **Show long-term consequences.** Every solution to a problem can carry long-term consequences with it. For example, oil contributes to our country's economy, so the tar sands project has short-term benefits. However, the tar sands can have long-term consequences for Alberta's environment.
- **Acknowledge opposing viewpoints.** If you acknowledge opposing arguments and then address them, you strengthen your position. For example, if you argue that handguns should be banned, address the arguments of those who like to shoot guns in shooting ranges. Try to refute some of the strongest arguments of the opposition.

TIP

Using Emotional Arguments

In an argument essay, sometimes the most effective way to influence others is to appeal to their sense of justice, humanity, pride, and even guilt. However, do not rely only on emotional arguments. Also, do not mistake an appeal to emotion for an appeal to base instincts. If you use emotionally charged words such as *wimp* or *idiot*, or if you make broad generalizations about racial, ethnic, linguistic, or religious groups, you will seriously undermine your argument.

WRITING EXERCISE 3

Read the following thesis statements and think of a supporting argument for each statement. Use the type of support suggested in parentheses.

1 University tuition rates should not be increased.

(Emotional appeal) ______________________________

____

2 The legal age required for marriage should be raised to twenty-five.

(Logical long-term consequence) ______________________________

____

3 To reduce obesity levels, fast food should be banned.

(Acknowledging an opposing viewpoint) ______________________________

____

4 Political leaders should not be able to run again after two consecutive terms.

(Anecdote) ______________________________

____

Avoiding *You* in Argument Essays

In some essays, the pronoun *you* is unavoidable. For instance, if you are telling the reader the steps to take to complete a process, it makes sense to use *you*. Look at this example.

> After **you** have finished building the frame, cut the canvas to fit the frame. **You** should leave about two extra inches around the edge of the frame.

However, when you write an argument essay, *you* is unnecessary. Look at this example from an essay about beliefs.

> Death is a frightening prospect. **Everyone** wants to feel like **he or she** will live forever. Religions provide **believers** with answers to the unanswerable questions.

Answers will vary.

WRITING EXERCISE 4

Edit the following paragraph by replacing all occurrences of the pronoun *you*. Use a variety of replacement words and adjust the verbs where necessary.

Digital media has turned a lot of ordinary people into thieves. Now, instead of going to a music store, [consumers] **you** can download material illegally. As soon as one file-sharing site is closed, another one comes online. [Music lovers] **You** can easily find such sites. Also, [nobody has] **you** don't have to pay for cable channels such as HBO. Instead, pirated films and television shows are available online. It's so easy, [most people] **you** probably don't even feel guilty about it. As my friend Victor said, "It doesn't really feel like stealing, but I suppose it is."

Using *I* in Argument Essays

In argument essays, you should not use the first-person pronoun *I* in your thesis statement or topic sentences. However, it is perfectly acceptable to use *I* in an anecdotal introduction. It is also acceptable to use personal stories when you provide supporting details.

Read these paragraphs with your students. Point out that the main arguments do not use the first-person pronoun, but some examples and the anecdotal introduction do.

WRITING EXERCISE 5

Read the following student essay. Underline the thesis statement and the topic sentences. Highlight or circle any use of the pronoun *I*, *me*, or *my*.

Daniel Joly
English 604-102-03
10 Nov. 2013

Problems with Political Idealism

Two years ago, when I turned eighteen, I was excited because I was old enough to vote in our nation's election. My father was interested in politics, and I became passionate too. That year, I tried to convince other students to vote for the party that I supported. One day, I got into a very big fight with two close friends who didn't agree with me. Today, I have some regrets about my arrogant attitude. <u>Political idealism can cause people to make unwise decisions and develop narrow views.</u>

Idealists can undermine their cause when they become too fanatical. In Montreal, during the 2012 student strike, three students put smoke bombs in Montreal's metro system. Many people panicked, and innocent citizens could have been hurt. The action didn't help the student movement, and those three students now have criminal records. In "Snitch," Jan Wong describes her experiences as a political idealist in the 1970s, when she betrayed two people who wanted to leave China. In my case, during that election campaign two years ago, my criticism of those who didn't agree with me probably turned some students against the party that I was supporting.

Furthermore, idealists develop tunnel vision and ignore uncomfortable truths. In "Snitch," Jan Wong admits that she did not want to see the dark sides of China's Communist government: "I did not know that the reason I enjoyed biking down the empty streets of Beijing was because so many of its seven million residents had been sent down to farms and communes for thought reform" (122). When I was a radical idealist, I ignored what the leader of my party said when it felt uncomfortable. For instance, she divided people instead of uniting them. She sometimes made intolerant generalizations about ethnic groups that I ignored because I wanted to like the leader.

Having strong beliefs is important, but youthful idealism can also cause problems. People can undermine the cause that they support, and they might develop tunnel vision. As Mark Reed, a teacher, once said, "It's great to be politically active, but keep an open mind."

TIP

Argument Essay Recap

When you write an argument essay, remember the following points:

- Your thesis statement must express an argument, not a fact or opinion. Avoid using phrases such as *I think* or *I believe*.
- Avoid using the pronoun *you* in an argument essay (unless absolutely necessary to explain something to the reader).
- Do not use the pronoun *I* in your thesis statement or topic sentences. (If needed, refer to yourself only in an anecdotal introduction or in supporting details.)
- Your topic sentences should support your thesis statement.
- Include supporting details in your body paragraphs. Refer to texts or videos that you've studied in this course. You could also include specific anecdotes from your life, from the lives of people you know, or from media events.

Compose It

Create an Argument Essay Plan

On a separate sheet of paper, develop an argument essay plan. Choose a topic from one of the Take Action! sections at the end of Chapters 1 to 8. You can also develop your own idea. Ensure that your thesis can be supported with evidence from this book.

Responding to a Story

For this workshop, choose one of the following short stories or narrative essays. You will then use this story or essay to complete the Writing Exercises. You will also have the option of comparing and contrasting two stories from this list.

- Cyclops (Chapter 3, page 49)
- My Prison Story (Chapter 4, page 67)
- Anonymous Strikes Back (Chapter 5, page 81)
- Big Brother (Chapter 6, page 100)
- My Visit to Montreal (Chapter 7, page 118)
- Snitch (Chapter 7, page 122)
- How to Be Good (Chapter 8, page 139)
- The Most Dangerous Game (online)
- As It Was in the Beginning (online)
- Shooting an Elephant (online)
- Your own choice (Do an online search for "classic short stories.")

In the list of stories provided, five are fictional ("Big Brother" and "How to Be Good," as well as the three online stories). The others are based more or less on true events; thus, they are non-fiction, although the distinction between truth and reality in writing is not always sharp. You can have a discussion with students about the value of fiction versus non-fiction.

For this workshop, you could ask students to choose a story that they have not previously read.

Fiction Versus Non-fiction

Stories can be fictional or non-fictional. A work of **fiction** is created in the writer's imagination. For instance, the stories "Big Brother" and "How to Be Good" are excerpts from fictional books. A work of **non-fiction** presents factual events. For instance, "My Prison Story" and "My Visit to Montreal" are narrative essays about true events.

Keep in mind that the line is sometimes blurred between the two genres. Many fiction writers incorporate elements from their lives in their work. Similarly, non-fiction writers may embellish the truth to make their stories more compelling or to make themselves more sympathetic. For instance, David Sedaris, who writes about his childhood in his story "Cyclops," calls his work "real-ish." In an interview with the *Christian Science Monitor*, he said, "I've always thought that if 97 percent of the story is true, then that's an acceptable formula."

Identifying the Main Elements in a Story

A well-written narrative essay, story, film script, or novel has certain elements. The plot, character, setting, and theme make the text resonate with people from different places and eras. When you read a story, consider the following elements.

COMPANION WEB+ Visit the Companion Website to read classic works of fiction. Enjoy George Orwell's descriptions in "Shooting an Elephant." E. Pauline Johnson writes a compelling story about a native girl who was removed from her home in "As It Was in the Beginning." Richard Connell's "The Most Dangerous Game" is an exciting tale about a deranged hunter and his prey.

The Characters

Often, the most memorable element of a short story is the characters. The **protagonist** is generally the character that the reader most identifies with. The **antagonist** struggles against the protagonist and may provide some of the sources of conflict in the text.

Although characters vary tremendously from story to story, they can also be categorized into those who evolve and those who remain static. **Dynamic characters** evolve during the course of a story. They may learn something new or behave in a different manner. **Static characters** do not evolve and their personalities do not change. When you consider character, ask yourself the following questions:

- What is the main character's background and personality?
- What are the main character's values, ambitions, hopes, and fears?
- Does the main character evolve or learn something new?
- Who or what is the main character in conflict with? For example, the character can be in conflict with himself, with other characters, with the state, or with the forces of nature.
- Who are the secondary characters, and how important are they to the story?

WRITING EXERCISE 1

Write a paragraph describing the main characters of the short story or narrative essay that you chose from the list on page 169.

The Setting

All stories are based in a particular time, place, and culture. The setting has an important influence on a story. When you read a short story, think about the time and place in which the story occurred. Also reflect on the social or historical context of the story. Ask yourself the following questions:

- Where does the story take place? Note the specific location (house, office, park, etc.), as well as the more general location (suburb, inner city, town, country).
- When does the action occur? What was happening politically and socially at that time?
- What was going on culturally? Does the story address gender, class, or race issues?

WRITING EXERCISE 2

Write a paragraph describing the setting of the short story or narrative essay that you chose from the list on page 169.

The Plot

When you discuss the plot, you describe what happens. A plot generally develops in the following manner, as illustrated in the plot timeline below.

- In the beginning of the story, we are introduced to the characters and the time and place of the action.
- A problem arises that makes the events more complicated.
- Generally, the problem includes some type of conflict (a struggle between opposing forces).
- The conflict generates a series of events that build tension and suspense; it may end in a climactic scene.
- Events take place that partially resolve the conflict. The central character may go through a transformation.
- The story concludes and the situation stabilizes.

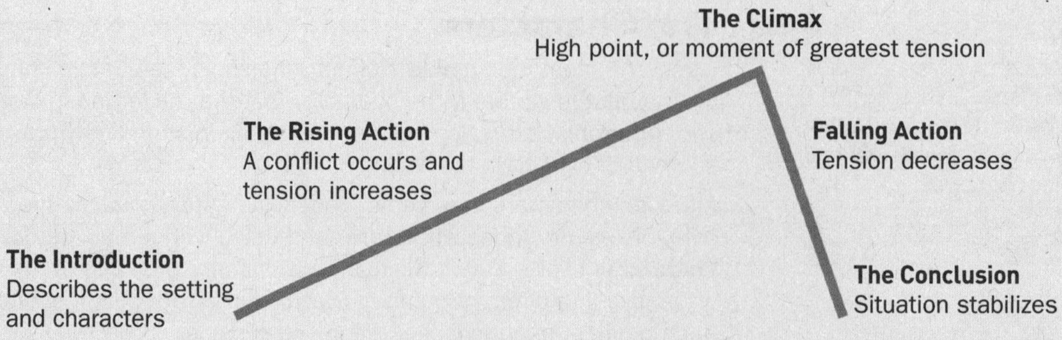

TIP

Writing about the Plot

When you summarize the plot of a story or movie, it is important to boil down the story to its most important events. Your entire summary should be about five sentences. Do not divulge the ending of the story.

WRITING EXERCISE 3

Look at the short story or narrative essay that you chose from the list on page 169. On a separate sheet of paper, make a diagram of the plot. Place the main events from the story on your timeline.

The Theme

In a short story or narrative essay, the plot tells us what happens, the setting describes the time, place, and social context, and the people form the characters. The **theme**, or principal topic of discussion, reveals the underlying meaning. The theme is a statement that provides insight into human existence. Thus, themes represent universal ideas or truths.

Most authors do not tell you explicitly what their story signifies. Instead, the situations that occur and the reactions of the characters allow the reader to discover the central meaning (or theme) of the story.

MAKING A STATEMENT OF THEME

The theme must be expressed in a complete statement and it must make a point. For example, a student wrote, "'The Most Dangerous Game' is about *hunting*." However, that is not a statement of theme because it does not express a point of view. A statement of theme must make a clear point. A better statement of them would be the following: "'The Most Dangerous Game' illustrates that hunting of living creatures is cruel."

The statement of theme must express a universal truth. Don't make narrow or overly generalized statements of theme. For instance, a student suggested that the theme of "How to Be Good" is "People are really very evil." But is that true? Your statement of theme must express a universal truth.

Some stories may have more than one theme. One story may express several universal truths. Most importantly, a statement of theme can be supported by referring to elements in the story.

Ask yourself these questions before you write your statement of theme.

- Does the title have a deeper significance?
- How does the main character evolve? Does he or she develop a new understanding about life?
- Does one of the characters make a comment that might express the author's views?
- How do the central events illustrate a universal truth?

WRITING EXERCISE 4

Once again, using the short story or narrative essay that you chose from the list on page 169, generate one or more statements of theme. Then write a paragraph describing the theme or main message of the story.

TIP

Consider Symbols

Look at the symbols in a story to help you discover the theme. A symbol is a person, place, thing, or event that has an underlying meaning. For example, in "Big Brother," the posters of the staring man symbolize the power of the state.

Creating a Thesis Statement

After you have thought about the short story or narrative essay you read, the next step is to create a thesis statement. Determine the central idea of the story or essay. You can then develop this main idea by referring to the plot, characters, setting, symbols, or theme. To create a thesis statement, you can do one of the following:

- Show that the plot, setting, or characters help illustrate the theme.
- Do a cultural analysis. What does the story tell us about gender, class, or race?
- Do a character analysis. What does the main character reveal about the human condition?
- Compare two texts and identify how they have a common message.
- Contrast two texts and identify how they look at an issue from different points of view.

Remember that your thesis must sum up the content and direction of the essay, and it should be expressed in one sentence.

EXAMPLE: Both "Cyclops" and "How to Be Good" demonstrate problems people face with parenting.

Writing Exercise 5 can be a final writing test. Students can prepare for the test by doing the other Writing Exercises in this workshop.

WRITING EXERCISE 5

Generate a thesis statement for at least one story or narrative essay that you have read. You can look for ideas in the previous Writing Exercises.

Writing an Essay about a Story

When you write your response essay, consider the next points.

- **Do not write a long plot summary.** It is boring for your reader if you explain everything that happened in a story. Instead, give a broad outline of the plot. For example, explain how the plot advances the theme. Remember to keep your plot summary short!
- **Keep yourself out of the essay.** Use third-person pronouns, and not *I* or *you*. For instance, instead of saying "*I think* the main character changes," simply write "The main character changes."
- **Support your points with quotations.** In your body paragraphs, include the exact words from the story that advance your main point. Put the page number in parentheses after the quotation.
- **Use the present tense to discuss the events in the story.** For example, "In 'How to Be Good,' GoodNews influences Molly when he suggests that beds are evil." When writing about true historical events, you can switch to the past tense.

- **Punctuate the title* of the work correctly.** If you are discussing a short story or essay, put quotation marks around the title and capitalize the main words in the title. If you are discussing a longer work such as a film or novel, italicize the title (or underline it in a handwritten text).

"Snitch" "Cyclops" *The Lord of the Rings*

The Lord of the Rings

* Note: When you title your own essays, simply capitalize the major words. Do not use underlining or quotation marks.

Compose It

Write a Response Essay

On a separate piece of paper, write an essay of about 450 to 550 words. Choose one of the following topics.

1. Choose a short story or narrative essay from the list on page 169. Develop a thesis statement and then support your main point with evidence from the story.
2. Compare and contrast two texts from the list on page 169. Explain how they examine a theme in similar or in different ways.
3. Explain which type of story you prefer: fiction or non-fiction. Fiction deals with imaginary events, whereas non-fiction deals with true events. Why do you prefer one type of story over the other? Provide supporting evidence from the stories and narrative essays in this book.

APPENDIX 1

How to Do Oral Presentations

There are a few points to remember when you make an oral presentation.

Planning Your Presentation

- **Structure your presentation.** Include an appealing introduction. Use facts or examples to support your main points. Remember to conclude your presentation to leave a final impression with your audience.
- **Practise.** Your teacher will not be impressed if you must frequently pause to think of something to say, or if you continually search through your notes. Practise and time yourself before your presentation date.
- **Use visuals.** Complement your ideas with visual support, such as a video, photo, drawing, poster, object, or PowerPoint presentation. If you use information from another source, acknowledge the source.
- **Don't memorize your presentation** or you'll sound too unnatural. It is better to speak to the audience and occasionally refer to your notes than to rattle off a memorized text.
- **Time yourself.** Ensure that your oral presentation respects the specified time limit.
- **Use cue cards.** After you have prepared the final draft of your presentation, identify some key ideas. On a cue card, write only a limited number of key words and phrases. For example, for a five-minute presentation, prepare about twenty keywords. Look at the example provided.

Rough Draft of Presentation

Before you book a place to stay in a foreign country, check out *TripAdvisor.com*. You can input the name of a youth hostel, bed and breakfast, or hotel, and you can read reviewers' comments. Go to the most positive and negative reviews, and see what people have said. Keep in mind that the owners of some tourist lodgings may pay people to write reviews.

Cue Card

TripAdvisor
hostel, hotel, b&b
comments + / -
pay reviewers

Giving Your Presentation

- **Look at your entire audience**, not just the teacher.
- **Don't read.** Use cue cards to prompt yourself through the presentation.
- **Speak clearly.** Pay particular attention to *th*, plurals and verb endings. Note that you may lose points if your teacher doesn't hear your final *-s* on verbs, for example.
- **Remember your visual supports.** A visual support will enhance your presentation.
- **Respect the time limit.** Ensure that you follow the teacher's guidelines. You might lose points if your presentation is too short or too long.
- **Use formal language.** Don't use words or expressions such as: *stuff*, *it sucks*, etc.

APPENDIX 2

Pronunciation

Pronunciation Rules

Review the pronunciation rules. You can visit the Companion Website to practise your pronunciation.

Present Tense: Third-Person Singular Verbs

Rules	Sounds	Examples		
Most third-person singular verbs end in an *–s* or a *–z* sound.	**s**	eat**s**	hit**s**	say**s**
	z	goe**s**	learn**s**	work**s**
Add *–es* to verbs ending in *–s*, *–ch*, *–sh*, *–x*, or *–z*. Pronounce the final *–es* as a separate syllable.	**iz**	fix**es**	reach**es**	touch**es**
		plac**es**	relax**es**	watch**es**

Past Tense: Regular Verbs

Rules	Sounds	Examples		
When the verb ends in *–s*, *–k*, *–f*, *–x*, *–ch*, or *–sh*, the final *–ed* is pronounced as *t*.	**t**	asked	kissed	watched
		hoped	touched	wished
When the verb ends in *–t* or *–d*, the final *–ed* is pronounced as a separate syllable.	**id**	add**ed**	fold**ed**	wait**ed**
		count**ed**	relat**ed**	want**ed**
In all other regular verbs, the final *–ed* is pronounced as *d*.	**d**	aged	killed	moved
		cured	lived	played

Past Tense: Irregular Verbs

Demonstrate the various *th* sounds to students. For instance, show them the difference between *breath* and *breathe*. They can practise pronouncing more *th* words on the Companion Website.

Rule	Sound	Examples		
When the verb ends in *–ought* or *–aught*, pronounce the final letters as *ot*.	**ot**	bought	caught	taught
		brought	fought	thought

Silent Letters

Rules	Silent Letters	Examples		
Gn: In most words, when *g* is followed by *n*, the *g* is silent.	**g**	benign	foreign	sign
		design	resign	Exception: signature
Mb: When *m* is followed by *b*, the *b* is silent.	**b**	clim**b**	dum**b**	thum**b**
		com**b**	plum**b**er	
Kn: When *k* is followed by *n*, the *k* is silent.	**k**	**k**nee	**k**nife	**k**not
		knew	**k**nit	**k**now
L: Do not pronounce the *l* in some common words.	**l**	calm	should	walk
		could	talk	would
P: Do not pronounce the *p* in most words that begin with *ps* or *pn*.	**p**	**p**neumonia	**p**sychedelic	**p**sycho
		pseudonym	**p**sychiatrist	**p**sychotic

T: Do not pronounce the *t* in some common words.	**t**	castle Christmas	fasten listen	often whistle
W: Do not pronounce the *w* in some common words.	**w**	who	write	wrong
Gh: In some words, the *gh* is silent. (Note that in some words such as *laugh* and *cough*, *gh* sounds like *f*. In other words such as *ghost*, the *gh* sounds like *g*.)	**gh**	bought daughter	light though	thought weigh

Th

Rule	Sound	Examples		
To pronounce a "voiced" *th*, push your tongue between your teeth and blow gently. Voice the sound.	**th** (voiced)	breathe that the	them there these	this those thus
To pronounce a "voiceless" *th* sound, push the tongue between the teeth and blow gently. Do not voice the sound.	**th** (voiceless)	breath death moth	north south strength	think three throw

H

Rule	Sound	Examples		
Pronounce the initial *h* in most words that begin with *h*.	**h**	hair hand handsome hangover happy	heal height help her/his hero	history home homeless hospital hurt
In some common words, the first *h* is silent.	–	heir heirloom	herb honest	honour hour

Pronunciation Help with Online Dictionaries

Many dictionaries are available online. On *dictionary.reference.com*, the stressed syllable is indicated in bold; by clicking on the loudspeaker, you can hear the word being pronounced. (Note that *dictionary.reference.com* also has a "Thesaurus" tab.)

de • vel • op [de-**vel**-*uh*p]

From *dictionary.reference.com*

APPENDIX 3

Citing the Source

When you paraphrase, summarize, or quote someone else, you must cite the source in the body of your essay. If your teacher requires it, you should also add a "Works Cited" page. Note that the most commonly used citation style is MLA (Modern Language Association).

Citing the Source in Your Essay

Mention the author's name and the title of the article in the sentence. Include the page number in parentheses. If you are using a website, no page number is necessary.

Print: In "The Case for Debt," Virginia Postrel writes, "On the subject of credit, bad news sells" (44).

Web: On his site *The Odyssey Expedition*, Graham Hughes calls himself "an adventurer, filmmaker, travel blogger, and TV presenter."

If the site has no author, then simply mention the title of the article and/or the website.

According to *Statistics Canada*, "In 2008, 244,380 students received a degree."

If your course does not include formal research essays, you can ask students to simply mention their sources in the text. They could skip the section on "Works Cited" pages.

Making a "Works Cited" Page

- Write *Works Cited* at the top centre of the page.
- List the sources alphabetically according to the authors' last names.
- Indent the second line and all subsequent lines of each entry five spaces.
- Double space all lines.

Carefully review the examples. Remember to separate items with periods or commas as shown.

Book

Last name, First name. *Title of the Book*. Place of Publication: Publisher, Year. Print.

Gaetz, Lynne. *Avenues 3 English Skills*. Montreal: Pearson, 2013. Print.

Newspaper or magazine

Last name, First name. "Title of the Article." *Title of the Magazine or Newspaper* Date: Pages. Print.

Geddes, John. "Canadian Combat." *Maclean's* 20 Mar. 2006: 21-22. Print.

Munro, Margaret. "Return of the Hooded Warbler." *Gazette* [Montreal] 27 Aug. 2012: A8. Print.

Internet sources

Last name, First name. "Title of the Article." *Title of Site or Online Publication*. Publisher/Sponsor, Date of most recent update. Web. Date of access.

Llewellyn Smith, Julia. "The Truth about Lying." *The Telegraph*. Telegraph Media Group, 15 Aug. 2012. Web. 14 May 2013.

If the site doesn't list an author's name, begin with the title of the article.

"Avoid Toxic Plastics." *SimpleSteps.org*. Natural Resources Defense Council, 2009. Web. 5 May 2010.

APPENDIX 4

Transitional Words and Expressions

Transitional expressions are linking words or phrases, and they show the reader the connections between ideas in sentences, paragraphs, and essays. A sentence can begin with a transitional expression. You can also combine sentences with a semi-colon and a transitional expression. **Always put a comma after transitional expressions.**

The plane crashed. **However,** everyone survived.

The plane crashed**;** **however,** everyone survived.

Common Transitional Expressions

Additional argument

additionally	furthermore	next
also	in addition	then
besides	moreover	

Chronology (sequence of ideas)

after that	first of all	next
afterward	formerly	subsequently
currently	in the meantime	suddenly
eventually	last	then
finally	later	these days
first,* second, third	meanwhile	

*Do not write *firstly*.

Comparison and contrast

conversely	in the same way	on the contrary
equally	instead	on the one hand
however	likewise	on the other hand
in contrast	nevertheless	similarly

Example

for example	in particular	specifically
for instance	namely	to illustrate

Emphasis

above all	in fact	principally
certainly	in particular	of course
clearly	indeed	specifically
definitely	more importantly	undoubtedly

Summary or conclusion

as a result	in conclusion	thus
consequently	in other words	to conclude
evidently	in short	to sum up
finally	on the whole	to summarize
hence	therefore	ultimately

Index

Credits

Chapter 1, p. 8 Audio text "Bear Attacks" © Canadian Broadcasting Corporation. pp. 8–10 "Redefining Who Lives" by Kathryn Blaze Carlson reprinted with the express permission of National Post Inc. p. 11 Video segment "Surviving a Plane Crash" © ABC News. pp. 12–14 "Memories of 9/11" by Douglas Quan reprinted with the express permission of Postmedia News, a division of Postmedia Network Inc. pp. 15–17 "The Rules of Survival" by Laurence Gonzales reprinted from *Deep Survival: Who Lives, Who Dies, and Why*. W.W. Norton. Copyright © 2003 by Laurence Gonzales. Used by permission.

Chapter 2, pp. 23–25 "Riff-Raff" by Heather O'Neill reprinted with the permission of the author. p. 26 Video segment "How Canadians See Americans" © Canadian Broadcasting Corporation. pp. 27–29 "Small Differences, Large Conflicts" adapted from Kim, Paul K. "Greeks and Turks." Paul's Travel Blog. paulstravelblog.com, 2008. Used by permission. p. 30 Audio text "Gay Heroes" © Canadian Broadcasting Corporation. pp. 31–33 "How the World Has Changed" by Robert Fulford reprinted with the express permission of National Post, a division of Postmedia Network Inc.

Chapter 3, pp. 39–41 "Why We Make Mistakes" reprinted from *Why We Make Mistakes: How We Look without Seeing, Forget Things in Seconds, and Are All Pretty Sure We Are Way above Average"* by Joseph T. Hallinan, copyright © 2009 by Joseph T. Hallinan. Used by permission. p. 42 Audio text "Neuroscience and the Law" © Canadian Broadcasting Corporation. pp. 44–46 "Amnesia Is the New Bliss" by Chuck Closterman reprinted with permission. p. 48 Video segment "Endless Memory" © BBC Motion Gallery. p. 49–52 "Cyclops" by David Sedaris reprinted from *Naked*. Copyright © 1997 David Sedaris. Used by permission of Little, Brown and Company. All rights reserved.

Chapter 4, pp. 58–61 "Why Are Canadians Afraid?" by Ian Brown reprinted by permission. pp. 63–65 "The Causes of Wrongful Conviction" adapted by permission from *The Innocence Project* (www.innocenceproject.org). p. 66 Video segment "Inside the Interrogation Room" © Canadian Broadcasting Corporation. pp. 67–69 "My Prison Story" by Yirga Gebremeskel reprinted by permission. p. 71 Audio text "Superhero Justice" © Canadian Broadcasting Corporation.

Chapter 5, pp. 77–78 "The Problem with Anonymous" by Andres Guadamuz reprinted by permission. p. 80 Video segment "Hackers' World" courtesy of Global News. pp. 81–86 "Anonymous Strikes Back" reprinted from *We Are Anonymous: Inside the Hacker World of LulzSec, Anonymous, and the Global Cyber Insurgency* by Parmy Olson. Copyright 2012 by Parmy Olson. Used by permission of Little, Brown and Company. All rights reserved. p. 88 Audio text "Dark Market" © Canadian Broadcasting Corporation. pp. 88–91 "A Romanian Town Is Cybercrime Central" by Yudhijit Bhattacharjee reprinted by permission.

Chapter 6, pp. 96–98 "Peep Culture" by Amanda Fortini reprinted by permission. This article first appeared in Salon.com, at http://www.Salon.com; an online version remains in the Salon archives. pp. 103–104 "Viral Vigilantes" by Matthew Fraser reprinted by permission. p. 106 Video segment "Geotagging" courtesy of Global News. pp. 107–108 "I Can Find Out So Much about You" by Ada Calhoun reprinted by permission. This article first appeared in Salon.com, at http://www.Salon.com; an online version remains in the Salon archives.

Chapter 7, pp. 114–117 "Bystander Apathy" by Mark Tyrrell reprinted by permission. p. 121 Video segment "The Power of Social Roles" © ABC News. pp. 122–124 "Snitch" excerpted from *Red China Blues: My Long March from Mao to Now* by Jan Wong. Copyright 1996 Jan Wong. Reprinted by permission of Doubleday Canada.

Chapter 8, p. 134 "what if no one's watching" by Ani DiFranco courtesy of Ani DiFranco/Righteous Babe Music. p. 136 Video segment "Good News" courtesy of Global News. pp. 137–138 "We're Not All Bad" by Diego Pelaez reprinted by permission. p. 139 Audio text "Voluntourism" © Canadian Broadcasting Corporation. pp. 140–145 "How to Be Good" by Nick Hornby, copyright 2001 by Nick Hornby. Used by permission of Riverhead Books, an imprint of Penguin Group (USA) Inc.

Photos

Alamy
p. 13 © PCN Photography; p. 16 © Photos 12; p. 38 © B.A.E. Inc.; p. 51 © D. MacDonald; p. 85 © TP; p. 89 © D. Pearson; p. 123 © S. and R. Greenhill.

iStockphoto
p. 9 left: © C. Dewald; p. 17 © J. Pauls; p. 22 © P. Kline; p. 50 © Vetta Collection; p. 100 © Juanmonino; p. 103 © RyanJLane.

McCord Museum: p. 119: M5030.

National Transport Safety Board, USA: p. 40.

Photothèque PEARSON-ERPI: p. 81.

Shutterstock
pp. 1, 19 © N. Armonn; p. 2 © AZP Worldwide; p. 5 top: © D. Brimm; middle: © V. Nesterchuck; p. 6 © Ferenz; p. 7 © zeber; p. 8: © creativex; p. 9 right: © Monkey Business Images; p. 12 © T. Szymanski; p. 14 © A. Correia; p. 15 © J. Czenke; pp. 21, 35 © R. Byron; p. 24 © majeczka; p. 25 top left: © R. Jegg; top centre: © iofoto; top right: © pzAxe; middle left: © S. Peterman; middle centre: © A. popov; middle right: © L. V. Nel; bottom left: © A. M. Tanasescu; bottom centre: © Blend Images; bottom right: © Majesticca; p. 26; p. 28 © P. Prescott; p. 30 top: © dutourdumonde; bottom: © Rikke; p. 32 © O. Yarko; pp. 37, 54 © photobank.kiev.ua; p. 42 © K. Sutyagin; pp. 45, 67, 104 © A. Danti; p. 46 © bds; p. 47 © D. Baker; p. 48 © B. Rolff; p. 52 © S. Bonk; pp. 56, 73 © J. Steidl; p. 57 © F. Gregory; p. 59 © R. M. Jethani; p. 60 © Blend Images; p. 62 top: © RAR de Bruijn Holding BV; bottom: © Lisa S.; p. 63 © rockey; p. 64 © C. D. Vitalevich; p. 66 © Phase4Photography; p. 71 © Malchev; p. 72 top: © H. Almeida; middle: © am piacquadio; pp. 75, 93 © Photosani; p. 76 © V. B. Varona; p. 78 © R. Kints; p. 80 © photomak; p. 82 © haak78; p. 83 © P. Rufo; p. 87 © Kuzma; p. 88 © F. Berti; p. 90 © M. Damkier; pp. 95, 110 © T. wang; p. 96 © bloomua; p. 97 © Pixel 4 Images; p. 98 © Kooda; p. 99 © conrado; p. 106 © O. Mark; p. 107 © am piacquadio; p. 109 © Nata Sha; pp. 112, 129 © Sideways Design; p. 113 © V. Daragan; p. 114 © Nomad_Soul; p. 116 © Lisa S.; p. 118 © P. McKinnon; p. 121 © D. Ercken; p. 122 © J. Lock; p. 127 top: © C. Kolaczan; bottom: © R. R. Beiler; pp. 130, 147 © antoniomas; p. 131 top: © D. Evison; bottom: © Rd; p. 132 © Mny-Jhee; p. 133 © red-feniks; p. 135 © Lisa S.; p. 136 © withGod; p. 137 © mangostock; p. 138 top: © Goodluz; bottom: © D. Berkut; p. 140 © Dhoxax; p. 141 © E. Bruns; p. 142 © E. ray; p. 143 © olivier.

Thinkstock: p. 31.